LOVE WOULD CRY INSIDE

Dreaming with God;
Prophetic Revelation

KAREN WRIGHT

LOVE
WOULD CRY
INSIDE

Dreaming with God;
Prophetic Revelation

KAREN WRIGHT

For Zion's sake I will not keep silent,

And for Jerusalem's sake I will not keep quiet,

Until her righteousness goes forth like brightness,

And her salvation like a torch that is burning.

—Isaiah 62:1, NASB

Dedication

Silent Gratitude isn't much use to anyone.[1]
—GB Stern

I dedicate with heartfelt tribute.

I begin with my heavenly loving Father and the Trinity, who are Ones who allowed this possibility.

I am thankful for my earthly family and my spiritual one whom God has given me.

To those who helped make this project come true: friends Marilyn, Brenda, Bill, Angie, LaShund, Pastor Walter Hallam, the editor, and my publisher, Kevin Basconi, with King of Glory Printing & Publishing.

My greatest support, my husband, David Wright, Sr. His faithful dedication can't be compared. He is steady in kindness, loyal, and generous. He sacrificed everything to help raise our sons together. He is my smaller rock (compared to Christ).

I honor you inside my heart.

ISBN: 978-0-9960217-4-6

King of Glory Ministries International Printing & Publications 2015

King of Glory Ministries International
PO Box 903, Moravian Falls, NC 28654, 336-818-1210
www.kingofgloryministries.org

Scripture quotations taken from the Holy Bible, English Standard Version, copyright © 2001 by Crossway Bibles, a division of Good News Publisher. Used by permission.
Scripture quotations marked AKJV are from the American King James Version of the Bible.
Scripture quotations marked AMP are from the Amplified Bible. Old Testament copyright © 1965, 1987 by the Zondervan Corporation. The Amplified New Testament copyright © 1954, 1958, 1987 by the Lockman Foundation. Used by permission.
Scripture quotations marked CEV are from the Contemporary English Version, copyright © 1995 by the American Bible Society. Used by permission.
Scripture quotations marked GNT are from the Good News Translation, Second Edition, Copyright 1992 by American Bible Society. Used by Permission.
Scripture quotations marked HCSB are taken from the Holman Christian Standard Bible®, Copyright © 1999, 2000, 2002, 2003, 2009 by Holman Bible Publishers. Used by permission. Holman Christian Standard Bible®, Holman CSB®, and HCSB® are federally registered trademarks of Holman Bible Publishers.
Scripture quotations marked ISV from the Holy Bible: International Standard Version©. Copyright © 1996–2012 by The ISV Foundation. All rights reserved internationally. Used by permission.
Scripture quotations marked KJV are from the King James Version of the Bible.
Scripture quotations marked MSG are from *The Message: The Bible in Contemporary English*, copyright © 1993, 1994, 1995, 1996, 2000, 2001, 2002. Used by permission of NavPress Publishing Group.
Scripture quotations marked NASB are from the New American Standard Bible–Updated Edition, Copyright © 1960, 1962, 1963, 1968, 1971, 1972, 1973, 1975, 1977, 1995 by The Lockman Foundation. Used by permission. (www.Lockman.org)
Scripture quotations marked NET are from the New English Translation, NET Bible® copyright ©1996-2006 by Biblical Studies Press, L.L.C. http://netbible.com All rights reserved.
Scripture quotations marked NIV are from the Holy Bible, New International Version. Copyright © 1973, 1978, 1984, 2010, 2011, International Bible Society. Used by permission.
Scripture quotations marked NKJV are from the New King James Version of the Bible. Copyright © 1979, 1980, 1982 by Thomas Nelson, Inc., publishers. Used by permission.
Scripture quotations marked NLT are from the Holy Bible, New Living Translation, copyright © 1996. Used by permission of Tyndale House Publishers, Inc., Wheaton, IL 60189. All rights reserved.
Scripture quotations marked NRSV are from the New Revised Standard Version of the Bible. Copyright © 1989 by the Division of Christian Education of the National Council of the Churches of Christ in the USA. Used by permission.
Scripture quotations marked TLB are from The Living Bible. Copyright © 1971. Used by permission of Tyndale House Publishers, Inc., Wheaton, IL 60189. All rights reserved.
Greek and Hebrew definitions are derived from *Strong's Exhaustive Concordance of the Bible*, ed. James Strong, Nashville, TN: Thomas Nelson Publishers, 1997.

Table of Contents

Preface

Behold, the eye of the LORD is on those who fear Him, On those who hope in His mercy, To deliver their soul from death, And to keep them alive in famine. Our soul waits for the LORD; He is our help and our shield. For our heart shall rejoice in Him, Because we have trusted in His holy name. Let Your mercy, O LORD, be upon us, Just as we hope in You.

—Psalm 33:18-22, NKJV

I'd relish the recognition for the title of this book, but it was given in a dream many years ago. Daniel of the Bible had great understanding in visions and dreams (Daniel 1:17).

Title Dream

In my dream, I viewed a vivid blue sky on a clear day. Surprisingly, a plane appeared flying from outside my peripheral vision from the mid-right side of my view, eventually exiting out toward the left side pulling a long, white banner. I saw each black letter sequentially spaced as each became enlarged before my sight. It was as if the signage came forward closer to my face, so I could see each single magnified letter. The first letter "L" followed by… wait, wait; then another letter "O," then "V," and "E." Then there was a blank space that I thought ended the message. It was a separation instead, and the letters kept coming until the entire message was given and the plane flew away from sight, banner in tow.

I pondered briefly as to exactly what these words, *love would cry inside*, precipitated. I knew this was the title of the book. It would be birthed from the unveiling of my life's experiences. When the time was right, it would come. This transcript is not manufactured, duplicated, or prefabricated. I personally lived out the experiences revealed.

God speaks to us on a heart level. God visits us on a first name basis directly into our ears, often during the night. This intimate impression feeds directly to our conscience. He engages us with what is going on in our lives. We respond by searching out these hidden messages and meanings in exploration of His revealed truths.

> *For God does speak—now one way, now another—though no one perceives it. In a dream, in a vision of the night, when deep sleep falls on people as they slumber in their beds, he may speak in their ears and terrify them with warnings, to turn them from wrongdoing and keep them from pride, to preserve them from the pit, their lives from perishing by the sword.*

> —Job 33:14-18, NIV

Notice the message above emphasizes four areas we are to perceive for the intention of *preserving our life.* The first set of words has to do with WARNING us of our WRONGDOINGS; while the last cluster tells us to avoid PRIDE that traps us in a PIT of debauchery. Who but our Daddy God would care enough to help us avoid worsening consequences?

Since the title was specific in its context and content, I wanted to find out what each word conveyed according to Strong's Concordance. For any avid student of God's Word, this will reinforce your digging skills.

Love is translated from the Greek word *agape*. It is a meaning filled full of a bouquet of affection. It expresses a love feast of endearment. I envision a trampoline of love—jumping with sheer abandon in the air and then knowingly falling into His lap of love, which stretches wide in every direction of grace to catch me from the enemy's grasp.

> *Who shall separate us from the **love** of Christ? Shall tribulation, or distress, or persecution, or famine, or nakedness, or peril, or sword?*
>
> —Romans 8:35, emphasis added

Would in Greek means "properly," as if assigning a reason to something. It can be used in an intensified debate, argument, or explanation. It is like a "seeing word," as we are willingly disposed to something. In Hebrew it conveys our contentment to rest in God.

> *On the morrow, because he **would** have known the certainty wherefore he was accused of the Jews, he loosed him from his bands, and commanded the chief priests and all their council to appear, and brought Paul down, and set him before them.*
>
> —Acts 22:30, KJV, emphasis added

Cry in Greek is *kraugazo,* as in a notifying outcry of tumult or grief. People cry for various reasons, which can be summed up to proclaim, pronounce, and publish one's intentions. In Hebrew it's the word *shava,* meaning to be free from some form of trouble as in a shout out loud for rescue or freedom.

> *O Lord, how long shall I **cry** for help, and you will not hear? Or **cry** to you "Violence!" and you will not save?*
>
> —Habakkuk 1:2, emphasis added

Inside in Hebrew is *bayith,* which refers to a house or family. It can take on the form of a great palace containing priceless treasures or a modest abode or a confined, concrete prison within its walls of restricted freedom.

We *are* the vessel or house in which God desires to live. All those intricate things we hold inside ourselves that are unique and unseen at times make the difference in what makes us and what we make of ourselves with God's grace. It is all part of the journey only we can walk through.

> *And he built the walls of the house within with boards of cedar, both the floor of the house, and the walls of the ceiling: and he* **covered** *them on the* **inside** *with wood, and* **covered** *the floor of the house with planks of fir.*

> —1 Kings 6:15, KJV, emphasis added

Universally put together, I believe this speaks a love greater than ourselves; one that is willingly seen and most desperately read within a vast heart of what is most important to us, a value of indescribable knowledge, and an inexplicable place of hope and longing nestled in the crevices of our soul. It expresses that deep place inside of us that holds onto a love so tightly woven there are no words that can be spoken, only a heartfelt cry.

Confirmation: 3.24.06 (My Birthday)

While attending a conference by the name of Open My Eyes, Lord, at Calvary Community Church in Houston, Texas, I was lifted in a time of luxurious praise and worship. My eyes became open to a vision from the Lord.

Lily Vision

I envisioned a brown treasure box with large gemstones on top in a set of three. The largest of the three formations in the center stack came to a high point. There were hands holding the box underneath and over the top. These were long hands and fingers that held the box tightly. I came close to it and extended my hands upwards toward the treasure box when the lid spontaneously lifted open.

There were pieces of paper (2" x 1") with soft edges that began floating toward my hands. The papers began to pile up as my hands became as if in the shape of a dustpan to allow all of them to be held, without losing one piece.

When all the papers were received, they began to float toward my heart and then upwards to my mouth as I consumed them within. They all fell in line in an orderly manner as they entered my mouth. The tail end of these papers took on the shape of a lily or some type of flower. But, I consumed them all.

The lily, our lady's tears, conveys a feminine message of purity, life, and hope to the church. The fruitful bulb bears robust, white petals as a humble picture of Christ's resurrection. One of its medicinal virtues is the "restoration of a lost voice."[1] As the chapters of the book unfold, I believe we will find that the Body of Christ is once again being positioned to have a *profound* voice.

Lilies grow but do not labor or spin as a beautifully dressed body of adornment to Christ's affection. We are His lily of the valley, a mystery to behold as a reflection of Christ's splendid glory. This is a season of Christ moving in a greater capacity in the Body of Christ. It is happening exponentially throughout the Earth as we are called to hear, listen, and discern His voice beat.

Then I will heal you of your faithlessness; my love will know no bounds, for my anger will be gone forever. I will be to Israel like a refreshing dew from heaven. Israel will blossom like the **lily;** *it will send roots deep into the soil like the cedars in Lebanon. Its branches will spread out like beautiful olive trees, as fragrant as the cedars of Lebanon. My people will again live* *under my shade. They will flourish like grain and blossom like grapevines. They will be as fragrant as the wines of Lebanon.*

—Hosea 14:4-7, NLT, emphasis added

The dustpan is a cleaning utensil used to sweep up all the dirt and messes that collect right where we live, and then we dispose of its debris in a trash container. It is very reminiscent of the sea of forgetfulness. Trash is meant to be taken away from our resting places.

As I relayed this vision to a woman I knew, she asked me what I felt the papers were. All I could think of were pages to a book, and she concurred. God had put His book inside of me. Then she laid her hands on my ears and asked the angels to make the words very clear and visible to my understanding.

Also, on the front cover of the main journal used for writing this book, I taped a Chinese cookie reading. I think these are whimsical and read them for amusement. This one, of course, was just for me, as it read, "You are a lover of words; someday you will write a book." Ah, what encouragement tucked inside the yumminess of Chinese cuisine!

Dreams and Visions

*In a dream, they were **warned** not to report back to Herod. So they worked out another route, left the territory without being seen, and returned to their own country.*

—Matthew 2:12, MSG, emphasis added

As you read this book, you will find many instances of dreams and visions that are as relevant today as those in the Bible. God has consistently used these in my life for warning, encouragement, and direction. Later on, I took dream courses that helped me learn their application and understanding. I strongly encourage anyone with this interest to seek out John Paul Jackson's web-site training information at www.streamsministries.com.

> [Zechariah] *saw in the night, and behold, a man riding on a red horse! He was standing among the myrtle trees in the glen, and behind him were red, sorrel, and white horses. Then I said, "What are these, my lord?" The angel who talked with me said to me, "I will show you what they are." So the man who was standing among the myrtle trees answered, "These are they whom the LORD has sent to patrol the earth."*

> —Zechariah 1:8-10

The mysteries revealed in this dream stance are dynamic. The prophet Zechariah was standing in a *dark place hidden* by myrtle trees, which can be seen back then as it is today for the church. Christ is prepared on His red horse. The adjoining angels anchor His message to the Earth. The symbolism shares intercession, hope, covenant, and deliverance. Captivity was stolen in the night, but a new Knight is here to stay.

Dreams carry the voice of the Lord (Genesis 31:24). They can be integrated in our lives against the attacks of the enemy. Insignificant, scrawny satan is always on the prowl to stifle, deter, and kill God's vision for our lives. I would recommend journaling your way to the truths God sends our way. Unravel and uncover these dreams effectively as you find out the symbolism, numbers, and colors.

Some dreams are from bad food; but as you dedicate and consecrate your night dreams and day visions, more of them will come. Study to show yourself approved (2 Timothy 2:15), as the revelation that comes will astound you. Be diligent and proactive to search out the layers of meaning revealed in each one.

In the last days we are told that dreams and visions will increase. I believe they will be utilized more in order to know what the very next step will be to avoid entrapments of various kinds. They will be used to deliver us from certain harm by avoiding wrong decisions with dire consequences. Seek God in this area so we can be used of Him to help mankind.

Dream of Security: In Him I Have Need of Nothing!

I saw a long tube that was encapsulated on either end. I was inside the center of the tube as it surrounded me. Both ends of the tube were secure and sealed. The front end looked like a flashlight, which was Jesus shining forth to protect, shield, and bring light to the situations ahead of me. The metal end cap held a thick, white round cord centered in it's middle that flowed outward (my lifeline to the Holy Spirit).

This is also the central resonating vibration of His Spirit. We are connected by shared sacred consecration to the New Covenant. He is my source; I am contained in His presence. He is all around me. I'm immersed in His wavelength of love, as the light beams from the head of a flashlight spreading out into a wider array of light output ahead. This makes all the difference in what we actually see.

A cord can be expressed as a chain, such as Psalm 2:3: *"'Let us break their chains,' they cry, 'and free ourselves from slavery to God'"* (NLT). The world thinks God's cord is an oppressive restraint to their feverish freedom of will. They forcefully cast off their lifeline to Christ as a prisoner's shackle. They aren't casting off chains of depravity but cables of virtue. They exercise cord cutters, refusing any rulership, holding tightfistedly to the corruption of man's bondage.

The LORD is my light and my salvation; whom shall I fear? The LORD is the stronghold of my life; of whom shall I be afraid?

—Psalm 27:1

Halfway Point—It Happens

About halfway towards the completion of this book, I was wondering, "Will I ever finish? Will I ever make it through to completion?" I had been told for many years, with several revelatory confirmations from prophetic individuals, that I would publish a book. It was a desire of mine since meeting a book author, Yvonne M. Wilson, in my teen years. Her small hardbound book was called *Sifted Gold*. Her testimony titillated me with her dramatic experiences of pain, life, and death.

I struggled, getting only bits and pieces here and there. This wasn't satisfying. I wasn't scoring big, getting large chapters written. There was more I needed to write, but it wasn't coming easily. I wanted to get all that I needed to do accomplished. I wanted this book to help others and equip them better than myself. I wanted it as in Jeremiah 30:2: "*Write in a book all the words I have spoken to you*" (NIV).

At this point, I had a **warfare dream**:

> One of my mentors from years past, "RY," and I had an encounter. This female mentor was a senior officer in God's army. We found each other with a group of women at an "encampment" spiritual facility. She took my hand, and said to me, "The enemy is very interested in you." Always the curious one, I said, "How so?" She shrugged my question off, not impressed by the content of it. I told her I was writing a book. She said, "Oh," in a nonchalant tone. She began to lead us downstairs and outside toward a military-type motor vehicle where she opened the hood. She took a tool in order to open up a quart of motor oil. It was for me.

The word *encampment* is meaningful because typically it is used as a military term referring to a place set up for soldiers' lodging. This was a military-based dream befitting the elements in it. The "motor" is our power for motivation and anointing.

Doesn't this get one to wonder of the application? I set off in my research mode looking for more insight. What is motor oil used for and what are the benefits to a vehicle? I found several uses:

- Lubricates all moving parts (Holy Spirit)
- Cleans away debris by preventing blockages of important pathways (like in my brain)
- Cools the engine from intense heat (life processes)
- Protects it from rust and corrosion (misuse/ distractions)

A major function for motor oil is to *reduce friction*. Intense heat is produced between all moving objects, thus the oil prevents wear and tear. Motor oil *increases fuel mileage*, allowing for a *smooth ride*. The efficacy of this slick oil *gives power and performance*.[2]

All right! I needed God's Holy *motor oil* so I don't wear out from hindering friction—obstacles from daily living that would deter my mission/vision; then overheating from exhaustion, triggering parts of my life to grind against each other, and ultimately causing everything to come to a halt. What can I accomplish by using God's holy motor oil? I will get a smoother, more effective stride; increased vital power from the Holy Ghost; and a cool, refreshing transition from place to place I could not attain on my own.

God anointed Jesus of Nazareth with the Holy Spirit and with **power**. *He went about doing good and healing all who were oppressed by the devil, for God was with him.*

—Acts 10:38, emphasis added

Without frequent oil changes, the cares and burdens of life can build up in our personal soul where old polluted oil won't lubricate the moving parts as well as fresh new oil. Dirty oil keeps us defunct and out of commission! The ride of life becomes rough and smelly. Fresh oil keeps us alive, purposeful, and powerful to complete our journey.

And why did my friend open the hood of the vehicle? That's the brain, where all the mechanisms of operation exist. Man, does that need refreshing daily!

> *For I will satisfy the weary soul, and every languishing soul I will replenish.*
>
> —Jeremiah 31:25

"A Call for Books": a Message by Pastor Walter Hallam, 8.18.13

Pastor Hallam asked those who felt they were anointed for books to lift their hand. He then prayed for those who lifted their hand to receive the anointing—for God to release that anointing on them.

- Books that set captives free
- Books that instruct
- Books that inspire

He prophesied that these books would not just sit on a shelf, but would be used by God to touch the masses for Jesus. He said these books would help establish men and women in the house of God and the ways of God.

He said these books would separate people "from the clutch of the devil and from the lure of this world and its social order" and set them on the path that's to fulfill the call of God. These books would help families become strong and powerful, be spirit-filled, word believing, Christian life style, Kingdom language books.

He prophesied that some people would move into the anointing and not hold back. These people, he said, will see the blessing of the Lord and will open up the flow. "For just like I showed Adam the river with the gold in it, and the precious stones, surely when you obey God, you'll see a river of provision coming your way, too!"

He then encouraged them to act on it, to go thru the door the Lord opened, and watch the blessing of God multiply, expand, and strengthen them.

Revelation 3:8

I know your works. Behold, I have set before you an open door, which no one is able to shut. I know that you have but little power, and yet you have kept my word and have not denied my name.

Introduction

In the beginning, God created the heavens and the earth. The earth was without form and void, and darkness was over the face of the deep. And the Spirit of God was hovering over the face of the waters. And God said, "Let there be light," and there was light.

—Genesis 1:1-3, KJV

Here, straight from the get-go, is the setting for this book you are embarking to read—the distinction of declared darkness split apart by a penetrating, powerful light source from the eye of our Creator God.

In this environment saturated with the richness of God is where the first family entered in. First was Adam whose rib was necessitated for the making of Eve's body. They were given markers in the Garden of Life. Everything was permissible to relish and enjoy while taking dominion over the substance of the Earth, except for that darn apple tree that was beckoning to be noticed. The placement of it was an irritant; smack dab in the center of that perfect place.

But I am afraid that as the serpent deceived Eve by his cunning, your thoughts will be led astray from a sincere and pure devotion to Christ.

—2 Corinthians 11:3

That tree just happened to bear rosy red, vibrantly luscious apples in the making. Red is the color most used by restaurants today in order to attract the attention of its potential customers. Smoking red causes the saliva glands to go full blast into dining mode. It begins to speak to our brain, "Eat me; eat me."

Of course, the enticer of the brethren lurched around the perfect spot, waiting for just the right moment to seduce his victims into an eternity of seductive alluring sin. What method would the serpent use? This would be too easy. The formula was simple. What an ingenious advertising ploy! Offer them something they can't have; then tell them they're gods of the universe. They are BIG enough to make their own decisions. Cunning, cleaver, so crafty!

The bite got sunk! It changed our lives forever. At least, until one Lamb changed that turn of events. Romans 6:10 tells us: *"For the death he died he died to sin, once for all, but the life he lives he lives to God."*

What did Adam and Eve do in the midst of such exposure? They ran under the radar of God's presence. They hid from view. They camouflaged themselves with shrouded leaves. They lied about it! Subversive sin is still in charge of these behaviors today.

Do we think we can cunningly obscure ourselves from our Creator? Disguises, masks, and tattoos don't work! We might pretend there is a place He cannot go to or see, or that He cannot know what we are thinking inside our heart. That's why Jonah chose to escape inside a horrific whale's stomach instead of confronting his God. Despicable deception tells us all these things, and we believe them for a time.

Ephesians 4:14 implores us to *"no longer be children, tossed to and fro by the waves and carried about by every wind of doctrine, by human cunning, by craftiness in deceitful schemes."*

Face to Face

> *For now we see only a reflection as in a mirror; then we shall see **face to face.***

> —1 Corinthians 13:12, NIV, emphasis added

I used to sell reading glasses to people who had once seen clearly in their close viewing range early on in life. But now, because of age, elements, and a hardening of the lens of the eye, they saw with dim cloudiness. They needed plus sign designated readers to "see" again, up close and personal. Images became bright and precise as the light sparkled back to them.

Many avenues in life are a cluster of darkened confusion in a bewildered place of inadequacy, inlayed with peaks and valleys. But when that reflection of light comes from His face, it effervescently shows us all things new.

One day our sight will be enlightened perfectly, having no need of glasses to have full view of our Savior. All darkness will be eliminated permanently, as if pressing our faces to the glass of His majesty.

> ***If you prepare your heart,*** *you will stretch out your hands toward him. If iniquity is in your **hand**, put it far away, and let not injustice dwell in your **tents**. Surely then you will lift up your **face** without blemish; you will be secure and will **not fear**. You will forget your misery; you will remember it as waters that have passed away. And your life will be **brighter** than the noonday; its **darkness** will be like the morning. And you will feel secure, because there is **hope**; you will look around and take your **rest** in security. You will lie down, and none will make you afraid; many will court your favor. But the*

eyes of the wicked will fail; all way of **escape** will be lost to them, and their **hope** is to breathe their last.

—Job 11:13-20, emphasis added

God told Job how it really is, as recorded in Job 38:4-7:

Where were you when I laid the foundation of the earth? Tell me, if you have understanding. Who determined its measurements—surely you know! Or who stretched the line upon it? On what were its bases sunk, or who laid its cornerstone, when the morning stars sang together and all the sons of God shouted for joy?

The Earth hangs out on a limb without any visible support, levers, or beams. We are all being held together by the fabric of God's Word. Who can measure the height of the sky or the face of the deep seas? The dimensions of the Earth are unsettling at best. The circumference and dimension have been debated for centuries. Where were any of us when God's secret plan was at work in creation?

*Therefore, having this ministry by the mercy of God, we do not lose heart. But we have renounced disgraceful, underhanded ways. We refuse to practice cunning or to tamper with God's word, but by the open statement of the truth we would commend ourselves to everyone's conscience in the **sight of God**.*

—2 Corinthians 4:1-2, emphasis added

Tears

And what of our tears? What is the significance of these clear, tender drops?

*He will wipe away every tear from their eyes, and death shall
be no more, neither shall there be mourning, nor crying, nor
pain anymore, for the former things have passed away.*

—Revelation 21:4

According to Strong's Concordance there are 697 references
for verses in the Bible associated with crying (weep, cry, tears).
That's not chump change; that's significant reference to a tear-
drop. British psychiatrist Henry Maudsley, among others, is
quoted as saying: "The sorrow which has no vent in tears may
make other organs weep."[1]

Our tears represent the heart's overflow of emotion that can
no longer be contained. They're releasing a mechanism that
lightens the weights we carry. God is so intimately acquainted
with our tears; He collects each one in a bottle. Tears are an
unavoidable reaction to stress, sorrows, and the painful real-
ities of this life. God treasures and redeems every seen and
unseen tear.

I believe the depth of David's many tears built the reservoirs
of an enduring, lasting relationship with his Lord. He soaked his
couch with rivers of weeping. David's kingdom therefore lasted
through many generations of his bloodline.

It's been said the stars *of our tearlets* don't come out until it
gets dark outside. Most weeping is done at nighttime. At least
that's how it was for me. The lack of daylight and the reflection
of matters at night brought on conditions that led to tearfulness.
They would saturate my pillow at night by swelling up, then
leaking out on their own. The pain was so deep a pit that my
face did not wrinkle up or move, but the overflow of tears came
without invitation.

She weeps bitterly in the night, with tears on her cheeks; among all her lovers she has none to comfort her; all her friends have dealt treacherously with her; they have become her enemies.

—Lamentations 1:2

David felt completely forsaken by God as his enemies encroached upon him. It was then he wrote Psalm 42:3: *"My tears have been my food day and night, while they say to me all the day long, "Where is your God?""* David waited on God with tears.

One day there shall be no more need for tears. They shall be done away with for eternity. On the other side there will be no more darkness to overcome. There will only be the visible light of His presence. The worst place in the world is to be shut out of God's presence, so cry out more tearfully than ever, "Here is my Lord."

How can we SEE the light if we never shed the tears that embody His life? Without tears this world would wax rock hard like the dark crevices spoken of in this book. There would be no hope whatsoever. Compassion, mercy, and all forms of love would die off. Love requires a decision. Make it count, choose the precious twinkles in life and let them stir up inside of you to everlasting life.

The following selection is by Charles Spurgeon based on Acts 9:11:

Prayers are instantly noticed in heaven. The moment Saul began to pray the Lord heard him. Here is comfort for the distressed but praying soul. Oftentimes a poor broken-hearted one bends his knee, but can only utter his wailing in the language of sighs and tears; yet that groan has made all the harps of heaven thrill with music;

that tear has been caught by God and treasured in the lachrymatory of heaven. "Thou puttest my tears into thy bottle," implies that they are caught as they flow. The suppliant, whose fears prevent his words, will be well understood by the Most High. He may only look up with misty eye; but "prayer is the falling of a tear." Tears are the diamonds of heaven; sighs are a part of the music of Jehovah's court, and are numbered with "the sublimest strains that reach the majesty on high." Think not that your prayer, however weak or trembling, will be unregarded. Jacob's ladder is lofty, but our prayers shall lean upon the Angel of the covenant and so climb its starry rounds. Our God not only hears prayer but also loves to hear it. "He forgetteth not the cry of the humble." True, he regards not high looks and lofty words; he cares not for the pomp and pageantry of kings; he listens not to the swell of martial music; he regards not the triumph and pride of man; but wherever there is a heart big with sorrow, or a lip quivering with agony, or a deep groan, or a penitential sigh, the heart of Jehovah is open; he marks it down in the registry of his memory; he puts our prayers, like rose leaves, between the pages of his book of remembrance, and when the volume is opened at last, there shall be a precious fragrance springing up therefrom.

Faith asks no signal from the skies,
To show that prayers accepted rise,
Our Priest is in his holy place,
And answers from the throne of grace.[2]

CHAPTER ONE

Inside the Circle

I hate all this silly religion, but you, GOD, I trust. I'm leaping and singing in the circle of your love; you saw my pain, you disarmed my tormentors, You didn't leave me in their clutches, but gave me room to breathe. Be kind to me, God—I'm in deep, deep trouble again. I've cried my eyes out; I feel hollow inside. My life leaks away, groan by groan my years fade out in sighs. My troubles have worn me out, turned my bones to powder. To my enemies I'm a monster; I'm ridiculed by the neighbors. My friends are horrified; they cross the street to avoid me. They want to blot me from memory, forget me like a corpse in a grave, discard me like a broken dish in the trash. The street-talk gossip has me "criminally insane"! Behind locked doors they plot how to ruin me for good.

—Psalm 31:6-13, MSG

Roots and Tentacles

It all starts in our roots—always! It starts in the root systems that lead one generation to another through a compilation of behaviors. Mine were intricately woven into suppressed but factual events. Early on I wasn't aware of its isolation type affect on me. Teenage years matured into secretively protecting my concealed world that caused considerable pain—that hidden place I wouldn't dare let others see inside much less openly reveal to them. I wanted everything to be all right, vividly and imaginatively pretending it was. Although imperceptible to me early on, I lived out this false reality. But it was a lie.

Who wants to be an insignificant outsider? As most teens, I wanted normalcy in my world. I tried to project a flawless dignified image around me, wanting to look perfect and act and dress perfect. We all have an image we want to project. But nothing in it was close to real. I needed to understand things, and even more to feel real love. Why did it have to be this way? Where did I fit into all this nonsense I was experiencing? There had to be something better than this. What I lived resembled a critical counterfeit of my broken home environment.

Many women and some men use foundation or concealer to camouflage flaws. The scars, redness, and unwanted blemishes we have experienced, we diligently try to cover up. We might use a brush, a sponge, or our fingers; but however it's done, the objective is to privately hide that sucker so it's not visible to outside observers. This is the motivation for disguising the ugliness we see in ourselves. The focus of our intended dissatisfaction is not to be seen.

My family moved across town when I was eight into a larger prestigious house, which acclimated into an increasingly hostile home life. My parents eventually ran their own company. It seemed as our financial prosperity increased, so did the escalation of daily manifestations of alcoholic arguments, yelling, and fighting. Many nights I could hear alarming sounds that could range from pounding on the kitchen counter to cabinet doors slamming repeatedly, screeching, or the final door shutting with forceful volatility.

My mother enrolled me in art classes at an art studio in Spring Branch, TX. There I had a warm natured art teacher who taught me the skills with passion that I still use today. I revel in acrylic medium paint applied to just about any surface imaginable. I also became an avid swimmer and did competition racing with neighborhood teams. In school I enrolled in journalism and found an outlet for my spiraling emotions. This is where my journaling diaries began that evolved to this juncture.

At home I wanted to somehow control or stop the craziness. In my sophomore year I began to gain weight, which did not fit well in my small squad uniform. That summer I found I could control what I ate or didn't eat. I lost thirty-five pounds in two months time. It was a drastic weight loss, but I could control something in my life. While it seemed everything else was out of control, this was something I could handle myself. When I went back to school in the fall, all my new skinny clothes were falling off of me.

At the lowest, I was about ninety-three pounds, which was too low for my height. I also experienced anemia with dizziness on this extreme diet. My friends told me that I needed to gain weight. This suggestion freaked me out. Why would you **not** control something that benefited you? I was baffled by needing to eat more after achieving my goal, an objective that made me feel good about myself. This was going to mess with my routine of controlled restrictions. Even though I loved the attention I received from guys and girlfriends, alike, it eventually clicked that I should stop the new crazy I created because nothing fit me.

Are you tired? Worn out? Burned out on religion? Come to me.
Get away with me and you'll recover your life. I'll show you how

to take a real rest. Walk with me and work with me—watch how I do it. Learn the unforced rhythms of grace. I won't lay anything heavy or ill-fitting on you. Keep company with me and you'll learn to live freely and lightly.

—Matthew 11:28-30, MSG

Secluded Sides

*For you formed my inward parts; you knitted me together in my mother's womb. I praise you, for I am fearfully and won- derfully made. Wonderful are your works; my soul knows it very well. My frame was not **hidden** from you, when I was being made in **secret**, intricately woven in the depths of the earth. Your eyes saw my unformed substance; in your book were written, every one of them, the days that were formed for me, when as yet there was none of them.*

—Psalm 139:13-16, emphasis added

The enemy would like to have squelched my life at birth. As my mother relayed it to me, my neck was in an awkward position in the birth canal, as it extended out instead of my forehead. Upon seeing the problem, one of the attending nurses passed out on the floor. Forceps were used to rotate my head to the correct position. I've always felt sensitivity in my neck, like when it's held tightly with a scarf.

*Save me, O God, for the waters have come up to my **neck** [they threaten my life].*

—Psalm 69:1, AMP, emphasis added

The Lord is close to us continually. In Psalm 139:5 it says, "*You hem me in, behind and before, and lay your hand upon me.*" This tells us the Lord is on every side of us; all around our being.

We are encompassed about with His complete knowledge and understanding of our whereabouts. His hand is upon us, upholding and encircling our very beings.

The first time I remember trouble in our family was while sitting on the modest kitchen counter in my childhood home. My mother stood next to the kitchen counter, while I sat upon it. My dad stood in the center of the kitchen yelling in an unusually harsh tone at my mom. I didn't understand why he was so angry or what he was really saying. Whatever it was, it caused my mother to cry—one of the few times in my memory. This upset me because I didn't understand the situation or what was causing it. I wanted the meanness to stop!

My family, like most, had well kept secrets, things you don't share or reveal to others outside of the family circle. On my mother's side was a tradition of keeping things to oneself, isolating the matter from the outside world. It was considered to be no one else's business. You couldn't give contradictory opinions on family matters to outsiders. They were secluded, private issues. Many of us have heard people speak of a "well guarded secret" that runs in families.

On my father's side, there seemed to be a pretense of acting as if the most obvious blatant problems weren't problems at all. It was as if some family members were blind to things that were right in front of them. It seemed that while my father may have been a drunken mess, no one wanted to deal with the issue seriously. Some seemed to just pretend it away, look around it, play with it, but not call it what it really is! There was no one to speak up, take action, or get him necessary help. It was forbidden to speak of it when the dysfunction was so obvious.

Both of these collaborated family behaviors worked deeply into my life, causing me to fear known things while guarding the hidden agendas played out before me daily. This produced an instinct to project the exterior of perfection with a seemingly normal image. Everything was okay as long as I acted, even pretended, it was. But this was not what I felt on the inside. I used this façade mechanism to exercise some control to my out of control family life, continually functioning out of hidden repressed pain.

We did not use or hear the word "love" very often, if at all. I saw the word occasionally in a birthday card. Encouragement and hugs were rare. Accusations and judgments were common. There were conversations of degradation toward others. I don't remember forgiveness being taught or displayed. The most positive attribute I remember was one of pride in who we were and what we had materially.

> How prosperous Israel is—a luxuriant vine loaded with fruit. But the richer the people get, the more pagan altars they build. The more bountiful their harvests, the more beautiful their sacred pillars.
>
> —Hosea 10:1, NLT

Our family moved to a more illustrious neighborhood. This is when our home environment began to escalate into more destructive tendencies. My father began to make a higher income and his alcohol usage increased with it. There would be alcohol-based bouts of chaos on a continual basis. When circumstances deteriorated, my father began to yell loud vulgarities. There could be the opening, then slamming of every single kitchen cabinet door. He was tormented. We had to bear this tirade so often, as I tried to cover my ears with a pillow from the terrible sounds emanating up into my bedroom.

Psalm 139:5 says, *"You hem me in, behind and before, and lay your hand upon me."* This is saying the Lord is on every side of us; all around us. He is close to us continually. We are encompassed about with His complete knowledge and understanding. His hand is upon us, upholding us, and encircling our very beings. Nothing escapes His knowing eye.

Excluded

> *Drug yourselves so you feel nothing. Blind yourselves so you see nothing. Get drunk, but not on wine. Black out, but not from whiskey.*

> —Isaiah 29:9, MSG

My father would travel away sometimes when I was a young girl. By week's end he would come home surprising me with something special from his travels. He would come get me and bring me to the trunk of his car. I always looked with great anticipation of the goodies that laid in store for me. It might be a comic book or other treat.

Sometimes my dad would go to the middle of the street where all the neighborhood kids would gather and play games. One time he made up a game for us to play, dividing up teams; but he didn't include me. I was left out of the game while my friends were all included. I came inside our home tearfully explaining this to my mom. This was the first time I remember feeling injustice as well as persecution from my father. It was so hurtful to be left out by him on purpose.

The importance of fathers in society is significant. Our relationship with our father is how we first learn to relate to our heavenly Father who loves all His children securely. We are fully cherished by Him. We're not designed to be separated from this Triune life source. Separation, rejection, and loss of identity as a result of our earthly father's model can lead to self-hatred, fear, hostility, insecurity, and promiscuity. What we insatiably crave is the eternal, unconditional love of our earthly and heavenly Father.

In school I encountered an experience with a group of girls who formed a close clique but of which I wasn't a part. I believe everyone has experienced being snubbed in some way, child or adult. That feeling of exclusion is one most of us bury away deep inside. We may try to brush it off as if it doesn't affect us, but it is still there.

Exclusion prevents someone from doing something or being a part of a group, leaves someone out, infers that someone is not worth attention. Countries can bar other countries from entrance, just as families can shut out certain individuals. God created us for social interaction and intimacy.

Social studies have found that isolation causes premature death and impairs immune function, with the same comparative risk as a smoker or obesity.[1] A large part of the popularity of social media is due to loneliness; people are trying to find a connection.

> Look to the right and see: there is none who takes notice of me; no refuge remains to me; no one cares for my soul. I cry to you, O LORD; I say, "You are my refuge, my portion in the land of the living."
>
> —Psalm 142:4-5

The First Family

We read in Genesis 3 about the first family to hide secrets. It was Adam and Eve in an attempt to escape the shame they felt stripped naked. They ran into the outer garden looking for shelter to placate the loss of covering they felt. Before this catastrophic event, they were covered in God's glory. Now that light of divinity was vanquished from them because of their disobedience. Hiding behind bushes did not thwart God, who couldn't seem to locate their whereabouts at first. Genesis 3:9: *"But the Lord God called to the man and said to him, 'Where are you?'"*

It's not as if God didn't know; it's just that the communion between the two had been darkened. The lifeline of glory once brightly cascading around them had been cut off. The tangible glow that had emanated outward was cancelled out as the default of sin engaged. Satan's agenda devastated God's plan for fellowship, blessing, and protection.

Their diversion tactic called justification began the blame game. Adam blamed Eve, she blamed the snake, and the serpent got sacked, limbless to the dirt. Just like someone who's caught in a lie of deception, they looked for a way out by using people or circumstances to cast their guilt upon. They became immersed in a shame sauna of unholiness.

Eve's objective was outside of God's boundary of obedience. How unreasonable, she thought, of God not to allow their eyes to be opened to the good stuff. Why was He holding out on them? It must be awfully special to keep them from God's secret goodies. Our *all seeing* Light-giver saw the connection of light to those He loved was no longer visible.

Adam now saw himself at his very worst. Bewildered; his most vulnerable place! The safety net was relinquished. He no longer saw himself in God's image but in his own incapable, soured image. He was a lesser man, torn from his authority to rule and reign with Godly purpose. Eve was right there too. No fig leaf could cover the damage.

Even today, men and women choose to go their own pathway. We have been given extended options in our thinking. Unfortunately, it is usually focused within ourselves, holding us to the past mindset. We are also given the liberty for blessing or cursing by design. We have been given a key to unlock this mystery.

The Father promised a day when a Seed descending from the woman would "crush the head" of satan, destroying his work and reclaiming from him what had been stolen by treachery and deceit (Genesis 3:15). Business as usual, these are still satan's methods; nothing has changed since the beginning. But God's Triune meeting had a mysterious plan ahead.

Adam's presumptive contract overridden in the first person, the place of victory was now replaced by an unnatural vacancy on all levels. Imagine a place of purest love, security, and everlasting fulfillment. It had fallen down below their feet, the shackles of slavery taking its place. How utterly strange to feel loss, lost, and abandoned. Their dominance over the Earth had been taken captive. Led astray!

Lost forever it seemed, until a later Savior. They were their own betrayer headed up by *the betrayer of us all*. Confusion ensued as they were led out of that luxurious garden into an unnatural place of abode. They were set outside of those perfect boundaries.

The pinnacle of relationship had spiraled downward. Adam and Eve were shafted relationally and broken spiritually by their enemy—the same enemy who today seeks to break and tear in half relationships. In order to stay in that heartless shape, we willingly enter those hidden dark places of false covering. We need to dismiss those who demand our demise, along with their inventory of lies.

There is a way. We can be delivered of the weaknesses as well as destructive tendencies passed down to us generationally. Psalm 107:20 says, Jesus *"sent his word and healed them, and delivered them from their destruction."* In pure humility release them to the Lord, our life preserver. This will infuse within us a greater place of authoritative power in the Spirit.

> *A Man of sorrows and acquainted with grief. And we hid, as it were, our faces from Him; He was despised, and we did not esteem Him.*
>
> —Isaiah 53:3, NKJV

Jesus took upon Himself every disease and affliction as Matthew 4:23 accounts. He took the painful wrath of all we have gone through upon His living flesh. Whatever our particular need, Jesus already captured it, bearing our burdens and delivering us free from it by our faith in Him.

Never confuse Jesus Christ with religion. They are two separate entities all together. One focuses on a personal encounter of enduring intimacy while the other forces conformist rules of rigidity that one must perform to minute perfection. There is a thrust to trust without going bust on the backside of the desert. Draw near to our God and do not refuse Him.

> *She listens to no voice; she accepts no correction. She does not trust in the LORD; she does not draw near to her God.*
>
> —Zephaniah 3:2

Jesus doesn't beat us to the Cross; He woos us, ever calling our name to His remembrance, His most loved of all creation, you and me. He counts our plentiful hairs (or some not so plentiful). God longs to bring us His favor and blessings. He adoringly collects our most tender tears. Nothing is lost in His sight.

Who among you fears the LORD and obeys his servant? If you are walking in darkness, without a ray of light, trust in the LORD and rely on your God.

—Isaiah 50:10, NLT

Cosmos Question

For he knows our frame; he remembers that we are dust.

—Psalm 103:14

What started churning on the inside of me in my teenage years drove me to find some answers. Desperation pushed me to ask questions about life and existence.

Whirlwind Visions

I started having recurring images of a huge whirlwind in the atmosphere of my mind. I would see a rotating swirl of glowing white cloudlike material go past the stars and planets in the night. Sometimes, I would see people's faces who I knew counting back in time past from our generations of grandparents and their parents.

I was trying somehow to find how my life came from a starting point in time. Where did all the people in my lineage come from and how did life start. Who was there? Who started it all and how did "they" come into existence without being created themselves? You can't just "poof" into appearance?

Hebrews 11:3 says, *"By faith we understand that the universe was created by the word of God, so that what is **seen** was not made out of things that are **visible**"* (emphasis added). God commanded a thought and it became a formation; like a rocky mountain terrain. Those impacting vibrations coming out of His mouth made something new. The sky had no limits. The invisible became seen with a spoken syllable of reckoning.

It was mind-boggling. Many times as I closed my eyes, this whirlwind appeared taking me back through the cosmos of time. I kept searching the circular motions as the rings became smaller in the center. I was looking for that finite pinpoint. It continually provoked me. These visions seemed irritating and irrational; but the search continued.

I was groping for someone to heal all the hurt inside of me. I wanted to be loved; in a real way, the right way. The substitute of material things I'd received wasn't enough. Who would love me like a daughter needing to be loved? It brought me to my inner knees, rejecting the deception satan painted for me. The issues I had hidden in a deep well, what had intimidated me, I still never told a soul.

I wanted the truth: "*You will know the truth, and the truth will set you free*" (John 8:32). And that's when God got a hold of me. All the false pretense didn't matter. It served no purpose to heal my toothpick built façade. The shambles of my world had to crumble and then totally disintegrate into His reality. That was the start of living without falsehood.

Therefore we do not lose heart. Though outwardly we are wasting away, yet inwardly we are being renewed day by day. For our light and momentary troubles are achieving for us an eternal glory that far outweighs them all. So we fix our eyes not on what is seen, but on what is unseen. For what is seen is temporary, but what is unseen is eternal.

—2 Corinthians 4:16-18, NIV

Outer Visitations

> *A bruised reed he will not break, and a faintly burning wick he will not quench; he will faithfully bring forth justice. He will not grow faint or be discouraged till he has established justice in the earth; and the coastlands wait for his law.*
>
> —Isaiah 42:3-4

I quietly accepted the Lord as Savior right after my sixteenth birthday. A friend's church group went to stay at the Flagship Hotel in Galveston, Texas, for a weekend beach retreat. Not really comprehending what was going on during the retreat, some of us acted pretentious. When I got home, I took the information pamphlet about how to accept Christ as Lord. It was a no brainer.

In my bedroom alone, I would talk to the Lord about my private concerns. I pressed deeply into reading the Word of God from my new Bible, borne from a dire need for truth and comfort. The Bible, which had completely disinterested me before, had now come alive to my viewing.

I had an ornate lamp in my bedroom which held golden angels swinging around the middle of it. There were times I began to experience movement of large, glowing, outlined figures that were in close proximity to this lighted lamp. I had been reading about the visitation of angels and began to experience them for myself. This was a divine experience that reoccurred during a time of routine turbulences in our home, which distressed me. Knowing that the angels of the Lord were there to guard and protect me let me know I wasn't alone in the spiritual warfare around me.

God sent a neighbor to encourage me when I relayed to her a few things I was going through. One day she called and invited me to her church and spoke about the things of the Holy Spirit. I was enthralled about this new and different dimension of the *parakletos*, our Comforter. When I got off the phone, I came downstairs and sat on the third step from the bottom. All of a sudden I felt an impression toward my left side. I turned to look; on the stairway wall was Jesus staring right at me. The artist in me looked long enough to take in His olive facial tones, warm brown hair, gentle intense eyes, and long nose shape. He did not appear ugly to me, as I'd been told.

I jumped up from where I sat and began to circle my mother who was sitting square in the middle of our living room's high back chair, watching. I ran around her chair three times exclaiming loudly, "I know you think I'm crazy, but I just saw Jesus." My physical body was wrecked by the spiritual charge that was electrically flowing through me. I could not contain the magnificence of who Jesus was, right there in our home! I couldn't shake it off, so I rushed up the stairs where I'd just seen Jesus (not looking in His direction) and collapsed in my bed, covers high in shiver mode. That experience has stayed with me still to this day!

> For my father and my mother have forsaken me, but the LORD will take me in.

> —Psalm 27:10

Keeper of Secrets

> You are my hiding place; You shall preserve me from trouble; You shall surround me with songs of deliverance. Selah.…Many are the sorrows of the wicked, but steadfast love surrounds the

one who trusts in the LORD. Be glad in the LORD, and rejoice, O
righteous, and shout for joy, all you upright in heart!

—Psalm 32:7, 10-11

The only time I remember laughter and celebration in our home was when my parents threw a party. That's when the alcohol flowed everywhere. It was just another excuse to overindulge in excessive drinking. It turned my stomach, as it felt staged and fake. It wasn't a real celebration; it was a pretender's binge party.

One time the alcohol bouts had became so frequent that my mother was deeply concerned. We discussed the issue, and I came up with a plan. I remember telling my mom that we should get all the alcohol bottles in the house and garage and pour them all down the sink. We did it; then we disposed of the evidence in the outdoor trashcans. We filled an entire large trash container as it overflowed the top.

One afternoon my parents were fighting verbally. It was getting loud, and it seemed I heard scuffling. I heard the loud, crashing sound of a large decorative lamp downstairs. It was enough to get my attention as I hurriedly dashed downstairs. By the time I got down to our den, I saw my parents on the floor. My dad had his hands around my mother's neck, which sent shivers down my spine. I yelled at my dad to stop, but he did not let go. So I threatened to call the police, and then darted out of the front door running across the street to a neighbor's house to cry for help.

I sounded frantic at the front door of my neighbor's house. We waited until a police car drove by as things seemed to get real quiet. Eventually, jittery, I went back home. Our house was empty when I returned, all was silent. This was a shocking episode, as I felt scared and angry at the same time. It never happened again while I lived there.

Another time my girlfriend and I and my family went to a high-class private restaurant behind iron gates. We were in a secluded room while waiters came from everywhere. My father was very high on alcohol, laughing and carrying on with the exclusive wine list selections. We ordered our meals as I observed my father taking twenty dollar bills out of his wallet and tossing them around the room toward any server who got close. I was indignant at this; but my friend just laughed it off, which relaxed me somewhat. As soon as we finished our meal, I got out of there as fast as I could, driving separately from my parents.

Shortly after arriving home, my mother called me, using a desperate tone of voice. She said my father had given all their cash away from his wallet and had no credit cards. She asked me to retrieve a credit card she had and bring it back to the restaurant so they could leave. This prestigious restaurant asked our family to never come back again.

During my college years, when a guy came to our home I would try to make sure my dad was out of sight, as I didn't want my date to see my father drunk. I didn't want him to interact with them in any way because I didn't know what to expect from him. I didn't want the shameful drunken antics seen by my companion.

When my family took me out to eat for my birthday with a special date, I had to make a firm request that my father not drink while we were out. Though he was sober, it seemed a very stiff occasion without wine taking over the atmosphere. I remember having to tell my boyfriend that my dad drank too much. He almost backed out in coming, but I assured him that it would be all right and not to worry.

The eyes of the LORD are in every place, keeping watch on the evil and the good.

—Proverbs 15:3

Circle of Friends

As the mountains surround Jerusalem, So the LORD surrounds His people.

—Psalm 125:2

A minister spoke this to me:

> As you would see your circle of friends gathering around you, know that this is what I would want for you. I would ask you to take one person's hand and say, "God has chosen you to help me. I will allow you to help me in my walk." For as the hand is outstretched before you, it is like My own hand outstretched to you. You can get off your knees now and start rejoicing. Help is on the way. The change that you've asked me about is here. But it shall be smooth, so do not fear it.

A man of many companions may come to ruin, but there is a friend who sticks closer than a brother.

—Proverbs 18:24

Friendship is the depth someone will walk with you and not turn back. At the shoreline of the ocean, the waters are shallow. It would be very difficult to drown in a few inches of surf. But as you head toward the deeper waters of friendship, there is more susceptibility to the depth of conditions that are mysteriously inside.

Proverbs 27:6 tells us, *"Faithful are the wounds of a friend; profuse are the kisses of an enemy."* When a person bleeds, applying pressure will stop the bleeding. A true friend will be gut-level honest with you for your betterment. Be careful if people always agree with you because something is suspicious. Those who show one face to you and hide another are double minded. Don't be deceived.

C.S. Lewis said, "Is any pleasure on earth as great as a circle of Christian friends by a good fire?"[2] A good friend is truly priceless. We should seek those that will benefit our lives while we benefit theirs, too. Seek Godly twosome friendships that will stick to us for a lifetime.

Praying for friendships is vital; don't take them for granted. Pray for those who God wants in your life and those He knows will buffet you. I have known several people in my life whereby prayer saved their life, literally. One of them, a cancer survivor, became a kindred spirit whom I cherish to this day.

Philippians 2:3 says, *"Do nothing from rivalry or conceit, but in humility count others more significant than yourselves."* People who are out for their own great cause are not out for the Great Commission. Self-serving recognition, elevating oneself over others, and boasting are not Kingdom attributes. These attitudes divide relationships and churches.

Jesus taught us that true greatness is in laying down our life for another (John 15:3). We need to give up preconceived ideas contrary to God's Word. Pride causes people to want to be right regardless of the context. They will argue their way to rightness. It's a do or die battle of the mind.

Deceit is in the heart of those who devise evil, but those who plan peace have joy. No ill befalls the righteous, but the wicked are filled with trouble.

—Proverbs 12:20-21

We don't count anything as being our own, but we share what God has given us. Humility opens the door for character resources to develop. It builds the church into one unifying force. This is what will open new doors awaiting our entrance.

Therefore, as the elect of God, holy and beloved, put on tender mercies, kindness, humility, meekness, longsuffering; bearing with one another, and forgiving one another, if anyone has a complaint against another; even as Christ forgave you, so you also must do.

—Colossians 3:12-13

We Have What?

Does not the ear test words as the tongue tastes food?

—Job 12:11, NIV

I learned a humorous lesson about calling things into the here and now with my words that worked in a reverse situation. I remember feeling panic while searching frantically in our bathroom for a misplaced item. It's how we respond when we need something at a moment's notice, like a blow dryer with soaking wet hair and not being able to find it readily. After a lengthy search, I responded with a euphemism to express my exasperation.

Then it happened again in my bathroom area while getting upset over another dilemma. That's when I momentarily thought about my choice word for expressing myself. Then a third time I was on another hunt for something I needed quickly. But this time I heard the Holy Spirit caution me about speaking things that are not as though they were. I was calling things into existence that had not been before.

Within a few days after this third episode, I started to hear sounds in the ceiling above me in the bathroom. It sounded like scratching; only the sound was slowly migrating around above my head. How bizarre, what could that possibly be? I asked my husband to check out this weird situation. He grabbed his flashlight to investigate inside our attic.

I received the report from the evidence that he'd found for me. It was the thing I'd been calling out in the atmosphere of our bathroom; it had manifested right above our head in that specific vicinity of our home. My husband announced to me, "We have rats."

Rats in the natural world are unclean, vile critters that have been the carrier of plagues in past centuries. Spiritually, a rat can indicate a wicked person, a devourer, or a betrayer (as in someone "ratting out another"). See Proverbs 17:13.

Words portray pictures in our mind, which elicit feelings and emotions. They build our thought processes, ideas, and decision making for the future. When we are around negative words frequently, they can fracture into a disturbing pattern in our thinking. I needed a buffer zone from the disturbing words I'd heard and images I observed. The Word of God began to cushion me from the negativity while building up a reservoir in my thinking.

I believe it is absolutely true that we become a part of what we experience or we completely break free from it in absolute determination to change what we have come up against. I didn't despise my family, as I developed His love for them. I only wanted to be free from the consequences of that toxic environment.

We are to be imitators of God as His much loved children. The Word doesn't say to imitate those who were raised by the conditions of men. The highest standard is always found in the Word of God. That is our reasonable service to live by for a reality change. I was a virtual candidate for righteous change.

In Isaiah 6:1-6 is an account of the prophet Isaiah with the Lord while He was sitting on His throne. It's significant that the Lord's robe is seen as filling the entire temple; just as the Lord should fill our entire being. Jesus embodies the temple wall to wall. Above Him, seraphim are flying around.

Each seraph or "burning one" has three sets of two wings. One set is to cover their faces, the other to cover their feet, and two were for flying. These celestial beings made blasting sounds that shook the temple entirely, causing it to fill with smoke.

> *And they were calling to one another: "Holy, holy, holy is the LORD Almighty; the whole earth is full of his glory.*
>
> —Isaiah 6:3, NIV

As Isaiah observed this scene, he responded: "*'Woe to me!' **I cried**. 'I am ruined! For I am a man of unclean lips, and I live among a people of unclean lips, and my **eyes** have seen the King, the LORD Almighty'*" (Isaiah 6:5, NIV, emphasis added). Whereby, one of the fiery angels flew to Isaiah with a living coal that touched his mouth. The heavenly seraphim then said in verse 7, "*See, this has touched your lips; your guilt is taken away and your sin atoned for*" (NIV).

Once Isaiah's sins were cleansed, his ears became open to the voice of the Lord. The King is looking for a choice group of people He can send out as His representatives. Isaiah is ever ready to be used, responding in verse 8, "*Here am I. Send me!*" (NIV). What does the Almighty Father convey to that generation of people that looks like us now?

> *Be ever hearing, but never understanding; be ever seeing, but never perceiving. Make the heart of this people calloused; make their ears dull and close their eyes. Otherwise they might see with their eyes, hear with their ears, understand with their hearts, and turn and be healed.*

> —Isaiah 6:9-10, NIV

Playtime is over! It is time to get hooked into the present with open eyes and ears. We are long overdue for the grandstand of seasons presiding over us now. The seraphim are flying above us preparing the last, great harvest. The canopy of darkness we see is calling us out with intensely held, blasting, brilliant torches. The Light is coming for the entire world to see.

Imagine oneself as a lamp that needs electricity (the source) to perform its function of producing light in every direction. When plugged into an outlet, we receive current (information) that functions (produces of its kind) when the switch is turned on. Like an LED light, it produces an efficient, cool, long-lasting light source. If the light source is poor quality or worn out, it produces a dim light that makes it difficult to see visibly or discern images.

> *Whoever desires to love life and see good days, let him keep his tongue from evil and his lips from speaking deceit; let him turn away from evil and do good; let him seek peace and pursue it. For the **eyes** of the Lord are on the righteous, and his **ears** are*

open to their prayer. But the face of the Lord is against those who do evil.

—1 Peter 3:10-12

Butterfly Beater Dream, 8.28.2014

To set the mind on the flesh is death, but to set the mind on the Spirit is life and peace.

—Romans 8:6

My initial dream view highlighted a small rectangular pond filled with magnificently exquisite, large-winged butterfly insects in various rich colors with glorious detail.

There were two predominant butterflies at the back left side of the pond. They were twice as large as the other butterflies. I was amazed at their splendor and beauty. The reflecting light bending on their scales produced an amazing sight. One butterfly was blue turquoise in color and the other, to its right, was a medium blue shade.

The two grand butterflies began a commotion and started to beat their wings against one another. I discovered an unusual attribute in butterfly behavior; they're not always peaceful. They will fight each other over a warm, sunny spot of territory. The butterflies ensued in battling it out.

I could not bear to watch the dual and turned my head away. After a short time, I turned my head back to see the conclusion. The medium blue butterfly sank to its death, out of sight. The turquoise one was lying inside a semitransparent plastic cup.

I carefully picked up the plastic cup with a stick, as the butterfly fell out of it like hot butter into the murky waters below.

I have always associated butterflies in a positive view, so this was very disturbing for me. Colors in dreams can have a Spirit dominate view or a soulish viewpoint. The turquoise or aqua light blue is interpreted on the negative side as a strong willed characteristic. Basic blue is likewise interpreted with depression, sorrow, and anxiety.

The butterflies were circumvented with strongholds that caused a caustic reaction. Despite their outward adornment, nervous anxieties and a strong-willed nature were victoriously put to death. Their earthly, vainglory was no longer visible as the Spirit life prevailed.

These characteristics used to be prevalent in my life. It has taken literally decades, but I no longer succumb to severe sorrows or rampant anxiety, as I rely all upon Christ the majority of the time. My strong-willed nature has a better cause entrusted into His insights. Let's lean into the Lord for our virtual reality of life, steeped into His goodness, knowing what is best for us every moment.

1 Corinthians 14:20

Brothers, do not be children in your thinking. Be infants in evil, but in your thinking be mature.

CHAPTER TWO

Hide and Seek

*When the godly succeed, everyone is glad. When the wicked take charge, people go into **hiding**.*

—Proverbs 28:12, NLT

Moving On

For everything there is a season, and a time for every matter under heaven.

—Ecclesiastes 3:1

I was able to avoid the tyrannical atmosphere of our home after I transferred to a university in another city my junior year. I was relieved to leave the negatively-charged environment behind. I wanted to have some fun as I tried to escape the built-in memories inside of me.

When I came home to visit on weekends, my mother told me of how my father kept control of all the money, not allowing her to purchase groceries until right before I showed up. That's when the pantry shelves became full and all looked normal on the outside again.

She told me how my brothers were pushed in the bathtub one night and kicked by my father. She refused to tell me everything; only that things had gotten worse since I left. I wasn't there to witness the dreadful conditions and was grateful to be away from it.

> Don't define yourself in a picture of your past. You have new adventures, so know this won't last. I'll see to it that you leave this place. Don't worry nor panic! Don't you see? Just lean on Me for all you need. So gather your strength, your fortunes won't shrink. Don't quit now! No hurry or squeeze. Tomorrow will take care of itself. Don't be concerned for the future, as I have the keys. The answer of course is found in Me. I'm a Servant to all and delight in your needs. I'll prepare you and wake you, when the time is right. So straighten your desk, keep things real tight. I'll define this all later; just don't squander your dollars.

> —A rhyming word from the Lord to me

Therefore go out from their midst, and be separate from them, says the Lord, and touch no unclean thing; then I will welcome you.

—2 Corinthians 6:17

Man Cave/Woman Cave

There he came to a cave and lodged in it. And behold, the word of the LORD came to him, and he said to him, "What are you doing here, Elijah?"

—1 Kings 19:9

Elijah was not in the right place at the right time. He was having a supersize pity party. Elijah did not come to the cave to meet with God but to complain of his task and circumstances. Elijah replied in verse 10, "*I have zealously served the LORD God Almighty. But the people of Israel have broken their covenant with you, torn down your altars, and killed every one of your prophets. I am the only one left, and now they are trying to kill me, too*" (NLT).

The Lord told Elijah to get out of that dark cave and "*go out and stand on the mount before the LORD*" (v. 11). Jesus generously showed Elijah how to hear Him. He wasn't to be found in the noise of rocks cracking, or wind howling, or a fiery earthquake. He was found in the soft, gentle breezes. And the Lord told Elijah to go back where he started, return to where he should be and finish his assignment (vv. 11-12, 15).

In Bible days, caves were typically holes in the ground built as tombs to enshrine the dead as a burial site. Caves were a hideaway for the dead, not the living. Life was over for those that had passed on; it was now a place of darkness.

When we hear the expression today of a "man cave" or woman's, it may cause a chuckle. We can *veg out* undetected. However, in our story in 1 Samuel 30, it's not a desirable place for David and his fighting men.

The foundation of our story finds David's hideout in a darkened hollow. He was reeling from emotions ranging from anger to distressing depression. His own men were contemplating stoning him because they were bitterly grieved over the loss of their families who had been ambushed. While David was away from his home, their enemy torched their beloved city to the ground. They took hostages including everything they possessed. This onslaught grieved David's soul, as the assault was aimed intimately at him. In his terms, it was an invasion of the Kingdom of God.

David and the men with him lifted up their voices and wept until they had no more strength to weep. David's two wives also had been taken captive, Ahinoam the Jezreelitess and Abigail, the widow of Nabal the Carmelite. David was greatly distressed, for the men spoke of stoning him because the souls of them all were bitterly grieved, each man for his sons and daughters. But David encouraged and strengthened himself in the Lord his God."

—1 Samuel 30:4-6, AMP

What turned it around were David's directed emotions, making a choice decision to lift the situation up toward the Lord as he both encouraged and strengthened himself in his Jehovah God.

David did not stay in a rut, but turned himself over to the Lord instead. That was the smartest thing he did. We can revitalize the present by pressing into the future. He allowed God to enter his dilemma. The best part is the Lord answered him right then. The answer was clear in verse 8 saying, *"Pursue, for you shall surely overtake them and without fail **recover all**"* (AMP, emphasis added). Now that's a restorative promise!

Restitution is the act of restoring to the rightful owner something that has been taken away, lost, or surrendered.[1] This is an incredible promise to receive. So, take it for the virtue it is in whatever life's situation is right now.

We can stand to benefit by posturing ourselves to be in the same position to RECOVER ALL!

1. In the midst of our trials we must seek God first.
2. God has the answer we need for the losses, turmoil, and injustices we experience.

David deliberately decided to cast himself over to the Lord. Instead of allowing others to beat him up mentally, he let his faith take over. The best place to build faith is in the Word of God. He spoke to himself what he should give place to in his thoughts. He had an intellectually spiritual discourse with himself.

Have you ever called out your name, and then started speaking something out loud? You might say something like, "Margaret, how in the world did you forget to pick up the laundry?" Even better would be, "Ms. Content, you are highly favored of God." So, David chose to pick the right thoughts for himself, choosing NOT to get bitter. He alone leveraged himself towards God. In verse 7 the ephod (equivalent of our Bible) was brought to him as he inquired of God's Word. It lifted him above his circumstances.

There is a difference between the source of the attack and its effect on us. We must determine in advance which direction to go. God is our guide, so seek Him as such. David sought the Word for encouragement like a champion. He was not performing, but living truth for the fruit of life.

If someone tries to prevent your success, don't drop out, get engaged. We are *more* than conquerors through Christ Jesus: "*No, despite all these things, overwhelming victory is ours through Christ, who loved us*" (Romans 8:37, NLT)

Bitterness is like cancer to the soul. It stores itself in human jars and remains there until we pour it out. We must get it out for God's pure refreshing to pour in. Remember, oil and vinegar don't mix. They can't combine; they stay separate. So make a choice—the oil of the Holy Spirit or the sourness of the world. Stay connected to Christ, His Word, and the Holy Ghost to overcome adversity.

> *Men will go into caves of the rocks And into holes of the ground*
> *Before the terror of the LORD And the splendor of His majesty,*
> *When He arises to make the earth tremble.*

—Isaiah 2:19, NASB

Acid Hole

> *Though evil is sweet in his mouth And he **hides** it under his tongue, Though he desires it and will not let it go, But holds it in his mouth.*

—Job 20:12-13, NASB

While attending a healing conference a few years ago, I saw an image in my mind.

Acid Hole Vision

I envisioned an enormously enlarged white tooth with a huge black "cavity" inside of its carved-out center. I saw a tiny black silhouette of a person on top of the tooth's outer edge who began to teeter, falling inside this black hole of "captivity."

Notice the parallel in spelling and meaning in "cavity" and "captivity." I quickly drew a picture in my notes of what I was seeing.

Later, I looked up "cavity," which can be an empty or hollow space or a pit in a tooth, commonly produced by decay. This hole can grow bigger and deeper over time. It's a body cavity, but more commonly refers to holes or "structural" damage in the teeth.[2] Also, having a low PH level (acidic) is an *unhealthy, weakened state causing susceptibility to decay.*[3] *Acids* have character attributes like the quality of being sour, sharp, or biting; as in an acidic reaction.[4]

Think about the Body of Christ relating to the hollowed out cavity and the affect of acids, spiritually. Acidity in the human body is an *unbalanced condition* just as it can lead to the susceptibility of diseases in the Body of Christ, the church. Acids are a symbol of destructive words that burn long after they have been spoken.[5]

These "acids" demineralize (break down) tooth structure (enamel, cementum, and dentin). Dental caries or cavities are the result of bacterial processes that change carbohydrates (sugars) left on teeth to acid.[6] Spiritually, acids represent sin that breaks us down leaving incriminating evidence in its place. The darkened depression left compromises what we're intended for with a mission specific to our purpose and function.

I believe the sugar or carbs left on the teeth represent the lust of the flesh we have indulged in our soulish (mind, will, emotions) areas. We may feel justified for feeling the way we do, so it remains on the teeth without being flossed, cleansed, or rinsed away. It stays with us, while we pay the price *unnoticed* to our senses.

Symptoms: There may be no symptoms! What? No symptoms to indicate the existence of something carving away our pearly whites! Destructive stuff is happening and no one is paying attention to it. Structural damage is being done without any known invasiveness. We are losing our protective enamel like a broken shield as people are falling victim to these divisive holes in their spiritual armor (teeth).

We can also lose our resistance to decay relating to Christ's Body. We must pray for discernment in this arena. It's a new battle for us; as we engage ourselves we can use potent strategies to win. The power of discernment and yielding to Christ's Spirit is essential to unravel the powers of darkness in our coming future generations.

Remember that acids wreck havoc on the enamel of our teeth producing a weakened state of being. God put enamel on our teeth for protection against the corrosive effects around them. When these negative elements aren't washed away, flossed out, and cleansed with toothpaste; then corrosion sets in, creating hollow black holes. This acidic state of sin spiritually destroys our healthy foundation.

As Christ's ambassadors, we have gotten out of sync, unable to detect or recognize an eroding acidic condition right in front of us. We may not realize our lack of sensitivity to discern these symptoms. Unintended destruction is silently maneuvering itself in the white structures of our soul, hearts, and nation. It's time to remove those devices that are penetrating a people who have harvested black holes.

Lord, help us discern the full dimension of the symptoms afflicting us today. No matter the extent, proportion, reason, range, or scope of undetected sins; give us insight now, so we don't take our brothers and sisters in an unholy place we've unknowingly permitted. Remove us from the prostitution of slavery we've allowed ourselves to fall into unwittingly. Let us not succumb to the harm and depletion of corrupt living. Take away the bondages that have kept us captive. As we've allowed resentments, harshness, brutality, viciousness, caustic words, cutting remarks, hatred, irreverence, anger, bitter begrudging, scorn, offenses, ridicule, mocking, abuse, or cynicism to creep into our lives, absorb them away from us and set us free to love each other as Christ loves us. We honor You as Judge and Lord. Let us never pass this way again. We thank You, Lord, for a permanent deliverance from all filthy works of the flesh, knowing we must be washed from all toxicity daily in our walk. Restore our minds anew from the ravages of polluted ways and indulgences! We are new creatures designed to live new purposeful ways. We have been separated to live a distinct destiny of strength in Christ today!

Read in Isaiah 42:22: "*But this is a people robbed and plundered; they are all of them snared in* **holes** *[the cavity of captivity] and* **hidden** *in houses of bondage. They have become a prey, with no*

*one to deliver them, a spoil, with no one to say, **Restore them!***"
(AMP, emphasis added)

To be SNARED is something that serves to entangle the unwary, to trap them.

What are these people NOT getting? The ability to recognize the Lord in the day of His visitation. They aren't interested in hearing His voice. To hear Him means they would be responsible for what they heard. They plug up their hearing processes. They get busy, numb themselves, add noise, get distracted, and then conceal themselves from discovery. They don't want to know what He's saying. They have lost sight of the message, rejecting Christ, unable to notice their rotting condition or plight.

> *And when he drew near and saw the city, **he wept over it**, saying, "Would that you, even you, had known on this day the things that make for peace! But now they are **hidden from your eyes**. For the days will come upon you, when your enemies will set up a barricade around you and surround you and hem you in on every side and tear you down to the ground, you and your children within you. And they will not leave one stone upon another in you, because you did not know the time of your visitation."*

—Luke 19:41-44, emphasis added

Scripturally, we must remove the black shades off our eyes to be able to see what Christ is seeing. With His eyesight all cloudiness and distortions are removed. Then we must unplug our ears from the waxes of the world that have hampered our ability to know the voice of the Lord. His voice of distinction has a sound like no other. There's a reverberation that's been designed into our spirit to recognize His voice as supreme above all else. We can flow in that significant variance to be Christ's active agents of sight and sound.

Poison Pockets

> *So that there will not be among you a man or woman, or family or tribe, whose heart turns away today from the LORD our God, to go and serve the gods of those nations; that there will not be among you a root bearing poisonous fruit and wormwood.*

> —Deuteronomy 29:18, NASB

There was a time I began to have various health issues. It wasn't about one area, but included female issues as well. It seemed to be a combination of things that made me not feel right. What distressed me the most was terrible acute acne on my face and chin that caused hard inflamed boils to develop. It would take months for them to clear up, and then they would reappear in another spot.

On a spiritual note, acne can be the underground affect from issues with fear of mankind. It boils up on our face, neck, and chin as an attribute to a physical condition festering from within. I believe this was a part of the issue, along with an acidic diet and yeast overgrowth.

I sought the Lord for the right healing pathway for me. I prayed, searched, and waited. A friend of mine had been healed of cancer twice; once by traditional surgery, but the second time through a technical device called an electro-dermal machine that determined the body's levels of normal or out of normal ranges. She told me the name of her research scientist contact who had helped her.

I decided to make an appointment and get a thorough test done. Our testing took half a day, with time for inquisitive questions. By the end of our session, I was told that my body toxicity age range was that of an eighty-two-year-old woman. I was in my early forties, but I had double the normal toxicity levels expected in someone my age.

It was explained that I had around sixteen hidden "trash cans" in various sites inside of my body where the toxicities that my immune system was unable to handle were stored away. This information scared me. I was prepared to do what was required to get rid of these festering silent bombs of poison locked out of sight.

The first appointment I made was with my dentist. We had all the ancient, deteriorated fillings removed, and then replaced them with a new material that tested safe for my body. I had a wonderful dentist who took the time and care to do the process of protected removal, cleaning, and checking everything out in advance. He answered all of my questions and put my mind at ease.

I was given an assortment of homeopathic concoctions and other remedies to help speed up this cleansing process. With this program and another one I'd been working on with another doctor, I began a slow recovery of health. I stuck to the regiment for a year and a half. By the end of it, I was retested and it was determined that my toxicity level was around the range of an eighteen-year-old.

Those hidden pockets of poison had evaporated. Whatever painful pocket you may carry inside, release it to our heavenly Father. Don't hold onto it, as it only gets progressively worse. Let go of bitterness, indignation, or any destructive attitude or behavior. Be rightness conscious. Hold onto Christ, our Redeemer Deliverer.

The people of the city said to Elisha, "Look, our lord, this town
is well situated, as you can see, but the water is bad and the

land is unproductive." "Bring me a new bowl," he said, "and put salt in it." So they brought it to him. Then he went out to the spring and threw the salt into it, saying, "This is what the LORD says: 'I have healed this water. Never again will it cause death or make the land unproductive.'" And the water has remained pure to this day, according to the word Elisha had spoken.

—2 Kings 2:19-22, NIV

Jesus Could Not Be Hidden

Not even Jesus could hide Himself! In Mark 7:24 Jesus entered the borders of Tyre and Sidon into the house of a *certain* woman. It was Jesus' desire that no one know where He was. He desired privacy and rest. But the Word says, "*He could not be hid*" (KJV, emphasis added).

If Jesus, who had all possible options open to Him, could not even hide His whereabouts, how can you and I possibly think we could hide anything in our lives from the Lord Almighty? He can penetrate anything in His creation knowing the substance from which we are made. Don't be found trying to hide in a baggage claims area, such as we read in 1 Samuel 10:22. Be found on your knees of heartfelt surrender.

*So they asked the LORD, "Where is he?" And the LORD replied, "He is **hiding** among the baggage.*

—1 Samuel 10:22, NLT, emphasis added

Some may hide from a sense of guilt or unworthiness. As the scripture above says, this man was *found* hiding in the present stuff of life; a place where people shove all their lost belongings together in an abandoned, dingy space. Jesus could still find him underneath all that debris of not being good enough. Jesus finds us out every time.

> You are **the light of the world.** A city set on a hill **cannot be hidden.** Nor do people light a lamp and put it under a basket, but on a stand, and it gives light to all in the house. In the same way, let your light shine before others, so that they may see your good works and give glory to your Father who is in heaven.

—Matthew 5:14-16, emphasis added

Hebrew Holes

In 1 Samuel 13, it tells the story of Saul fighting the Philistines. In his second reigning year, he chose three thousand men in Israel. Two thousand were with Saul in Michmash, meaning "hidden place," and the hill country of Bethel, and a thousand were with Saul's son Jonathan (God-given) in Gibeah. The rest of the people he sent home, every man to his tent. Jonathan had remarkably defeated the garrison of the Philistines that was at Geba, and the Philistines heard of it. And Saul blew the trumpet throughout the land, saying, *"Let the Hebrews **hear"*** (v. 3, emphasis added).

> And the Philistines mustered to fight with Israel, thirty thousand chariots and six thousand horsemen and troops like the sand of the seashore in multitude. They came up and encamped in Michmash.

—1 Samuel 13:5

The people were called together to Saul in Gilgal. As well, the Philistines gathered themselves together to fight Israel as a mob of well-equipped fighting machines. The Philistines were

47

disposed to metal making and swords, unlike the unprepared Israelites. Thus they had an arsenal of weaponry, while the Jews had only inferior farming tools at their disposal.

The Israelites thought their king would have solved all their problems, not realizing they had rejected the King of kings. The dwindling people, who followed Saul, trembled in fear because they lost sight of the One they could trust. The people fled in panic, venturing out into the countryside for a place to hide themselves. Even the most courageous men stole away from camp thinking this was a miserable venture.

> *When the men of Israel saw that they were in trouble (for the people were hard pressed), the people hid themselves in **caves** and in **holes** and in **rocks** and in **tombs** and in **cisterns**.*

> —1 Samuel 13:6, emphasis added

The Israelites were moved by what they observed. The commanding force of chariots, horsemen, and foot soldiers eclipsed the landscape everywhere they could see. They expected destruction! So they fled, not in faith but in absolute surrender to terror. They trapped themselves by hiding in dark and broken places as self-imposed prisoners.

They hid in **caves** (*marah*), which means "dark hole" in Hebrew; and **holes** (*chor*), a cavity, socket, or den. Isaiah 42:22 tells us, "*But this is a people plundered and looted; they are all of them **trapped in holes** and **hidden in prisons**; they have become plunder with none to rescue, spoil with none to say, 'Restore!'*" (emphasis added). Where has their Restorer gone? He was expelled from His Kingship for a human king. Those are bad odds!

Rock, in Hebrew (*cela*), is defined as lofty, a craggy rock (a fortress) or stronghold. The terrain in this region is full of broken, treacherous rock formations infiltrating the countryside.

> *Other seeds fell on **rocky ground**, where they did not have much soil, and immediately they sprang up, since they had no depth of soil, but when the sun rose they were scorched. And since they had no root, they withered away.*
>
> —Matthew 13:5-6, emphasis added

Tomb, in Hebrew (*qeburah*), means a grave for burial—not a place for the living but the dying. There is no hope for the future. A person's life has expired.

> *Woe to you, scribes and Pharisees, hypocrites! For you are like whitewashed **tombs**, which outwardly appear beautiful, but within are full of dead people's bones and all uncleanness.*
>
> —Matthew 23:27

Cisterns, Hebrew (*baar*), are pits or wells. Jeremiah 2:13 says, "*My people have committed two evils: they have forsaken me, the fountain of living waters, and hewed out **cisterns** for themselves, broken **cisterns** that can hold no water*" (emphasis added). Cisterns are receptacles built for holding water. People worshipped the object of their hands instead of the Creator who gave them the materials for such things. They made an idol out of it then worshiped their results. A broken cistern can hold nothing, it's worthless.

In 1 Samuel 13:7-10 it tells how the people lost confidence in their appointed king. Saul's army was damaged and disarmed because of their inadequate tools to fight. The spoilers (Philistines) came to overtake the land from three directions and the land became wasted. To make matters worse, Saul decided to take upon himself the sacred role of a priest out of haste and impatience. His prideful ambition to gain the glory reserved for God got the better of him. Samuel the priest shows up after the sacrifice was finished.

Samuel made it quite clear the consequences were abominable: *"'How foolish!' Samuel exclaimed. 'You have not kept the command the LORD your God gave you. Had you kept it, the LORD would have established your kingdom over Israel forever'"* (v. 13. NLT). Samuel then reveals Saul's replacement God had prepared in His own house.

> But now your kingdom shall not continue. **The LORD has sought out a man after his own heart**, and the LORD has commanded him to be prince over his people, because you have not kept what the LORD commanded you.
>
> —1 Samuel 13:14, emphasis added

Spoiler Dream, 8.15.90

I did not want to include this dream, but the Holy Spirit kept urging me.

> Look! Here I stand at the door and knock. If you **hear me calling** and open the door, I will come in, and we will share a meal as friends.
>
> —Revelation 3:20, NLT, emphasis added

This dream was set at a camp that I'd come to visit with some friends. There was a female minister present who was very pregnant. I asked someone how far along she was, and they answered, "In about a week and a half." This pregnancy was of a spiritual connotation.

I looked around the room containing a long banquet table nicely prepared with garnished food. Oddly, I noticed several large roaches floating in the punch bowl and in the food preparations. I yanked on the sleeve of the man in charge to show him what I saw. He responded, "Don't worry, they've been there awhile." I thought to myself, "How gross! It's still disgusting and dirty."

I looked up at the west wall closest to the entrance of this facility. Right at the beginning of the banquet table marched an army of roaches and bugs in military style order crawling in masses toward the banquet table.

In a flash vision I saw my hand holding a cup of water with a roach floating on top. That did it; I had to find out what it meant, as there was nothing on the subject in my dream material.

Then Jesus said to his host, "When you give a luncheon or dinner, do not invite your friends, your brothers or sisters, your relatives, or your rich neighbors; if you do, they may invite you back and so you will be repaid. But when you give a banquet, invite the poor, the crippled, the lame, the blind."

—Luke 14:12-14, NIV

This particular banquet in Luke speaks of the rich elite who rejected Jesus' invitation. They made excuses not to participate in His presence, which was a grave insult socially. Those with no significance, as common people, were invited instead. Those that needed deliverance and healing were the focal point. All people groups are in this category regardless of wealth.

Roaches are unclean pests that live in dark places, representing hidden sin. They can make hissing noises; and are defined by large bulging eyes with an offensive odor. They are one of the most resilient insects on the planet, surviving on limited human food resources. They can transport microbes that can potentially lead to allergenic asthma symptoms in people. Pregnant females will scavenge around for out-of-sight, protected crevices in which to insert their eggs. Adult roaches can even survive with their heads decapitated. A light (truth) turned on in a room will cause them to scurry and scamper to avoid the intrusiveness, seeking escape routes undercover.[7]

The Lord revealed to me they are "spiritual spoilers" of the fruit of the Spirit. A spoiler is one who has little or no chance of winning, but is capable of *depriving a rival of success*. It is also defined as "a long narrow plate along the upper surface of a plane that may be raised for reducing *lift and increasing drag*." On a car a spoiler can *reduce lift* off the road at high speeds.[8]

> *Now the works of the flesh are evident: sexual immorality, impurity, sensuality, idolatry, sorcery, enmity, strife, jealousy, fits of anger, rivalries, dissensions, divisions, envy, drunkenness, orgies, and things like these. I warn you, as I warned you before, that those who do such things will not inherit the kingdom of God.*
>
> —Galatians 5:19-21

So, roaches represent "fruit spoilers" of our character as demonstrated in our behavior. The price of forgiveness is spoiled when we rail on each other viciously. We serve tainted food and drink while polluting the Body of Christ with these contaminants. The spoiled fruit they deliver can misguide even church leaders.

We can't allow ourselves to be cut off from the Holy Spirit's operation of fruitfulness. Be willing to be infused by His immersion of love and grace. We can only thrive with living nourishment in the Word of God. We can no longer malign one another, as that deprives us of hope. We are relievers of burdens, builders of destiny, and healers in faith by love, the fruit of the Spirit.

*On this mountain the LORD of hosts will make for all peoples a feast of rich food, a feast of well-aged wine, of rich food full of marrow, of aged wine well refined. And he will swallow up on this mountain the **covering that is cast over all peoples**, the **veil that is spread over all nations**.*

—Isaiah 25:6-7, emphasis added

*He will swallow up death forever! The Sovereign **LORD will wipe away all tears**. He will remove forever all insults and mockery against his land and people. The LORD has spoken! In that day the people will proclaim, "This is our God! We trusted in him, and he saved us! This is the LORD, in whom we trusted. Let us rejoice in the salvation he brings!"*

—Isaiah 25:8-9, NLT, emphasis added

God is uncovering buried, rebel waste places for our benefit, not our detriment. We were destined to destroy works of wickedness, release the captives, and set at liberty all that are blinded. It is time to clean up the opposing operations of the flesh in our lives. We must have something to give back, not live for our own personal agenda. We are meant to transport the glory of God from within and spread it out to the upcoming generation. We are to bombard the gates of hell wide open. The description of God swallowing up the hidden veil spread over all nations is magnificent. God is on the move to remove all vile things from existence. Tears will leave us, along with all injustices, insults, and mocking.

Let's agree today that the roaches that once were active in our life walk are no longer alive in our fruit of the Beloved. I speak death to every contaminating cockroach that has invaded any of the affairs of our life! Let's dispose of those filthy perversions,

take them to the garbage can, and send them off to the inciner-
ators. Let His royal fruit come, sustain, and remain within us.

*And just as my Father has granted me a kingdom, I now grant
you the right to eat and drink at my table in my Kingdom. And
you will sit on thrones, judging the twelve tribes of Israel.*

—Luke 22:29-30, NLT

Come Out of Your Hole

*Seek the LORD while he may be found; call upon him while he
is near.*

—Isaiah 55:6

In I Samuel 14:1-10 we read where Jonathan took his armor-
bearer (his confidant) to check out the enemy camp of
Philistines, hoping the Lord would be with him. His father, Saul,
and his 600 brave men were resting on their laurels under a
tree at their camp in Migron. As Jonathan silently left their site,
he crossed over into their enemy's camp following a revelatory
plan. If the Philistines urged them to climb up to them to where
they were, that would be a sign from the Lord that the enemy
would be given into their hands.

These two men alone revealed themselves to the huge Philistine outpost. When they made themselves known to the Philistine garrison: *"The Philistines said, 'Look! The Hebrew's are
coming out of the holes in which they hid themselves'"* (v. 11).

What the Philistine's meant by *hiding in holes* was they were
"chicken"; too fearful to come out in the open and fight like men.
In essence they are calling them cowards. In foolish arrogance,
they asked both men to come up to them and they would teach

them a lesson. Surprisingly, the Philistines fell down prostrate before Jonathan (v. 13).

I love verse 15: *"Then panic struck the whole army—those in the camp and field, and those in the outposts and raiding parties—and the ground shook. It was a panic sent by God"* (NIV). Then Saul caught on, watching as the enemy camp jolted away in every direction. Even better, some Hebrews who had been with the Philistine camp (deserters) now went back to the Israelites to fight with them. All the Israelites who had **hidden** themselves in the hill country joined the battle in hot pursuit. So the Lord rescued Israel that day! (vv. 16-23).

We can see Jonathan, who left the protection of a large camp to venture out alone seeking God's will. Some may be considering leaving a secure situation to set out in a new direction. Don't recoil backwards looking back over your shoulder in trepidation or dread. God honored Jonathan's faith and rewarded his actions.

It's not the size of our enemy we are dealing with, but the size of our God. The various enemies in our life may seem to be thwarting or overwhelming our thoughts to the task. Pressures can build in us, ultimately causing us to want to hide from everything. We may want to abandon our post before getting started. We must put all of our trust in the Lord from the get-go. We cannot fail with our full reliance on the Lord of hosts. We need to designate Jehovah as the Captain of our soul and let Him guide us instructively, step-by-step.

> *From the ends of the earth, I cry to you for help when my heart is overwhelmed. Lead me to the towering rock of safety.*
>
> —Psalm 61:2, NLT

Getting Hitched

*Does a young woman forget her jewelry? Does a bride **hide** her wedding dress? No! Yet for years on end my people have forgotten me.*

—Jeremiah 2:32, NLT, emphasis added

When I was twenty-six, I went to a large church helping as a young adult with a youth group. I had a good paying job, a rented condo, and a "sweet" sports car to drive. Everything seemed to be falling into place. I was ready for a husband and kept it at the top of my prayer list. I found out about a man from the pulpit who was going to be a youth pastor. I heard his name spoken from the speaker and wondered who he was. I went over to the youth section and asked who this guy was, and someone pointed him out.

A short time later the youth leaders and volunteers went out after service to eat together. This was my first time to have a real conversation with the one whom I would later marry. I had a mutual male friend with me who observed our close interaction that night. From this point on, I will refer to him as Fred (not his real name; in order to protect the innocent, as they say).

Upon leaving, my close friend decided to question the veracity of this new acquaintance. While we were sitting in my car about to leave, he asked Fred exactly what his intentions were. The response was not exactly what I wanted, sounding somewhat elusive. He might have thought it confrontational or shocking. But I was flattered that my friend spoke up for me.

A short time later I had a unique dream I call:

Hands-Dirt-Bridge-Tree-Bird Dream

I saw hands digging in the ground. Then I saw a shovel digging up the ground more efficiently. As the hole grew deeper I saw a bridge being uncovered from a side view. It contained large stones at the base. The bridge railings were made from people instead of metal or wood. They stood at the outer edges of the bridge floor on either side. They were there as lookers and observers of what was happening around the crossing bridge.

The dream changed its course somewhat when the digging ended. The dirt pile grew upward into the shape of a half-part rainbow. At the top of this dirt heap was a barren tree (not having any fruit). To the side of the dirt rainbow was a large black crow that came to sit on the tree. The tree seemed to have no roots (not grounded in the Word of God or stable).

I saw a smaller blue bird fly to the tree and sit next to the large black crow. The blue bird plucked two of the crow's black tail feathers out and opened its mouth to allow the two feathers to fall to the ground, one at a time. The crow flew off.

I believe the understanding of this will become clearer later in the proceeding chapters, as it eventually did for me. The crow represents a spirit of confusion and can refer to an outspoken individual. Isaiah 34:11 says, "*The raven shall dwell in it: and he shall stretch out upon it the line of confusion, and the stones of emptiness*" (KJV).

When you put blue and bird together it describes a revelatory spirit that can fly to higher heights. The two different birds were completely opposite of one another in what they represented.

Fred and I had a season of dating followed by a December wedding. There was something that bothered me right from the start regarding my wedding ring. We had my ring custom made from gold and diamonds I already owned. I made a drawing; but when I picked up my ring, it was not what I expected. There was no time to make changes. It was a flattened version of a higher built design I desired.

After a month of marriage, I found a wedding ring design I liked at a department store. Although it fit my taste, it wasn't real gold or diamonds; it was costume jewelry. It had the look of being authentic, but it was fake. That would prove prophetic, as later our marriage had the look but it proved not to be the real deal.

I married straight into full-time youth ministry. Fred had received his youth pastorate position at a church in the inner city (which no longer exists today). We were on a roll, moving fast and furious.

New Start

Our beginnings as a married couple were on rapid fire. We began developing a youth group from the ground up. We soon became pregnant as we proceeded forward in activities all around us. I was still working at my full-time sales position. Dealing with the demands of outside work during this time proved difficult on my body, so toward the end of my pregnancy I resigned.

This was spoken to me from a traveling minister while pregnant:

> When you're going have a baby, things change. All sorts of things happen on the inside. Your feelings go completely haywire. Things trouble you that use to not trouble you. There's a new life. No matter how many times it happens to women, they just seem to go crazy. It'll be over when the baby's born; it's just something you go through with all these changes. It's not a normal time, but it's a wonderful time. Now, it's not your husband's

fault. Well, it is his fault! But these situations that are surrounding it are not his fault. Everything is going to work out fine with the baby. You're going to have a happy, healthy child. You've got some good news; it will all be paid for. Don't worry about that. God is your source!

Now, with the coming of this child you've been unsettled. You haven't known what to do. You haven't been yourself. You don't know what to do with yourself. You're just going to praise the Lord, quietly. Love Him, read the word, and pray. Rest a lot and enjoy yourself. Don't try to do all the things other people tell you to do. Do what God tells you to do and enjoy yourself. Just love God and trust Him. There's nothing you could do; it's all in God's hands.

If your husband didn't take care of you, you couldn't help it. So just throw yourself on God's mercy. He's never left anybody in the lurch. He's going to take care of you and the baby. He'll take care of the family. You're going to have more than enough of everything. Just rest in the Lord!

*Come to Me, all who are weary and heavy-laden, and I will give you rest. Take My yoke upon you, and learn from Me, for I am gentle and humble in heart; and YOU SHALL FIND REST FOR YOUR SOULS. For My yoke is easy, and My load is **light**.*

—Matthew 11:28-30, NASB, emphasis added

We served at many different churches in three different cities over the next several years. It began to feel like a ping-pong ball effect as we moved almost every year. There were so many adjustments in packing, moving, unpacking. There was the development of youth programs with new relationships.

There were plenty of closed doors and struggles. I wondered why we were on this track. Were we really in God's will or just following the next open door? Viewing ministry from all angles was not always a pretty picture. You got to know the good, bad, and ugly scenarios. People are just people no matter what their position. John Paul Jackson wrote:

> In the deepest, darkest shadow of night, God always has a plan. If we choose Him instead of fear, rage, or bitterness, He will unfold the rest of the story to us, and we will realize that if it had not been for the difficulty, we never would have walked into the promise.[9]

But he said to me, "My grace is sufficient for you, for my power is made perfect in weakness." Therefore I will boast all the more gladly of my weaknesses, so that the power of Christ may rest upon me. For the sake of Christ, then, I am content with weaknesses, insults, hardships, persecutions, and calamities. For when I am weak, then I am strong.

—2 Corinthians 12:9-10

Ski Trip Dream

I know, O LORD, that the way of man is not in himself, that it is not in man who walks to direct his steps.

—Jeremiah 10:23

I dreamt of a vacation trip to a cold weather area to snow ski with a group of people while staying at a hotel. There were three couples, totaling six people, which is man's way. Outside our window we saw a huge, impressionable looking but degenerate tree with a condominium built into it.

Sin cannot offer security! But if you live right, you will be as secure as a tree with deep roots.

—Proverbs 12:3, CEV

The foundation at the base of the tree was black with its roots exposed. Roots can only grow and stabilize in healthy soil (the word). The roots were coming out because the tree was not fully built on the Word of God. There was a dark cave at the bottom of the tree revealing an evil intent. It appeared to be a demonic stronghold in this region. The roots of generational curses to this entity were coming out of the ground. It had no stakes in the land.

For land that has drunk the rain that often falls on it, and produces a crop useful to those for whose sake it is cultivated, receives a blessing from God. But if it bears thorns and thistles, it is worthless and near to being cursed, and its end is to be burned.

—Hebrews 6:7-8

We were all wanting to ski this particular day, especially the leader. As we all loaded into a car, the leader drove us all to the large tree. The road was built in a cylinder shape around the tree, taking you up to the condominium level.

We drove up and around the tree, but we were driving in reverse. This meant looking in the mirror to see behind us (the past) to see our way. The leader had to maneuver slowly in order to steer carefully and not fall off the road. We finally landed at the upper level. I noticed everyone had their snow skis on except me. As we all exited the car, I told everyone that I left my skis at the hotel.

We had to pack our things back in the car and head back to our hotel. Instead of skiing around the cave tree, we skied down the roads of snow (favor) near the hotel.

The vivid tree appeared to be a marvelous adventure. Instead, it was entrenched with strongholds united with hindrances that would have caused us to go backwards when being mislead in an uphill battle. We could have easily been led astray by believing in a wrong perception.

> Even now the axe is laid to the **root of the trees**. Every tree therefore that does not bear good fruit is **cut down** and thrown into the fire.
>
> —Matthew 3:10, emphasis added

Soulish Ruts

> For you were called to freedom, brothers. Only do not use your freedom as an opportunity for the flesh, but through love serve one another.
>
> —Galatians 5:13

Within the first year of marriage, we were already seeking counsel. That's not to say this was a bad thing, but Fred did not seem to be on my side. The insinuation was we had a 50/50 relationship. It felt if I didn't do my part of the 50 percent see-saw scenario; then neither did he. It was a standard I could never measure up to; and when I failed, I was out.

Proverbs 13:10 tells us wisely, "*Where there is strife, there is pride, but wisdom is found in those who take advice*" (NIV). Pride leads to arguments, as it resists God. We can make all kinds of requests, but the Lord controls every decision.

You are jealous and covet [what others have] and your desires go unfulfilled; [so] you become murderers. [To hate is to murder as far as your hearts are concerned.] You burn with envy and anger and are not able to obtain [the gratification, the contentment, and the happiness that you seek], so you fight and war. You do not have, because you do not ask.

—James 4:2, AMP

To quench strife accommodate the following with James' advice:

- Recognize the Holy Spirit's powerful place in our life.
- Pray for God's grace to *lose our friendship* with the world that's hostile toward God.
- Put on a selfless subjection in Christ.
- Put a demand on the devil to get lost in Jesus' name.
- Take a step toward God as He takes one to you.
- Purify yourself—we have come to God with soiled hands and divided hearts.
- This is not a laughing matter. Godly sorrow must be wept over contritely. The heaviness of sin reflects in the casting down of the eyes.
- Humble yourself, and God will exalt you.
- Ask God everything!

When God joins a relationship together He designed a natural sandpaper effect toward one another for refining and improving our love walk. That isn't the same as a devouring wood chipper that shreds logs for igniting and burning. The Christian walk is not to consume one another. We are to seek out the best interests of each other.

I began to feel a devouring effect with a partner that wouldn't back me up or love me when I was down. More and more there was a competitive edge to the relationship. We mustn't leverage our rights over another. Instead of unity, there was a growing division. *"Can two walk together, except they are agreed?"* (Amos 3:3, NKJV).

We can be victimized by habit patterns when we allow them. Like ruts in the ground of the soul, they will trap debris that falls into those dark, hidden places. They hide there until swept out. Let the rains of the Holy Spirit come and wash us clean. Allow God to reveal those hidden ruts. There is no escaping God's Holy flames of purification. He's not there to condemn us; He wants to free us permanently.

> *But if you bite and devour one another, watch out that you are not consumed by one another. But I say, walk by the Spirit, and you will not gratify the desires of the flesh.*
>
> —Galatians 5:15-16

Ocean Dream

I dreamt I was on an airplane with **four** other people. Two men wearing parachutes (faith) jumped out casually while a third jumped without his parachute (no faith), so I had to throw it toward him. The fourth man was prepared, along with myself. The total of us was five. In dream terminology this means redemption, grace, and anointing. It's something that's been prepared for one to do.

Next scene: We all landed on the ground safely in a coastal area. We went to a hotel lobby as I requested a room closest to the coastline. I noticed the hotel's layout of the property by rooms. I requested a particular room wanting to be closest to the ocean view as possible.

Shift to another scene: I was with my cousins and my father. Three of us girls retained the coastal room, so I walked straight over and fell fast asleep feeling exhausted.

Early the next morning I awoke while my cousins were asleep in the lower part of the room near the windows. They were sleeping on smaller beds that fit that area. I went to one cousin and tickled her feet until she laughed. It was early so I didn't want to wake her.

I looked out of one of the windows, which were built long and wide having protective screens on them. The seawater flowed back and forth under the window. I put my feet in the water and it felt good for a moment. I found the room set-up interesting.

All of a sudden the water began to rise up above the window. There wasn't a storm; it just rose quickly bringing in waves from the ocean. There were buckets and kitchen paraphernalia with plastic ware and measuring spoons. They began floating all around me, knocking me into these various utensils.

It was as if the items were placed there on purpose. It began to get a little rough while the items continued to knock towards me. The second window also contained plastic items that came towards me. Although it wasn't dangerous, it startled me. Things began to crowd in on me quickly and in a strange way.

Then it stopped. I awoke, and then fell back asleep, as God wasn't done with His message. I heard the words, "Too much, too fast."

This was calling to my attention things coming in the future. An ocean in a dream is the church or masses of people. My capacity to measure the forthcoming wave would be inadequate on my own. Measuring spoons don't begin to touch the huge ocean. I can't do it alone in my own works. Circumstances and events would overwhelm and take me captive without Christ navigating the way.

> *Yet we know that a person is not justified by works of the law but through faith in Jesus Christ, so we also have believed in Christ Jesus, in order to be justified by faith in Christ and not by works of the law, because by works of the law no one will be justified.*

—Galatians 2:16

Hidden in a Tent

> *Joshua sent men from Jericho to Ai, which is near Beth-aven, east of Bethel, and said to them, "Go up and spy out the land." And the men went up and spied out Ai. And they returned to Joshua and said to him, "Do not have all the people go up, but let about two or three thousand men go up and attack Ai. Do not make the whole people toil up there, for they are few." So about three thousand men went up there from the people. And they fled before the men of Ai, and the men of Ai killed about thirty-six of their men and chased them before the gate as far as Shebarim and struck them at the descent. And the hearts of the people melted and became as water.*

—Joshua 7:2-5

What's happening here? Joshua and his men had just defeated Jericho. This little town Ai should be a piece of cake. They didn't realize yet that the Lord was angry with them. Joshua had sought the Lord preceding the battle of Jericho. But this time, Joshua didn't bother to ask the Lord. In his pride, he thought they could handle such a small matter without the Lord's assistance. They judged by their blinded eyesight and faulty reasoning.

Joshua is distraught over their defeat including the death of tribal members. He tore his clothes then grabbed dust to fling around his head. He goes into pity party mode, whining to God about why He bothered to bring them to Ai just to destroy them and ruin their reputation (vv. 6-8).

God does not mince words telling Joshua, *"Get up! Why have you fallen on your face? Israel has sinned; they have transgressed my covenant that I commanded them; they have taken some of the devoted things; they have stolen and lied and put them among their own belongings"* (vv. 10-11).

The consequences of disobedience are: (1) They will not win before their enemies without God's help. (2) They are committed to destruction and death. (3) The Lord's presence will no longer be with them while they defile Him (v. 12).

God doesn't totally abandon them but gives them instructions for the next morning. Why wait? The Lord always gives us an opportunity to repent first. Joshua is told to consecrate the people and separate them by tribes in order to draw lots to find the transgressor. The exact lot shall go to a clan, then further down to the exact household (vv. 13-15).

The next morning Joshua was motivated to find out who the culprit was. The lot chosen was the tribe of Judah to the clan Zerahites until the man Achan was taken (vv. 16-18). *"Then Joshua said to Achan, 'My son, give glory to the LORD God of Israel and give praise to him. And tell me now what you have done; **do not hide it** from me"* (v. 19, emphasis added).

At first Achan did not confess his sin willingly. After this long process of deduction he admitted he had sinned by covetousness (v. 20). *"And see, they are hidden in the earth inside my tent, with the silver underneath"* (v. 21). "Tent" is a shortened version of the word *tentative,* which means unsettled. God wanted a holy tent to dwell in, even as it moved about.

> *So Joshua sent messengers, and they ran to the tent; and be-hold, it was **hidden in his tent** with the silver underneath.*

—Joshua 7:22, emphasis added

The Israelites grabbed the man with his family out of the tent and brought them to Joshua before all the tribes. They laid them down before the Lord. They saw all the stolen silver, the cloak and the bar of gold, his oxen, donkeys and sheep and his tent and all that he had (vv. 23-24).

> *And Joshua said, "Why did you bring trouble on us? The LORD brings trouble on you today." And all Israel stoned him with stones. They burned them with fire and stoned them with stones.*

—Joshua 7:25

Achor (Achan) in Hebrew means trouble, muddy, turbid, gloomy and dejected—not what I would call a living legacy. How would you like to end your life gloomy and dejected? Me neither! That's why this story doesn't end here. God redeems this message in a transformative way on a later day. Pursue God to take our turbulent troubles and make a straight pathway of hope out of them.

> *I will return her vineyards to her and transform the Valley of Trouble into a gateway of hope. She will give herself to me there, as she did long ago when she was young, when I freed her from her captivity in Egypt*

—Hosea 2:15, NLT

Secret Service

A talebearer causes strife, injury and wounding as a false witness found in Leviticus 19:16 which says, *"You are not to go around slandering your people. You are not to stand idle when your neighbor's life is at stake. I am the LORD"* (ISV).

A talebearer gives us a negative connotation of a gossiping agent. But when we are in the "secret service" of hiding information under cover, this can be applied against sound reason. We may bask in the fact that we're a great friend because we would never deceive someone's confidence. After all, aren't we something special to guard other's secrets so tightly? But when we step over that safe boundary into a destructive one, not being able to tell what should be kept a secret and what should be confessed, it gets muddy quickly!

Double crossing friends or other relationships will sabotage our integrity. This will break down trust causing overwhelming agony. Slander is never an option as a believer. It is an excuse for dealing with a situation without prayerful love. The first person I'd take any matter to is the Lord, who has ears to hear and wants to know what's moving our hearts.

Solomon is our living testament example of how to approach God. Go to God first for wisdom, discernment, and admonition. We need to seek His Word supremely, like our life depends on it! Also, our pattern is to seek wisdom from a multitude of counselors (Proverbs 11:14; 15:22; 24:6, NKJV). The counselor we choose is of utmost importance. Anyone can throw out advice; today there's an absurd amount of it in the airways. We should ask the Lord to specifically lead us to the right advocate who is accountable and trustworthy; one that has a track record with credentials to help others in a Christ-like manner based on sound principles.

The seed promise follows the pattern laid down at creation for healthy lifestyle. Everything created has a seed from which it propagates itself after its "kind." Genesis 1:27 says, "*So God created man in his own image, in the image of God he created him; male and female he created them.*" Stand firm in Christ, never wavering under falseness. Be who God created you to be. Haggai 2:19 tell us, "*Is the seed yet in the barn? Indeed, the vine, the fig tree, the pomegranate, and the olive tree have yielded nothing. But from this day on I will bless you.*"

> *By the word of the LORD the heavens were made, and by the breath of his mouth all their host. He gathers the waters of the sea as a heap; he puts the deeps in storehouses. Let all the earth fear the LORD; let all the inhabitants of the world stand in awe of him! For he spoke, and it came to be; he commanded, and it stood firm.*
>
> —Psalm 33:6-9

A Guarded Heart

> *The LORD is a stronghold for the oppressed, a stronghold in times of trouble. And those who know your name put their trust in you, for you, O LORD, have not forsaken those who seek you.*
>
> —Psalm 9:9-10

I began to feel like a target in Fred's and my conversations. In a regular exchange of words, things would get twisted or taken the wrong way. When I tried to convey care or concern, it would often be taken with dejection, an unexplainable reaction. Words would be received completely different than what I had intended.

There was a lot of commotion about who was right and who was wrong. There was a demand placed about Fred always being right, but I was touted as "just thinking" I was right. There were dramatic mood swings from gregarious laughter to angry bouts or strange withdrawal. There was an increasing level of agitation personified.

I had so much teaching about not being an offense. We are to speak a blessing to our enemies. We are to heal the broken. We are to bind the enemy. We should want change in people's life, not wanting others to look bad. We shouldn't judge our brother but seek reconciliation to understand. But what if the other person doesn't respond long-term; and what about the downward spiral navigating me with it?

> *My son, fear the LORD and the king; Do not associate with those who are given to **change**.*

—Proverbs 24:21-22, NASB, emphasis added

I observed some behavior patterns I couldn't grasp. There was a hypersensitivity to what others said, while the interpretation was usually way off key. Insinuations, motives, perceptions, and questions were usually misinterpreted toward a negative impulse. It seemed there needed to be an enemy; which was usually me.

Journal: 7.5.90

> Both days have held great turmoil, tearing, control, and anger in our marriage. I want to put it all behind me and get rid of the pain he inflicts. He acts as a lone ranger, just for himself and just as miserable.

Hostilities began to erupt as areas of ministry began to come to an end while exposure came out. Outbursts and arguments began to ensue more often and from largely unknown places. I was bewildered at the high level of escapades unraveling before me. What was really causing this?

When we have our guard up, we're not listening to God. How else are we going to know if something is of God or not? Our defenses will deafen us to the point that we don't know what to do. Trauma will keep us on the fence; it builds a barricade around us that entraps emotions. It can cause a shock to our system. But nothing separates from the love of God.

John Paul Jackson once said that all people deal with rejection one way or another. It's an inescapable hindrance in life. It's a test of progress. Once we pass it, we will not be held captive by it any longer. The love of God will not be fully realized until we receive His healing touch of deliverance from rejection.[10] Remember, we are ACCEPTED of the Beloved (Ephesians 1:6). We are to come as we are, not fainting or concealing the pain. Reach out your hands and receive Christ's complete total emersion of love, acceptance, and purity. Be acquainted with our Father's loving embrace as He holds us closely. God will use our hands for others who are desperate to receive the same healing virtue we can give them.

> Then they **cried to the LORD** in their trouble, and he delivered them from their distress. He sent out his word and healed them, and delivered them from their destruction. Let them thank the LORD for his steadfast love, for his wondrous works to the children of man!
>
> —Psalm 107:19-21, emphasis added

1 John 1:1-5

That which was from the beginning, which we have heard, which we have seen with our eyes, which we looked upon and have touched with our hands, concerning the word of life— the life was made manifest, and we have seen it, and testify to it and proclaim to you the eternal life, which was with the Father and was made manifest to us—that which we have seen and heard we proclaim also to you, so that you too may have fellowship with us; and indeed our fellowship is with the Father and with his Son Jesus Christ. And we are writing these things so that our joy may be complete. This is the message we have heard from him and proclaim to you, that God is light, and in him is no darkness at all.

CHAPTER THREE

No More Power to Weep

I'm exhausted as I groan; all night long I drench my bed in tears; my tears saturate the cushion beneath me.

—Psalm 6:6, NET

Brief Reprieve

Peter began to say to him, "See, we have left everything and followed you." Jesus said, "Truly, I say to you, there is no one who has left house or brothers or sisters or mother or father or children or lands, for my sake and for the gospel, who will not receive a hundredfold now in this time, houses and brothers and sisters and mothers and children and lands, with persecutions, and in the age to come eternal life. But many who are first will be last, and the last first."

—Mark 10:28-31

For one year we moved away from the city to the outskirts of a small town in the countryside. This was my mother's property that included a small house, pump house, ponds, cows, and snakes. We added a trampoline and swings in the trees for our sons. This would be a short reprieve to uncoil from a business upset that left us owing a substantial amount of money.

I was hoping it would give us time to rebuild our business and our relationship. I helped with marketing sales and Fred expanded his business territory. Our two young children, joined by our dog Cody, seemed to love the serene outdoors. I needed the peaceful solitude longingly thinking this would bring the stability we needed.

We easily met people in the local area. We developed warm friendships and had people over for fellowship. Things started to feel like they were falling into place. My oldest son went to a private school and our youngest had day care when needed. Our business started to make a gradual turn around.

By the end of one year's stay, Fred spoke of taking two weeks to get away. He wanted to take a trip with funds we did not have saved. Then one day Fred left anyway. I did not know where he went or how to reach him. I called a family member who said they would try and talk to him about coming home. Eventually Fred returned, but I felt something was still not right. Shortly after, we moved back to the city.

While journaling at this time, I wrote a passage that told of what was happening to me spiritually. It reads as follows:

Journal: 2.20.94

God's showing me I've made an idol of my spouse. I've tried to command the order of things by what I believe to be right. It's all wrong. God's asking me to let go of my "perfect" input all the time and make the ultimate sacrifice—give Fred to God completely, even with all the justification and real problems.

*As for me, I will call upon God, And the LORD shall save me Evening, morning and at noon. I will pray, and **cry** aloud. And he shall hear my voice. He has redeemed my soul in peace from*

the battle which was against me, For there were many against
me. God will hear, and afflict them, Even He who abides from
of old. Selah Because they do not change, Therefore they do
not fear God.

—Psalm 55:16-19, NKJV, emphasis added

A New Year

On January 14, 1994, I had a vision I labeled "Trust." In my journal came this vision as a sign to help me "trust" the Lord even
when the path ahead is rough.

Trust Vision

I saw Fred and me together on a motorcycle. (At least we were
going the same direction and on the same vehicle.) I saw us
on a path in a mountainous area (could be hazardous). The
grass was green and beautiful to the right of us. We were on
an extremely high cliff and the sides were jagged and steep
with a full view to the bottom terrain. God showed me that if
we veered to the "looks right" of His plan, or an easy out, that
it would be "all downhill." We could only go forward. As we
headed forward the path behind us all caved in. There was no
going back either. I heard, "There's **no** easy way out!"

If God has anyone in a "hard" place right now and there is no
clear sign to change, then stay put! Go forward in God; don't fal-
ter, sway, or look another direction. Trust Him with everything,
and the circumstances will eventually line up.

I had no idea what the application of this would be and the
whole dimension of what it encompassed. It was a warning of
things to come while holding onto God for dear life. To be sure,
there would be NO EASY WAY OUT.

While in the country, we had begun to feel comfortable with the new relationships we'd made. We had neighbors to visit and laughter; and it was such a great bond of enjoyment. But my new girlfriend revealed that they did not care much for Fred. This was in stark contrast to what I thought. They could see through the exterior façade.

Journal: 2.25.94

> I feel Fred doesn't really take an interest in my heart, motives, or opinion or the "intent" of where my concerns are in matters I bring up to him. The defenses are so high. It gets twisted to such a degree that the issue is turned into an attack on myself. I need a companion, not a commander always looking for the next war.

I always wanted my dad to take his raging mannerisms and just... go away. I'm now saying the same thing inside my head about Fred when he gets hostile and out of control. He always needs a listening ear, but he shuts me off instantly by playing the devil's advocate and accuser.

My prayer

Lord, I pray You would take all deceptions and denial out of both our hearts. I pray for a gentle answer and breeze over our soul. We would take a serious note of how we would answer the heart, not the perception; to take the time to feel, to care about the other's real motive.

Lord, I'm realizing how very little I can really handle. I need Your help in everything.

(I drew a circle with arrows pointing to the next space like in a clock; the top, at 12:00, read "matters concerned about"; to 3:00, "defenses"; to 6:00, "accusations of me"; to 9:00, "blames me." This was how I perceived

the rotation of our relationship. This was the crux of our conversation much of the time).

To the side I wrote, "Lord, I'm petitioning Your backup." I was still in control here, only asking for God's backup instead of the whole collection of my being. I was the person taking the frontal attack on myself. Wrong! But God was showing me a very different attitude ahead.

Who delivered me from my enemies; yes, you exalted me above those who rose against me; you rescued me from the man of violence.

—Psalm 18:48

A Humble Way

I dwell...With him who has a contrite and humble spirit, To revive the spirit of the humble.

—Isaiah 57:15, NKJV

My then six-year-old son had a dream. I wrote down what he said the next morning on April 27, 1994.

Lamb Dream

There was a lamb that was little. There were these two guys that came around. And they did not read the stone of the Ten Commandments. They didn't read the whole thing. They saw the lamb and they got their big bow and arrow. They stretched it out, and they shot the lamb on the side, but not in the bone, just the wool. Then they backed up and saw the stone, and it said not to kill the sheep or animals. The sheep had a hole in his skin and they took the arrow out of the sheep's skin and they cut all the fur off. A little boy came out and lifted his hands up to Jesus, it was me.

Can one imagine such a revelation of my six-year-old son? The two guys had a temporary loss of revelation, but then truth came forward in clarity. They had only read in part; not seeing the whole image. Jesus, the lamb's naked and innocent flesh, became visible to my son. He was able to grasp the attack, the purpose for the wounds, and then exalted the true Savior—precious and humble revelations.

> *For now we see in a mirror dimly, but then face to face. Now I know in part; then I shall know fully, even as I have been fully known.*
>
> —1 Corinthians 13:12

In contrast, I had a distorted puffed up view of self-sufficiency. I thought it was the great American virtue. I had this idealistic determination that I could handle what life threw at me. Needing help outside of myself was almost foreign to me. I'd protected my independent self-focused pride for so long that it was my default key. It's what I always fell back on, my tenacious "see it through to the utter end" persona. I could perform well on the surface. I could keep everyone else's secrets, protect people's lies, and sustain myself completely while helping others.

> *Such is the confidence that we have through Christ toward God. Not that we are sufficient in ourselves to claim anything as coming from us, but our sufficiency is from God, who has made us sufficient to be ministers of a new covenant, not of the letter but of the Spirit. For the letter kills, but the Spirit gives life.*
>
> —2 Corinthians 3:4-6

Humility begins the process towards loving obedience. Presumption is pride in disguise. Without humbling ourselves we stay in a stalwart, stubborn-powered, will-driven, contrary obstinacy! Did anyone get that? We must recognize our need. We are not indispensible to God. In other words, life keeps going even when we don't obey Him. I don't have the power, authority, or rulership to lead our planet or city, much less my household. That's spelled DISASTER. But God is wholly indispensible to an entire world that can't rotate one minute without Him!

Journal: 5.28.94

> Stop! Wait! Hush yourself. Be still. No scolding. I'm only molding you into My character. Practice staying in My presence more and for longer periods of time. I am molding you, now! Even today. Be transparent, moldable, and resilient for Me. Thank you for loving Me tenderly, affectionately as I've loved you. Listen quietly to My voice and heartbeat. It may not look to you like much is happening on the outside, but it's the inside of people's hearts where things are happening. Be diligent and strong. Pray more, more, more. And more will be happening on the inside and outside. Visibly, you will see the results of prayer, because you care!

God has given each of us a capacity of purpose to fulfill. If we take on more than grace has allotted us, we will eventually fail. I need all the energy I can get for what I am called to do. I don't need any drainage tube sucking me dry outside of His gifting. Use the anointing God has for your life, function in it, and stay in the safety of humility. The fruit will show up!

God's protection doesn't allow us to push or back off. Stay centered; rest in the Lord. Satan doesn't sneak anything past God. We need to have our eyes wide open at all times, fixed on Jesus. God's will is always on time, and it's time we listen. As we do, God will raise up those in authority. Never do anything impulsively. Don't try to be a one woman or man show, as I used to be. Tear down those stumbling stones that lead to error and begin afresh.

Listen and give heed, do not be haughty, **For the LORD has spoken***.*

—Jeremiah 13:15, NASB, emphasis added

Repulsive Romance

You cover the LORD'S altar with tears, with weeping and groaning because he no longer regards the offering or accepts it with favor from your hand. But you say, "Why does he not?" Because the LORD was witness between you and the wife of your youth, to whom you have been faithless, though she is your companion and your wife by covenant. Did he not make them one, with a portion of the Spirit in their union? And what was the one God seeking? Godly offspring. So guard yourselves in your spirit, and let none of you be faithless to the wife of your youth. "For the man who does not love his wife but divorces her, says the LORD, the God of Israel, covers his garment with violence, says the Lord of hosts. So guard yourselves in your spirit, and do not be faithless."

—Malachi 2:13-16

One evening I approached Fred with a romantic notion, as I'd felt so scorned at that point. I thought intimacy would help, but he provoked me harshly asking, "What do you want?" This turned into more degrading language as he kept coming into our bedroom, then leaving it repeatedly. It turned into reviling insinuations that were repulsive, turning my stomach into knots.

After a short time, he came back flip-flopped on me and said he was now interested. I was sobbing over the demand he wanted something from me, as if I were a "thing." I went to the restroom, locked the door behind me, and told him to leave me alone. I felt totally unwanted and devalued. This was the first time I realized I did not feel like a wife. What resonated inside of me was this must be how a prostitute must feel from a pimp's treatment. I did not want to be touched.

Eventually, I opened the restroom door and locked the bedroom door. I stayed inside our bedroom falling asleep exhausted. I awoke sometime in the early morning hours to find Fred in bed next to me. He must have picked the lock. I went into the living room, and found my Bible on the sofa. I took it in my hand sobbing, then thrust it full force against the invisible God of the living room wall that I could see. I felt incredibly desolate, overcome by peculiar emotions including fiery turmoil mixed with sorrows.

What flew out of my throat towards God was why He had lied to me: "Didn't You say You would not let us be tempted beyond our ability?" (See 1 Corinthians 10:13.) The interpretation of scripture I used was with the word *tempted*. Temptation is a desire which is contrary to God's ways where the intended actions desired produce sin. All of us are tempted in one way or another; there is no escaping the test of faith in life. It requires our conscious forethought, our actions, avoidance when necessary, and confrontation.

I wasn't being tempted, but was dealing with a life struggle that consumed my whole being. It was beyond my ability to invest anything any longer. My mental and emotional resources were on empty. I could no longer bear the agony of a disparaging and destructive marriage. I was muddling through an existence that didn't seem to be mine; but it was.

> *O LORD my God, I cried to you for help, and you have healed me. O LORD, you have brought up my soul from Sheol; you restored me to life from among those who go down to the pit.*
>
> —Psalm 30:2

Separation

> *But whoever hates his brother is in the darkness and walks in the darkness, and does not know where he is going, because the darkness has blinded his eyes.*
>
> —1 John 2:11

Marked so clearly in my journal was the date March 29. It had been exactly five days since my birthday when Fred left us. That night I came home from work late. The single wilting red rose he'd given me for my birthday was still in its petite glass vase on the kitchen counter. Our sons had not been fed, though it was an hour past their bedtime on a school night. There, sitting front and center in our living room, was Fred with his dinner tray watching TV. My two young boys huddled around my legs telling me they were hungry. I could not fathom why these two little guys weren't taken care of.

In a distressed tone, I asked Fred why he was stuffing his face when our sons were hungry and crying past their bedtime. Up came the TV tray, food flying around the room. He was enraged at my charge to make such a demand on him. He stormed out of the house and into his car. He left for a few minutes while I followed outside with my oldest child. He drove back, honking at my son, calling out to him to get in the car with him.

I needed to talk, now! Fred rolled down his driver's side window for a moment, watching my every expression. He quickly closed the window while I was still pleading that it was a school night and to let our son stay home. He left with our son. I put our youngest child to bed comforting him not to worry.

After what seemed a long time because I was feeling desperate and frantic, my oldest son was returned. It had only been twenty minutes. I felt the waves of despair while sleeping in bed alone. Pastor Walter Hallam said, "You are never responsible for the pain caused from those that ignore your advice."

My days have passed, my plans are shattered. Yet the desires of my heart turn night into day; in the face of the darkness light is near.

—Job 17:11-12, NIV

Dark Shadows

*But if your eye is bad, your whole body will be full of darkness. If then the light in you is darkness, **how great is the darkness!***

—Matthew 6:23, NKJV, emphasis added

Calendar Dream

I had a vivid dream about two months before the separation of our marriage. I remember so clearly seeing a white calendar with numbers surrounded by the separating daily boxes. The calendar pages began flipping through the months landing on the month of April. A dark shadow gradually oozed from the top covering the entire month in dingy smokiness. It completely covered the month in a full dense black darkness. Then it leaped over into the following two months.

For it comes in vanity and goes in darkness, and in darkness its name is covered.

—Ecclesiastes 6:4

This blackness extended itself into the months of May and June. I came to realize as time went on that I was living this dreadful existence out to its fullness. I initially went from emotional shock to experiencing hot and cold sweats at work. Sometimes my head would just drop on the counter from mental exhaustion, unable to comprehend. My legs would quiver and get weak beneath me. I was living a paralyzing nightmare.

Let my eyes run down with tears night and day, and let them not cease, for the virgin daughter of my people is shattered with a great wound, with a very grievous blow.

—Jeremiah 14:17

There are a myriad of losses that can tap into our soul and emotions. My personal loss initially overflowed into feeling lack in the following areas; safety, hope for the future, companionship, friendships, dignity, power, authenticity, finances, physical endurance, and even my faith. Brokenness was all around me. That is something difficult to recover from quickly. I was facing a long-term reality that I could barely endure for just one day. It was hard to muster enough courage to wake up and take care of the simple needs of my children.

There seemed to be a continual cycle of feeling let down, being unsure of anything, having goals thwarted, and my life spent and spinning out of control. I felt fear, anger, and extreme disappointment as expectations of sacrifice and plans were stolen. The extended aggravations from displays of rejection, criticism, and accusations made me feel like a woman scorned by her lover. I felt isolated from within and did not want to share my painful situation while wrestling with these feelings of insignificance. Abandonment can bring self-worth and value spiraling into question.

I was not making it on my own with two sons to support. The ability to control situations and circumstances had come crashing down. The pressure of it all became too much for me to handle as I faced my own limitations. I felt utterly helpless, which opened up a valve of shame, despondency, and failure.

I felt trapped in a darkened time tunnel with limited options, except to plod along this depleted dirt road. I could not see where all of this was leading to. My future seemed like a contrary wall I had to push against. All felt like an empty hollow shell for this season, not knowing if there would be a different one ahead. The empty seashell has a sound we hear as we quietly listen.

What others wanted of me I could not produce as the reversals and losses sapped everything from me. I was at the end of many things in my life. My next step was transparency, as I had to expose my true situation in order to survive. I could no longer cover all the bases around me; it was time to let God move.

> For we were so utterly burdened beyond our strength that we despaired of life itself. Indeed, we felt that we had received the sentence of death. But that was to make us rely not on ourselves but on God who raises the dead.
>
> —2 Corinthians 1:8-9

Into the Haze

> We don't yet see things clearly. We're squinting in a fog, peering through a **mist**. But it won't be long before the weather clears and the sun shines bright! We'll see it all then, see it

all as clearly as God sees us, knowing him directly just as he knows us!

—1 Corinthians 13:12, MSG, emphasis added

Towards the end of my marriage, our life had become so unpredictable. We'd moved to a street that had the name "hazy" on the sign; this became an insignia to my plight. It even resonated in a dream I had during this time.

Fog/Mist Dream

I watched as a viewer in my dream, while seeing Fred with his back toward me. He was next to the street observing a grassy drainage ditch, which ran on the east side of our house. I watched as he ran full throttle into the thick, misty, gray fog ahead of him. He went headlong into it without flinching until I could see him no longer.

The land of gloom like thick darkness, like deep shadow without any order, where light is as thick darkness.

—Job 10:22

Remember the childhood nursery song, "Three Blind Mice?" Here are the lyrics, speaking of visual impairment in a bog fog.

Three blind mice. Three blind mice.
See how they run. See how they run.
They all ran after the farmer's wife
Who cut off their tails with a carving knife.
Did you ever see such a sight in your life
As three blind mice?

Blindness caused these poor, wicked mice to run as far and fast as they could. They got caught up with a mad woman with a knife in her hands. Their long, lost tails, which interprets as lies in dream interpretation, may have been the root cause of their blindness. The story teller ask us to see this sight in our mind's eye, which leads us back to the condition of the blind mice with no more tails or tale to tell.

> *The leaders of Israel are the head, and the lying prophets are the **tail***.

> —Isaiah 9:15, NLT, emphasis added

Fear, *phobos* in Greek, describes a person who flees from a battle. We can run from our enemies temporarily, but we can't run from God. Once we start running, confusion will continue to chase us away. We may try to escape pain, tormenting thoughts, relationships, and situations in life, but they'll remain until they are dealt with.

It's how we handle these types of encounters that bring change. Otherwise we will stay in a paralyzed position. Circumstances will dominate us instead of us taking dominion over them. We will not serve or fulfill our purpose with a "duck your tail" attitude. Life is meant to be pursued, while the love of God sustains us all the way. Go fight any necessary battles and allow God to be our Victor.

What's wrong with being a fighter? We're not trying to pretend. We're not playing church or God. We have a real existence that includes fighting an uphill battle at times. Put on His righteous armor and go for it! God has a strategic battle plan as He leads us by the hand.

Hebrews 6:18 tells us,

> *So God has given both his **promise and his oath**. These two things are inseparable because it is impossible for God to lie.*

Therefore, we who have fled to him for refuge can have great confidence as we hold to the hope that lies before us.

—Hebrews 6:18, NLT, emphasis added

There is only one place we can flee to, which is into the safe arms of our loving Father. Christ alone can be trusted, so grasp this hope with confidence as He vindicates our every stance.

If we cut the chain linked to Christ's strong anchor, we sink down, tumbling across the broad ocean floor of scattered debris. Christ is our safe house from all distresses. If we unplug from this trustworthy dependency, there is only peril ahead. Ungodliness takes root, as a spirit of death takes over. Danger is ahead for those who neglect the stronghold of Christ.

*For you shall not go out in haste, and you shall not go in flight, for the LORD will go before you, and the God of Israel will be your **rear guard**.*

—Isaiah 52:12, emphasis added

Fear Nothing

*Do not think like everyone else does. Do not be afraid that some plan conceived **behind closed doors** will be the end of you. Do not fear anything except the LORD Almighty. He alone is the Holy One. If you fear him, you need fear nothing else. He will keep you safe.*

—Isaiah 8:11-14, NLT, emphasis added

Fear is a robber, telling us what we can't have. It lies by stealing our dreams, actions, or vision. It will prevent the best in us from coming out. It kills vitality, creativity, and adventurous risks. It squelches our drive and desires. It's a roadblock sign that says no one can enter here. It makes us blind and deaf to God's transmission signals.

> Bring out the people who are blind, yet have eyes, who are deaf, yet have ears!

—Isaiah 43:8

There was a time the Lord dealt with me about the fear of becoming an alcoholic. This wasn't due to my own drinking; it was due to what I had lived with and seen. My desire to be the opposite of this made me hard on myself and others. The fear of addiction added to the pain. Don't allow fear from past experiences interrupt our walking in the light or interpret our future passages.

The enemy will try to get us to succumb to his lies when you feel most vulnerable. Let's close our ears to satan's defective, warped thoughts about us. God is leading us toward a different way.

I attended a conference titled Bold Love, where the speaker gave me a word of knowledge. He said, "I see the word 'SECURITY' over your forehead. Fear Nothing! Let nothing intimidate you. Let no one intimidate you. Trust God." Then he gave me this scripture, Matthew 14:27: "*But immediately Jesus spoke to them, saying, 'Take heart; it is I. Do not be afraid.'*"

Initially after the separation, I stayed in the Book of Isaiah, which helped me through my need for identification. Everything else seemed to be perishing, but the Word of God became my survival food. I wrote the scriptures below in my journal and read them repeatedly for assurance that God knew what I was going through and cared.

> Fear not, for I am with you; be not dismayed, for I am your God; I will strengthen you, I will help you, I will uphold you

*with my righteous right hand. Behold, all who are incensed against you shall be put to shame and confounded; those who strive against you shall be as nothing and shall perish. You shall seek those who contend with you, but you shall not find them; those who war against you shall be as nothing at all. For I, the Lord your God, hold your right hand; it is I who say to you, "**Fear not, I am the one who helps you.**"*

—Isaiah 41:10-13, emphasis added

Intimidation turns us into a puppet controlled by other people's attachments. They try to dictate what we're supposed to be or not. It controls our emotions. We can't be ourselves because of the fear it brings to us. Our gifts stay buried and dormant underneath this layer of trepidation. We don't belong to anyone but the Lord. Break those chains that bind us, tear down the darkness in Jesus' name!

But now thus says the LORD, he who created you, O Jacob, he who formed you, O Israel: "Fear not, for I have redeemed you; I have called you by name, you are mine. When you pass through the waters, I will be with you; and through the rivers, they shall not overwhelm you; when you walk through fire you shall not be burned, and the flame shall not consume you. For I am the LORD your God, the Holy One of Israel, your Savior.

—Isaiah 43:1-3

There is nothing anyone of us can go through that He has not already been aware of. His helping hands are outstretched to us constantly. Jesus understands the pain; He participated in it on this Earth. It's not something anyone willingly wants for their child. But it is there nonetheless. We are not to be consumed by it, but be transformed into His image through it. This season is passing away. A bright light is over the horizon.

The scripture below is speaking of no longer being held captive by fear. Shake off those stifling bands—we are not slaves to sins gone by or our former captors. Don't stay in the waste places of neglect, sorrow, and fear. Money doesn't buy this type of liberty! Jesus did not put us in bondage; and His nonnegotiable payment of blood for our freedom has already been paid. There is nothing left to pay for. Christ gave us a total fix on the cross; there are no substitutes. We can take His lasting freedom for all our afflictions. We are able to collect what is ours in Christ Jesus.

> Awake, awake, put on your strength, O Zion; put on your beautiful garments, O Jerusalem, the holy city; for there shall no more come into you the uncircumcised and the unclean. Shake yourself from the dust and arise; be seated, O Jerusalem; loose the bonds from your neck, O captive daughter of Zion. For thus says the LORD: "You were sold for nothing, and you shall be redeemed without money."
>
> —Isaiah 52:1-3

His Love Breaks Off Fear

> She is not afraid of snow for her household, for all her household are clothed in scarlet [think of His eternal blood clothing you in scarlet].
>
> —Proverbs 31:21

The Bible promises an abundance of *shalom*; our *peace, completeness, prosperity*, and *welfare* for those who reverently fear God. Fearing God in this manner does not mean we are to *hide* under a heavy, guilt-ridden blanket of insignificance. Our Creator deserves our most meaningful awe-inspired wonder for

His holiness. God's presence, favor, and power begin to increasingly encompass our life as we reach out to Him endearingly.

Jeremiah 1:8 relays to us, *"Be not afraid of them [their faces], for I am with you to deliver you, says the Lord"* (AMP). The more I confessed this scripture in my early years of outside sales, the more I realized we are all on the same level, as God made us all in His image. There is no grade A, B, or C levels in God's eyes. God doesn't call us by our earthly titles of chairman, director, manager, corporation executive, or CEO. We have the same access, acceptance, and terms with Him as all His children. We are loved in the same exact, monumental proportions by our loving, heavenly Abba, Dad.

> *For God did not give us a spirit of timidity (of cowardice, of craven and cringing and fawning fear), but [He has given us a spirit] of power and of love and of calm and well-balanced mind and discipline and self-control.*
>
> —2 Timothy 1:7, AMP

How fast does fear leave us? At the speed of His love; the One we have our hope, faith, and trust in is always present. Power without love renders us wholly unstable. Man's strength can shrivel in a moment. Fear robs us of the power of God, but faith activates God's love in us. Fear causes us to shrink in their mind, will, and emotions. We have been given the power to serve with a sound mind and His victorious love.

During my interim period, after a devastating divorce and believing for a pronounced future of hope as in Jeremiah 29:11, I had multiplied dreams and visions, including warning and encouragement types. One I will relay is a warning that could have caused a foreboding apprehension concerning my future; but it did not happen because I used the Word of God and actively applied it to my life. I hope this will help anyone who might be succumbing to the same type of adversarial attack.

Beam Gun Dream: Journal 1.8.97

I just dreamed of a spiritual force surrounding me over my bed. The force was like a throbbing, beam gun that came behind my head in a circular movement back and forth, then over my eyes several times. I tried to speak in prayer over it, but could not move my lips. My tongue seemed paralyzed. Then I thought on Jesus' name!

I spoke with my spiritual mentor who helped me determine what was behind the threat in my dream. She said, "Do not be afraid or disturbed as something was keeping close tabs on you." Then we took authority over the following areas in Jesus' name:

- We took captive "soulish prayers" and cast them to the ground.
- I was instructed to anoint my bed with oil, and then check it out.
- All projected thoughts against me were made void and incomplete.
- Destruction of all ungodly soul ties, false prophecy, and judgments that were spoken over me.
- All false council would be forgotten (erased).
- All mind control spirits were bound.
- Any areas of unforgiveness toward me or of me toward others were uprooted in Jesus' name.

Constructively, I needed to use the Word of God as my sword. I have the mind of Christ to uproot anything planted by the enemy. Numbers 14:9 tells us, *"Only do not rebel against the LORD. And do not fear the people of the land, for they are bread for us. Their protection is removed from them, and the LORD is with us; do not fear them."*

Future plans: God would run all relationships through a sieve (some stays, some goes) tightening up walls, refining my relationship with Him. This would be a time for refocus, discipline, and discipleship.

Jesus' desires:

> To be one with you as you do. Jesus is going to honor my request for more gifting, as well as more sensitivity in the Spirit. Cleaning out of your EARS (1 Samuel 3:19). Holding your EYES open. God created you with humor—bringing laughter back into your life. Your joy to be full and infectious to others as they will have fun, too! His daughter—the apple of His eye. No good thing would be withheld from you. He will be stretching Himself for you. He will resolve questions about your needs. My hand to be in His hand. Mercy and compassion to flow even though you've been through a lot. See Judges 12:1-6; Shibboleth means to flow like a river. You will be appreciated even though you haven't been.

September was the month that "lighted up," as something very different would happen during the last months of the year. It would not be an easy year, but would not be like the last five years. My instructions were to have a picnic with Jesus, as He's my best friend.

> *There is no fear in love, but perfect love casts out fear. For fear has to do with punishment, and whoever fears has not been perfected in love. We love because he first loved us. If anyone says, "I love God," and hates his brother, he is a liar; for he who does not love his brother whom he has seen cannot love God*

whom he has not seen. And this commandment we have from
him: whoever loves God must also love his brother.

—1 John 4:18-21

Marriage Wanted

Husbands, love your wives, as Christ loved the church and
gave himself up for her.

—Ephesians 5:25

After two months of separation, I put my thoughts together of
what I wanted in my marriage. *If that could not happen, then*
send another one God; preserve him for me.

Keep me safe, O God, I've run for dear life to you. I say to God,
"Be my Lord!" Without you, nothing makes sense.

—Psalm 16:1-2, MSG

- Strength to stand in the gap for the salvation and restoration of my marriage for a certain duration. If not, I
  will believe for another marriage partner.
- Need of a mutual partnership and companionship
  with respect. James 3:16: *"For where jealousy and*
  selfish ambition exist, there will be disorder and every
  vile practice."
- Not facilitating another separation or cycle of escape,
  running, or leaving unexpectedly—for my sanity's
  sake, but especially for the children, that they will not
  learn to deal with their problems the same way, for
  they would not be able to learn to fight their battles
  themselves and say no to the real enemy.

- The priest and ruler of the home needs to be established by actions not just words. A relationship built on God's love.
- Eyes to see real evidence that he would lay down his life for us and serve us completely without a begrudging heart; he needs to put us first.
- To be supported and provided for in a biblical way; not a half-way version, but completely.
- My vow to pray for and encourage my spouse and take care of our home and family.
- A happy marriage full of fun, harmony, joy, and goodness. Not a perfect one.
- We need to know what's important in life! I thought, if he doesn't know by now, he never will. I'm attractive, smart, and a giver. I have many great features to give someone. I need someone to appreciate me! I don't want to keep the marriage in limbo any longer.

This is either going to be a truth or tell with all the cards faced up on the table or it's not real. I didn't want a marriage built on lies and deception. I wasn't "in love"; but based on covenant, commitment, and responsibility, I chose to keep it together.

I desire the pure will of God in my life so God can get the glory, not man. Covenant with God is everything we desire. God will go back and answer our tremendous heart cries to restore those areas of our life. Don't allow the snares of the past to hold back any aspiration. The enemy will try to use them as devices against God's children. Resist any torturing thoughts that there is no future forward. In Christ all things are new again.

Likewise, husbands, live with your wives in an understanding way, showing honor to the woman as the weaker vessel, since they are heirs with you of the grace of life, so that your prayers may not be hindered.

—1 Peter 3:7

Breaking Point

By means of his one Spirit, we all said good-bye to our partial and piecemeal lives. We each used to independently call our own shots, but then we entered into a large and integrated life in which he has the final say in everything.

—1 Corinthians 12:13, MSG

I didn't realize it then, but my life up to this point was built upon my own "rule of might" to get things done. I'd idolized this area as being my best resource and all sufficient one. Oh, I loved God and made requests of Him frequently, but my necessity for life was built on my own strong will and sheer determination. I could harness self-control and discipline more because of family genes. I could accomplish goal-driven desires because of my sales background. I would make a way to get something done.

But I needed rescuing from myself. My life was wrapped up in how *I* was the central theme in order to make it work! I could press that little lever inside of myself and presto magic, the problem would be fixed or at least I could use "Plaster of Paris" to hold it all together. I was a die-hard trooper thinking I could outlast anyone in the battlefield of life. That was with my artificial, spiritual crown positioned perfectly.

The only real thing I surrendered to God was my sins; and that was a gift, easily received. I simply got rid of a barrier that was holding me down so I could do more about moving on with things. But in order to operate in life successfully, I relied on my own wits and a few muscles. It was my right of passage. I had pretty decent character quality and skills, so that was my mark. Only, that mark was always ME performing what I did so well. Up until now!

> Let me ask you only this: Did you receive the Spirit by works of the law or by hearing with faith? Are you so foolish? Having begun by the Spirit, are you now being perfected by the flesh? Did you suffer so many things in vain—if indeed it was in vain? Does he who supplies the Spirit to you and works miracles among you do so by works of the law, or by **hearing with faith**.
>
> —Galatians 3:2-5, emphasis added

Waiting on the Lord was out of the question. There were places to go and people to see. I'd become a speed spoiler, ever in a hurry. I did not treat God as my Helper or ally, the One who could uphold my life. Now, there seemed a stranger rising up against me, seeking and demanding my life. (See Psalm 54.) God alone is faithful.

Change is a product of growth. Ephesians 4:15 tells us, "*Rather, speaking the truth in love, we are to **grow up** in every way into him who is the head, into Christ*" (emphasis added). I was ready. I wanted to embrace the kind of change that would bring new life to me and my children.

An eagle is the only animal that can look directly into the sun. This trait symbolizes seeking the Lord in spirit and in truth. Isaiah 40:31 says, "*But they who wait for the LORD shall renew their strength; they shall mount up with wings like eagles; they shall run and not be weary; they shall walk and not faint.*"

Submit yourselves therefore to God. Resist the devil, and he will flee from you. Draw near to God and He will draw near to you.

—James 4:7-8

Suffering

I want to know Christ—yes, to know the power of his resurrection and participation in his sufferings, becoming like him in his death.

—Philippians 3:10, NIV

We are not being brought to an idea but the reality of the person of Christ, our head Mentor. Our identification, assurance, and justification are being conformed to Him. His death, then, raises us to spiritual life now.

None of us can avoid sufferings. It is all around us; it is all around the world. When we suffer it is suffering with Christ because He experienced it completely. It is a uniting of knowing, as He is *"touched with the feeling of our infirmities"* (Hebrews 4:15, KJV). We are being conformed to His image, not forsaken (Romans 8:29). It is not a pleasant road, but a necessary one.

For I consider that the sufferings of this present time are not worthy to be compared with the glory that is to be revealed to us. For the anxious longing of the creation waits eagerly for the revealing of the sons of God. For the creation was subjected to futility, not willingly, but because of Him who subjected it, in hope that the creation itself also will be set free from its slavery to corruption into the freedom of the glory of the children of God. For we know that the whole creation groans and suffers the pains of childbirth together until now. And not only this, but also we ourselves, having the first fruits of the Spirit, *even we ourselves groan within ourselves, waiting eagerly for our adoption as sons, the redemption of our body. For in hope we have been saved, but hope that is **seen** is not hope; for who hopes for what he already **sees**? But if we hope for what we do not **see**, with perseverance we wait eagerly for it.*

—Romans 8:18-25, NASB, emphasis added

Even though we live in a world of gross negligence, of degeneracy, and of hardships, we know there is a future place of glory right over the horizon. We are not just maintaining the status quo; we have a hope that can't be seen yet—it's our reality of faith. In the meantime, we are to take a strong stance before the Lord, not thinking difficulties are unexpected. Hold firmly to Christ allowing His attributes to stabilize us in shared fellowship.

Suffering is as valid today as in Bible times. It comes in all levels, formations, and entities. It can be national, local, or individual. Sometimes it lasts longer in duration or can be brief. Whatever you are in, do as Psalm 109:1-4 instructs us: *"Be not silent, O God of my praise! For wicked and deceitful mouths are opened against me, speaking against me with lying tongues. They encircle me with words of hate, and attack me without cause. In return for my love they accuse me, but **I give myself to prayer"*** (emphasis added).

Allow God to use the conflicts and trials we face as gliding momentum underneath our wings to lift us to new heights otherwise unattainable. Don't let a disparaging tone take over to incapacitate us into lower depths of discouragement. Second Corinthians 8:2 uplifts us: *"For in a severe test of affliction, their abundance of joy and their extreme poverty have overflowed in a wealth of generosity on their part."* God takes us up and over, not down and out, as Exodus 3:17 confirms: *"I promise that I will bring you up out of the affliction of Egypt."*

You then, my child, be strengthened by the grace that is in Christ Jesus, and what you have heard from me in the presence of many witnesses entrusted to faithful men who will be able to teach others also. Share in suffering as a good soldier of Christ Jesus. No soldier gets entangled in civilian pursuits, since his aim is to please the one who enlisted him. An athlete is not crowned unless he competes according to the rules.

—2 Timothy 2:1-5

Wisdom from 2 Timothy above tells us four things about our sufferings. (1) We will be able to teach and instruct others on how to handle the matters of combobulations in life. (2) We can share in sufferings as stalwart and faithful soldiers of Christ's cause. (3) We are here to please our Enlister, Jesus Christ. (4) We need to seek the #1 Rulebook to know what to expect and then follow accordingly. We can then apply traction to our faith; otherwise we'd all be worthless in our calling. Isaiah 48:10 says we've been refined in the furnace of suffering (NLT).

Those who chose not to fight the good fight of faith make themselves subject to the captivity of the world. We are either servants to Christ or slaves to the system of destruction. Those who leave the house of worship, get worldly counsel, and mingle with the elements of the flesh are being suffocated. Psalm 107:17 informs us: "*Some were fools through their sinful ways, and because of their iniquities suffered affliction.*"

The Lord said in Jeremiah 15:11: "*Have I not set you free for a good purpose? Have I not intervened for you with your enemies in times of trouble and times of distress?*" (ISV). Lower ranking Chaldean officers mistakenly put Jeremiah in chains. But the captain loosed him in the sight of them all. Where God has made us free, be free; take a stake in that freedom. Christ is our forever Captain, so declare this liberty out loud.

*In his kindness God called you to share in his eternal glory by
means of Christ Jesus. So after you have suffered a little while,
he will restore, support, and strengthen you, and he will place
you on a firm foundation.*

—1 Peter 5:10, NLT

Heartache of Two Women

Genesis 16 reveals the story of Sarai and her servant slave Hagar.
It's apparent both women suffered considerably. First, Sarai is
not able to bear a child. She condones her husband, Abram, in
having relations with her maid Hagar who becomes pregnant
with a son. This latter situation did not bring the solution Sarai
had hoped for. It brought even more anguish to have another
woman around the house having the promise in her belly.

In Genesis 16:5 Sarai says to her husband, "*You are responsible for my suffering! I put my slave in your arms, and ever since
she saw that she was* pregnant [with the prolific seed], *she has
looked down on me* [that snide look that a woman can wear].
May the LORD judge between me and you" (HCSB).

Sarai blamed her husband for the predicament. Women are
pros at blaming their problems on their husbands when it was
their decision that got them there. By saying Abram is responsible, she is referring to the fact that he had the greater authority
to stop this impregnation. But after all, Sarai thrust her own
slave into his loving arms.

Sarai is hot and bothered, and I can empathize with the outcome of her actions, being spurned. Hagar has the baby bump to
prove to Sarai that she has something that Sarai cannot deliver.
Most of us have been in a situation where another woman has
looked down and judged us; whether we deserved it or not is
not the issue.

Sarai is feeling the results of manipulating God's will in her life. She made something happen, but regrets the outcome. This was not a pleasant aftermath of her fulfilled wishes.

Abram finally pipes up and says the most convenient thing possible, *"Here, your slave is in your hands; do whatever you want with her"* (v. 6, HCSB). So much for a quick fix! Notice how they keep handing the supposed solution back and forth. Sarai to Abram and now back again. Hagar is tossed about as if a beanbag.

Sarai mistreated Hagar so badly that she ran away grieving. Sarai is hurting because Hagar has possession of her victory child, so she degraded and abused her. She caused Hagar mental and emotional torment because that was how Sarai had been suffering.

> *Let them curse, but you will bless! They arise and are put to shame, but your servant will be glad! May my accusers be clothed with dishonor; may they be wrapped in their own shame as in a cloak! With my mouth I will give great thanks to the LORD; I will praise him in the midst of the throng. For he stands at the right hand of the needy one, to save him from those who condemn his soul to death.*

—Psalm 109:28-31

What happened to Hagar as she scurried here and there in the dry desert? An angel told her to go back from where she came and submit to her mistress. She was told her son's name, Ishmael, because the Lord heard her misery. The promise of increased descendants was given for her lineage. In verse 13 we read, *"She gave this name to the LORD who spoke to her: 'You are the God who sees me,' for she said, '**I have now seen the One who sees me**'"* (Genesis 16:13, NIV).

Isaiah 33:24 declares, *"No one in Zion will say, 'I'm sick.' Best of all, they'll all live guilt-free"* (MSG). This is the opposite of shame; we are to live well and whole, fully healed. Don't accept the weights of condemnation that pull us down and make us less than we are. When people try to ring the doorbell of shame and blame, don't answer. It's the devil's trash to keep.

It's important to keep our sights on who we are in Christ, which keeps us guilt free. We are already in right standing with God; not based on our works, but our heavenly position. Let's cherish this privilege as His children. His requirement is unconditional, unending love.

Our thought life needs continual reviving to be rejuvenated. Isaiah 33:15-16 gives us a list full of hope. The answer is to *"live right, speak the truth, despise exploitation, refuse bribes, reject violence, and avoid evil amusement"* (MSG). Our motives need to be purified by continually bathing in God's Word. It makes all the difference in how we think, act, and feel. This will give us constancy to live a satisfying life of intimacy in the Lord.

Prophecy, 6.2.95

I received a revelatory word from an Arkansas minister that I will closely paraphrase. I believe this minister met Fred briefly at a meeting, in a natural way; he did not know much about him. This message was from the Spirit of God. It is shared below as I had written it down at that time from a recording device.

Referring to Fred, the minister said,

> He has personal problems and habits. He has a hard time with his mother, as she's domineering. This has been building up a good while. He has tried to plant little seeds to get you to move out. That lust spirit came back on him. He found out he can't justify himself. There is a lying spirit telling him to get back with you so he can be the one to

chase you off. It is miserable with the kids. The oldest one is tore up. Don't jump too soon! There is no relationship with you unless he has a repentant heart. But he is just justifying against you.

I convicted him so hard. Scripturally, you're right. It's okay to be away until he admits something is wrong. Tell him he takes things as condemnation, when it is not. There is no excuse for him. He will use anything to justify himself. He likes being single spiritually and have other women notice him, right now. Make it clear. I am having those in authority deal with him. They believe some of the things he says against you. They know in their heart it isn't so. He's going to be called on the carpet (and catch him) when he goes around with other women. Don't get upset and think you're less of a woman. You're much of a woman. It's a problem inside of him that's never been dealt with.

It's a problem of never really feeling he can live up to the things with women because of his mother. Then he tries to put everyone in line against her. There is a hate in his heart for his mother that he doesn't realize. He's got to get that out, distaste for women, in his heart and mind. He's got to be free of that. The only way for him to get free is for people to face him with it. Make it clear to him. We need to go to a neutral counseling center and get help. He needs to pay for it! He needs to move out of that apartment to help pay for it. If he can't do that, daughter, you don't need that kind of situation. He'll come back and make your life hell and miserable. He has a woman-hating spirit. He was trying to get you to leave. He can't justify himself now and has to go. There was no interest with the woman he was looking toward. The ministers will deal with him. He's going to try to get another woman involved with him. You will know something in seven weeks. It's his decision, too! Fast and pray once a week for him. After that, if you see change, then **wait** to make sure he's ready for commitment. Don't allow yourself to get under condemnation. The deep root is in him. You have tried to encourage him. It could go either way. If he files for divorce, you are no longer obligated. You can't make a man serve God. Demand to see something happen with him. He can't try to find fault with you. He's being convicted and that's why he's going back and forth. He got so mad. Don't accuse him of wanting another woman. See past the surface. Don't do anything rash. Obligate him once he decides on a divorce. Get your financial house in order. Don't be afraid to get legal matters in order. There will be a settlement of the kids! God will open the door for a lawyer.

Styrofoam Wakeup Call

For it is impossible, in the case of those who have once been enlightened, who have tasted the heavenly gift, and have shared in the Holy Spirit, and have tasted the goodness of the word of God and the powers of the age to come, and then have fallen away, to restore them again to repentance, since they are crucifying once again the Son of God to their own harm and holding him up to contempt.

—Hebrews 6:4-6

Not long after Fred left us, he moved into an upscale condo. I came by to drop off my sons on a gray, overcast afternoon. It had started to drizzle outside as I came to his front door, watching my little guys enter this foreign dwelling. Fred was holding his take-out order from a restaurant. The remainder of it was inside a white Styrofoam container that he held out for me. With the front door partially opened, he made an ingenuous offer that I could eat his *leftovers.*

First Samuel 21:6 says, *"So the priest gave him the holy bread, for there was no bread there but the bread of the Presence, which is removed from before the LORD, to be replaced by hot bread on the day it is taken away."* Every seven days, on the Sabbath, the holy bread was replaced with new fresh bread.

Jesus does not want us taking from the old wine or bread. It needs to be tossed out as spoiled. We are to take of the New Covenant of His life and provision of fresh baked bread representing the Lord's body. We are sanctified and set apart in Christ. His new mercies prevail over old ritual sacrifices.

Something broke loose in me! It was like a large metal coil inside of me that finally sprang, going haywire from its sturdy placement. My memories were rapidly clicking a succession of evidence about this moment. I surmised instantly what it meant. I took the lightweight container and opened the lid to stare at half-eaten spoils. I realized this half-empty package symbolized our marriage and what I meant to Fred.

The bell in my head revolted at the suggestion. I declared loudly, "No, I don't want your leftovers," throwing the box his direction. He stood there, seemingly stunned at my response as I walked down this stranger's sidewalk to my car. The rain started to pick up, splashing droplets on my face.

I no longer wanted a "leftover" marriage. Leftovers deliver dread from the past. I didn't want to acknowledge that was all I was worth to him. But the realization was so overwhelming and powerful. I briskly walked now, rain falling harder while I entered and closed my driver's door. I was shivering, but not from the wetness. I started the car and turned on the windshield wipers as the silent rain splashed outside my foggy windows.

All of a sudden, Fred jolted towards my car. He threw the Styrofoam box and its contents toward my car hitting my moving windshield wipers and they boomeranged the box right back towards him. I chuckled inside while tears emerged as I drove back to an empty house.

This event gave me a small validation of hope for freedom from the emotions I had cycled through. I did not have to take the insults or degradations from him. I could go a different direction. I desired to be a person of significance who was no less important than the one I'd been married to. It was time to put things in perspective. My tears planted seeds towards a revolution of hope!

The field is the world, and the good seed is the sons of the kingdom. The weeds are the sons of the evil one, and the enemy who sowed them is the devil. The harvest is the end of the age, and the reapers are angels.

—Matthew 13:38-39

Lighthouse Dream

And they will look to the earth, but behold, distress and darkness, the gloom of anguish. And they will be thrust into thick darkness.

—Isaiah 8:22

I had a dream set at the dark of night that I was bobbing in the ocean looking toward the shoreline ahead of me in the distance. I was holding onto a buoy for support, but knew I had to make a swim toward the land and the light. I saw a large **"lighthouse"** on the landscape. I tried to calculate how far it was from me and how long it might take to get there.

I finally made a swim for it, as I kept my eyes on the rotating light that increased its full spectrum before me as I got closer. When I made it to shore, I went into the lighthouse and found some friends I knew there. They wrapped me in towels to dry off. We went on a search to try to find Fred, as he was lost.

Someone said he left the lighthouse and went to another building close by where there was no light. We went to the balcony window upstairs to look outside at the darkened two-story building to the right of us. One of the men in our group shouted out that he saw movement at the building. He volunteered to go check it out; taking a flashlight to help him see.

We watched him leave the lighthouse door below and go towards the long, dark facility. We eventually saw shadows as one man chased the other about, then we observed a still conversation. My friend eventually came back to tell us that Fred refused to join us. He did not want to come back to the lighthouse.

I watched again, outside the balcony through the nighttime air. Searching, I observed a single silhouette prowl through the moonlight, further away in the distance, down a road. He was moving the opposite direction from us, but continued going. I felt significant sadness knowing what I had to do.

I bless the LORD who gives me counsel; in the night also my heart instructs me.

—Psalm 16:7

For a Mother

Search me, O God, and know my heart! Try me and know my thoughts! And see if there be any grievous way in me, and lead me in the way everlasting!

—Psalm 139:23-24

As I was experiencing a time of divisiveness in our family, one morning I heard in my heart, "You aren't a mom to your children or a daughter to your mother." I knew it was a lie of the enemy, but it still stung me to the core of my soul.

I then declared the opposite of what I heard, telling myself that I was a good mother and daughter despite the enemy's diversion tactics. My faith (belief) was what steered me correctly, as all the evidence around me seemed contrary to what I was seeing. Stay on course with what God says about you.

Isaiah 49:15-16 tells us, "*Never! Can a mother forget her nursing child? Can she feel no love for the child she has borne? But even if that were possible, I would not forget you!* **See, I have written your name on the palms of my hands**" (NLT, emphasis added).

God must have enormously wide hands to inscribe all of our names upon them, like a permanent tattoo that can never be removed. We are there for Him to recognize. He can never forget us. We are a constant reminder of His love for us. Commit the children God gave us to Him, as they belong there, too.

> *All your enemies rail against you; they hiss, they gnash their teeth, they cry: "We have swallowed her! Ah, this is the day we longed for; now we have it; we see it!"...Their heart cried to the Lord. O wall of the daughter of Zion, let tears stream down like a torrent day and night! Give yourself no rest, your eyes no respite! Arise, cry out in the night, at the beginning of the night watches! Pour out your heart like water before the presence of the Lord! Lift your hands to him for the lives of your children, who faint for hunger at the head of every street. Look, O LORD, and **see**! With whom have you dealt thus?*
>
> —Lamentations 2:16, 18-20, emphasis added

Weep No More

> *I will feast the soul of the priests with abundance, and my people shall be satisfied with my goodness, declares the LORD. Thus says the LORD: "A voice is heard in Ramah, lamentation and bitter weeping. Rachel is weeping for her children; she refuses to be comforted for her children, because they are no more." Thus says the LORD: "**Keep your voice from weeping**, and your eyes from tears, for there is a reward for your work, declares the Lord, and they shall come back from the land of the enemy."*

> —Jeremiah 31:14-16, emphasis added

The Assyrians are deporting captured Jews from the city of Jerusalem. They are sent out by way of Ramah. Rachel is weeping over the exile of her children, Joseph and Benjamin.

There is hope of restoration and joy by turning to God. To prevent backsliding and complacency, Ephraim is encouraged to set up "signposts" *to prevent the things that led to their downfall.* Jeremiah 31:21 tells them, *"Set up road markers for yourself; make yourself guideposts; consider well the highway, the road by which you went. Return, O virgin Israel, return to these your cities."*

The Lord is making a declaration, a promise of hope for their future. In verse 18, God's response to these heart-worn women is to come back to Him so they may be restored—satisfying their weary soul, while replenishing every sorrow they've experienced (v. 25).

The way out of bondage is like a highway or GPS that directs us in the right direction so we don't get lost again. God does not forget us even when we have been guilty of forsaking Him. God's love never fails, as His heart yearns for us with great merciful compassion.

The best part of Jeremiah's prophecy is the New Covenant prepared in advance for us. We can know the Lord for ourselves while He promises to forgive our sins. Hebrews 8:10 tells us, *"For this is the covenant that I will make with the house of Israel after those days, says the Lord: I will put my laws in their mind and write them on their hearts; and I will be their God, and they shall be my people."*

> *Come, let us return to the LORD; for he has torn us, that he may heal us; he has struck us down, and he will bind us up. After two days he will revive us; on the third day he will raise us up, that we may live before him. Let us know; let us press on to know the LORD; his going out is sure as the dawn; he will come to us as the showers, as the spring rains that water the earth.*

—Hosea 6:1-3

Get a Hearing Check

> *To whom can I speak and give warning? Who will listen to me? Their ears are closed so they cannot hear. The word of the LORD is offensive to them; they find no pleasure in it.*

—Jeremiah 6:10, NIV

People's ears have become uncircumcised, never having been brought into covenant with God. They find the Lord's sayings repugnantly bitter. Their ears have filtered out the words of life decreeing them despicable. There is no remorse for their deviant ways. Rejecting God has ruined them to the brink of despair.

Christ's true followers are joined to Him as part of the covenant price He paid. Psalm 71:2 says, *"In your righteousness deliver me and rescue me; incline your ear to me, and save me!"*

God admonishes us to stand at the crossroads, to look and see. Ask for the old paths *"by the new and living way that he opened for us through the curtain, that is, through his flesh"* (Heb. 10:20). This gives us guidance, salvation, and restoration.

Jeremiah 7:24 and 26 tell us, *"But they did not obey or incline their ear, but walked in their own counsels and the stubbornness of their evil hearts, and went backward and not forward....Yet they did not listen to me or incline their ear, but stiffened their neck. They did worse than their fathers."*

One generation becomes a detriment to another because they did not follow the Lord. The next generation gets their hearing plugged up by deceptive waxes. The inability to hear anything from the Spirit lends itself to a degeneracy of defilements and curses. They are lead astray so easily that all forms of evil attachments are birthed out.

Jeremiah 6:19 warns us, *"Hear, you earth: I am bringing disaster on this people, the fruit of their schemes, because they have **not listened** to my words and have **rejected** my law"* (NIV, emphasis added). There is a penalty for not listening to the Lord's sayings. Are we now a nation that has rejected even the most decent laws?

Psalm 58:4 says, *"They have venom like the venom of a serpent; Like a deaf cobra that stops up its ear"* (NASB). The snake is not easily enticed or influenced by those that would train it. This scripture tells us it willfully avoids compliance. Those who refuse to hear through heaven's window pane will eventually suffer the byproduct of a world of deadened grace.

Let's open our ears from the neglect of this age that refuses to acknowledge God's divine vocal cord. Ask God to mercifully remove all the insulation that stops the flow of His Spirit. All the areas that are clogged up need purging. Let's allow God to melt our hardened hearing. As He illuminates the plug of resistance, let go and let's flow!

> *The Lord GOD has given me the tongue of those who are taught, that I may know how to sustain with a word him who is weary. Morning by morning he awakens; he awakens my ear to hear as those who are taught. The Lord GOD has opened my ear, and I was not rebellious; I turned not backward. I gave my back to those who strike, and my cheeks to those who pull out the beard; I hid not my face from disgrace and spitting. But the Lord GOD helps me; therefore I have not been disgraced; therefore I have set my face like a flint, and I know that I shall not be put to shame.*

—Isaiah 50:4-7

The Battle Is Not Yours

> *You are a hiding place for me; you preserve me from trouble; you surround me with shouts of deliverance. Selah*

—Psalm 32:7

In the second Book of Chronicles, chapter 20, begins a threat of war from two tribes upon Jehoshaphat, as some men warned him: "*A vast army is coming against you from Edom, from the other side of the Dead Sea*" (v. 2, NIV). It states Jehoshaphat had an alarmed reaction and resolved to inquire of the Lord. That tells me he really considered his options on how to handle this matter. Judging the army's size and the possible duration and effects of a deadly war, he invokes the entire nation of Judah to a fast. Smart man!

This united effort to seek help from the Lord made a powerful determinant. After this nation came together as one to seek the One, Jehoshaphat *stood up* boldly in front of the temple before the people. He proclaimed their history with the God of their fathers, who rules over all the kingdoms of all the nations. He spoke of God's might and strength while encouraging the people in God in whom they believe. In verse 9 he states, *"If calamity comes upon us, whether the sword of judgment, or plague or famine, we will stand in your presence before this temple that bears your Name and will **cry** out to you in our distress, and you will **hear us** and save us"* (NIV, emphasis added).

Jehoshaphat takes the dagger to the heart by reminding God how they had obeyed Him earlier by not invading their enemy's land and how the enemy is now repaying them by attacking. This land is their possession as an inheritance. Who dare try to take it from God Himself? Initially Jehoshaphat wants judgment!

By drawing wisdom with insight, he humbles himself to the sheer reality that he has no strength to attack such a huge army. He further realizes what he'd said many times in situations that can overwhelm people: *"We do not know what to do, but our eyes are on you"* (v. 12). His helplessness causes him to pursue God above all else.

While the people stood there and waited for a response, the Spirit of the Lord found Jahaziel, a Levite descendant, who tells everyone there to *"listen"* (v. 15, NIV). How riveting the answer we all need to hear in critical situations, he said, *"Do not be afraid or discouraged because of this vast army. **For the battle is not yours, but God's**"* (v. 15, NIV, emphasis added). What a great association of relief as God tells them they will not even have to fight! God then reveals the enemy's whereabouts, saying they will find them at the end of a gorge in the Desert of Jeruel.

The battle plan is simple: (1) Take your position, (2) stand firm, and (3) see the *deliverance* the Lord will give you. This is followed by more encouragement. *"Go out and face them tomorrow, and the LORD will be with you"* (v. 17, NIV). Everyone great and small fell down before the Lord in worship following this example. What a great deliverance is about to proceed for them! Some Levites decided to give praise in advance of the power play of God about to be displayed the next day.

Jehoshaphat began early in the morning strengthening the people's hearts to have faith in God. He takes an interest in the people and even consults with them. He appointed some to sing and praise at the front of the army as a spiritual shield. It seems the tip of the rocket ship of worship will penetrate all barriers, as they say, "*Give thanks to the LORD, for His love endures forever*" (v. 21, NIV).

God went before them setting ambushes for their enemies as they began to invade and the enemy began succumbing to defeat. God confounded the Ammon and Moab group against the men from Mount Seir destroying them completely. After this slaughter the enemies all began to go after and destroy each other. Ouch! No one escaped!

Jephosphat's group pillaged equipment, clothing, and other valuables; there was even more than they could take away. This confirms Malachi 3:10 saying, "*I will...pour out so much blessing that there will not be room enough to store it*" (NIV). As far as their inheritance, it continues verse 12: "*Then all the nations will call you blessed, for yours will be a delightful land, says the LORD Almighty*" (NIV). Talk about redemption to the max! In Christ all things are possible.

A prior Pastor gave me a word of knowledge as I share it below (7.21.96)

> You are an intercessor. You have been an encourager to many others, so God is going to send encouragers to you. The biggest part of the battle is over! It is going to be easier now. There will still be some ripples and resistance. From here

on God is going to fight the battle for you. He is going to be giving back to you. You have been found selfless and God sees that. He is going to reward you!"

For I am with you, and no man shall assault you to harm you, for I have many people in this city.

—Acts 18:10, NET

Paul Refuses to Depart Secretively

The LORD is on my side; I will not fear. What can man do to me?

—Psalm 118:6

Acts 16 tells the story of how God allowed Paul and Silas a one night's pass to a Philippi prison, which was the right place at the right time. The magistrates sent officers to release Paul and Silas. As an earthquake shook violently, it seemed an environmental sign to motivate the royal Roman guard to get rid of these guys. To silently push the situation out of the back door, they excused Paul and Silas to depart NOW! But small Paul had a big mouth and he wasn't about to accept those terms. As Paul put it in verse 37, *"They have beaten us **openly**, uncondemned Romans, and have thrown us into **prison**. And now do they put us out **secretly**? No indeed! Let them come themselves and get us out"* (NKJV, emphasis added).

No sleazy sneaking around here! Paul not only knew who he was in Christ, he was a privileged Roman citizen of an elite class. By Roman law he was guaranteed a fair trial; wanting to expose the culprits who deceived the Roman officials into believing they were causing unlawful disturbing acts. Paul's *false charges* needed to be eradicated for his witness and for the Philippians who believed in his message. His testimony was at stake.

119

When the magistrates found out Paul was a Roman citizen, they became very fearful. They had overstepped their boundaries. Now, they rushed the matter to get them out of the way and keep from being uncovered. Confrontation is a form of love; we care enough to get to the bottom of what's true. Silent avoidance would have left Paul and Silas in a precarious situation discrediting the Gospel.

If anyone has experienced people giving them the silent treatment, that's a form of control. We don't need to tuck our tails and hide behind the shadows. In this life, confrontation is going to happen. Cultivate it for character building and not evil. Light always dispels darkness, so don't be fearful. Do what must be done to make the crooked places straight, turning wrong into right.

2 Peter 2:19-21

They promise freedom, but they themselves are slaves of sin and corruption. For you are a slave to whatever controls you. And when people escape from the wickedness of the world by knowing our Lord and Savior Jesus Christ and then get tangled up and enslaved by sin again, they are worse off than before. It would be better if they had never known the way to righteousness than to know it and then reject the command they were given to live a holy life. (NLT)

CHAPTER FOUR

The Escape—His Voice

Therefore let anyone who thinks that he stands take heed lest he fall. No temptation has overtaken you that is not common to man. God is faithful, and he will not let you be tempted beyond your ability, but with the temptation he will also provide the way of **escape**, *that you may be able to endure it.*

—1 Corinthians 10:12-13, emphasis added

Spider Expelled

Therefore let us stop passing judgment on one another. Instead, make up your mind not to put any **stumbling block** *or* **obstacle** *in the way of a brother or sister.*

—Romans 14:13, NIV, emphasis added

In dream terminology, a black spider is a symbol of the occult. It's something the dreamer may be involved in which negatively affects his life or spiritual destiny. A person may feel trapped or spiritually poisoned by the *venom* of words spoken over them. This is based on dream materials available from Streams Ministries International, www.streamsministries.com.

Spider Dream

My dream was set in a bedroom I was using temporarily. I saw a black widow spider on the floor of the bathroom, which was well lit while sunny outside. I decided to get some bathroom cleaner to spray it with. Notice the word *cleaner* while the bathroom area is for cleansing.

As I went to retrieve the cleaner, the spider followed me. I wasted no time to spray it immediately. It continued to follow me—persistent little black bug. I sprayed it all the way to the bed and night or "light" stand table. I see this as standing in the light whether we "see" it or not. We are to continually stand on God's promises regardless of the conditions.

First Corinthians 16:9 explains, *"For a wide door for effective work has opened to me, and there are many adversaries."* Opportunities to advance the work of God abound; but we must get to the door by passing through all obstacles, even those right on our tail, in the name of the Lord.

I stood back by the door (Jesus) and watched as the spider jumped on the bed (a place of intimacy). It started to take large jumps towards me on the bed, then to the floor. I grabbed a white Kleenex (clean-ex) tissue to snatch the little insect then wrapped it up tightly. I went back to the bathroom toilet, turned the flush handle and placed the tissue wad right into the draining water to make sure it exited in the bubbling forceful stream. It flushed away!

A nightstand represents God's promises will stand, even when all seems dark and daylight has not yet arrived.

Whoever isolates himself seeks his own desire; he breaks out against all sound judgment. A fool takes no pleasure in understanding, but only in expressing his opinion.

—Proverbs 18:1-2

I interpret this as a temporary season during which a negative force was imposing itself against me. It was a trap! The black spider was sending out poisonous words my direction, taking big leaps to do so. It was right on my trail. As it took its biggest shot in my direction, I trapped it with a cleaning cloth. The Word of God snatches evil words and disposes of them making them null and void. There was action for me to take. I had to use the sword of the Spirit. The evil works of the enemy became invalidated by flushing all its poison down the drain, led by the Spirit. Water symbolizes the Holy Spirit's work as it purges toxic waste. Cleansing had come as the spider *did not escape*!

That He might sanctify her, having cleansed her by the washing of water with the word.

—Ephesians 5:26

Prophecy: Fresh Start, 11.3.95

This prophet asked if I worked at a job, and I affirmed yes.

> I see changes, a shaking. There will be some layoffs, but it won't affect you. Regarding my work, I was told in the month of September, there was a promotion coming.
> He asked, "Are you not married?" I answered, "Yes, but I'm going to court."
> The Lord says you're not married. There will be a divorce. The Lord has prepared you. This is what that man will do. This is not the end of your life. This is just the beginning.

You've questioned what you didn't do right? How could this happen to you? God says you're beautiful on the outside and inside. This is just the beginning. You will begin to fly. The winds will come and help you fly.

That man will be grief stricken when he sees you.

Was there another woman? (I shook my head unknowingly.)

Do not think this fiery trial strange. It has happened to others. There has been a persecution that has come against you.

God wants you to know... you are innocent and blameless in this matter. Slap your hands up and down to cut yourself from the past. You're washed from the old so get on with the new. This is nothing more than an incident.

You will be replanted in new soil—a new birth, a birth. This is the seventh hour in your life; the beginning of a new fresh start, a completion of what was. Philippians 3:13-14 says, *"Brothers, I do not consider that I have made it my own. But one thing I do: forgetting what lies behind and straining forward to what lies ahead, I press on toward the goal for the prize of the upward call of God in Christ Jesus."*

Tonight marks the "NEW." Also, there is a new house for you!

Remember not the former things nor consider the things of old. Behold, I am doing a new thing; now it springs forth, do you not perceive it? I will make a way in the wilderness and rivers in the desert.

—Isaiah 43:18-19

Broken Yokes

What do you plot against the LORD? He will make a complete end; trouble will not rise up a second time. For they are like

entangled thorns, like drunkards as they drink; they are con-
sumed like stubble fully dried. From you came one who plotted
evil against the LORD, a worthless counselor. Thus says the
LORD, "Though they are at full strength and many, they will
be cut down and pass away. Though I have afflicted you, I will
afflict you no more. And now I will break his yoke from off you
and will burst your bonds apart."

—Nahum 1:9-13

When people come against God's children, it's as if coming against God Himself. The passage above is speaking of the Assyrian rebellion against the Jews. It's just as relevant to any of us being pursued by an adversary. When people continue to oppose and undermine God's will, they will run into a wall—the wall of Almighty God.

Those trying to torment and destroy will now experience the reverse effects of it. Those pursing us to bring defeat will be the defeated themselves. Let God arise and let His enemies be scattered, permanently (Psalm 68:1). The one who plots hostilities against you will have his plans broken. The yoke of your enemy's enslavement tactics are divided up, squandered, and torn.

Be fully set free using His majestic grace to propel your stance in fulfillment of His Word. Allow the divisive strategies of broken yokes to give the new breed generation a conquering, resolute voice that will be heard. Maintain His voice, as it's been activated by life's negative consequences and then turned upwards. Think of black charcoal, which, when lit, maintains a constant, glowing ember. Use that visual picture to power up our voices on full throttle.

Psalm 21:11 tells us, *"Though they plan evil against you, though they devise mischief, they will not succeed."* Our enemies are deficiently anemic against God's strength. Their end results will not prevail. It isn't saying we will not go through the trials of life. It's saying schemers will not win by going against our backside. Call on God's covenant to stand between us and the evil enemy. God is capable of being judicially heard as He determines our claim.

We are called as believer's to believe in a relationship greater than our own. If someone has been defeated by a wrongful foe, put complete trust in God. Our cognizant LORD will make a righteous ruling. Consecrate with Him; that trauma will not rise up again. Know the time of conflict and affliction has ended. Declare the end of it with your voice strings.

> *I will give them a heart to know that I am the LORD, and they shall be my people and I will be their God, for they shall return to me with their whole heart.*
>
> —Jeremiah 24:7

Prophecy, 5.3.97

> You have a lot of the Word inside of you and it needs to come out. You will have a ministry to small children; and a teaching ministry to children. Do not despise small beginnings!
>
> A bigger family for you; more children will be added to your family. Your future husband will be a "seven" to you this time — meaning perfect.
>
> You have another ministry that you move in and out of because of the doubt, fear, and unbelief. Some of this was put upon you, but we are going to cast it out tonight. (We took authority over it and I renounced the doubt and unbelief I'd let creep into my heart.)

After this meeting a friend came to me and spoke about what the prophet had just spoken. She said I had a more willing heart than my ex-husband; that I would no longer be last but be put first.

She said she understood why I didn't believe for my ex-spouse to come back because of the lack of repentance and the hell he put me through. Concerning teaching to small children, I became a substitute teacher in elementary schools for nine years after I remarried. It started as a commitment I made to my youngest son that we would go back to school together.

To have someone give you compassionate understanding during a trial like this one that extended out for a year of separation, was meaningful to the utmost. I recommend always looking for a way to encourage others, as you will need it back many times.

During the summer I took my sons to the beach. While I was sitting back relaxing, the Lord spoke to me about the hotel behind me in this distance—the same hotel that had been the last excursion of a past anniversary. I heard these words, "That was the beginning of the end and now this is the start of a new beginning for you!"

Then, I kept hearing three months inside my spirit. The Lord repeated, "Three more months for your harvest." Later I was to remember the prophetic word from my mentor friend with the month of "September" lighting up. God used this method to confirm and encourage.

And this, my best friend, betrayed his best friends; his life betrayed his word. All my life I've been charmed by his speech, never dreaming he'd turn on me. His words, which were music to my ears, turned to daggers in my heart.

—Psalm 55:20-21, MSG

Betrayal

*It was not an enemy who taunted me—then I could have borne it; I could have **hidden and escaped**. But it was you, a man like myself, my companion and my friend. What fellowship we had, what wonderful discussions as we walked together to the Temple of the Lord on holy days.*

—Psalm 55:12-14, TLB, emphasis added

Betrayal is one of the worst offenders of emotion bringing hurt and pain. We can't just bypass this conflict and move on easily. It creates a deep cut in the heart. Mark 14:21 says, *"But woe to that man who betrays the Son of Man! It would be better for him if he had not been born"* (NIV).

One story of betrayal is found in 2 Samuel 15:30, *"But David went up the ascent of the Mount of Olives, weeping as he went, barefoot [unprotected] and with his head covered. And all the people who were with him covered their heads, and they went up, weeping as they went."*

David was told that Ahithophel, the ringleader in this conspiracy, was advising David's son Absalom. David cried out to God all the more to turn the counsel of Ahithophel into foolishness (v. 31). Wisely, David sent his loyal servant Hushai, to go back and spend time with Absalom as a two edged sword of a visit. Hushai would keep his eyes and ears open to Ahithophel's divisive plans while playing the part of a servant to his son (vv. 32-34).

It was decided that any word of entrapment would be delivered to his loyal priests, Zadok and Abiathar. Their two sons, Ahimaaz and Jonathan, could be sent to report back to David the exact plans that would be instituted against David (vv. 35-26).

David spent the first part of his life hiding from bipolar, narcissistic King Saul. But now his own flesh and blood son Absalom was receiving council from Ahithophel, whose words were appealing to Absalom's arrogance and greedy desire for his father's kingdom. David had placated this son, not disciplining him in his youth. What manifested in his adult son came from a lack of training on honor, sacrifice, and loyalty. This came back to haunt David, having dealt himself a bad hand. As Galatians 6:8 reminds us, "*The one who sows to his own flesh will from the flesh reap corruption.*" As we honor the Lord, we harvest honor back (1 Samuel 2:30).

Matthew 24:10 informs us, "*And then many will fall away and betray one another and hate one another.*" Betrayal was preceded by a quiet listener looking for a way to trap its victim. The betrayers of Jesus were always around Him, straining to hear the language they could justifiably use against him. We see it of Judas in Mark 14:11: "*And he sought an opportunity to betray him.*"

> *Then Satan entered into Judas called Iscariot, who was of the number of the twelve. He went away and conferred with the chief priests and officers how he might betray him to them. And they were glad, and agreed to give him money. So he consented and sought an opportunity to betray him to them in the absence of a crowd.*
>
> —Luke 22:3-6

Jesus' own disciples temporarily betrayed Him by their silence, hiding themselves from their accusers in blatant denial of Him. Their fear of persecution later turned into a turbulent taking of the Kingdom by force. The demonstrative sacrifice of Jesus' resurrection love turned their world downside UP.

Their betrayal did not cut off their lifeline. God used these horrific forces for their own good. God will protect those that depend on Him. We must open ourselves up to the Lord who sees all and makes right judgments for us. Don't allow devastation or worthlessness to speak into our lives. Roll up those sleeves, get ready for battle; prepare for righteous action.

Revenge is never the answer or solution. Jeremiah 20:10-11 speaks to that:

> *For I hear many whispering. Terror is on every side! "Denounce him! Let us denounce him!" say all my close friends, watching for my fall. "Perhaps he will be deceived; then we can overcome him and take our revenge on him."*

Satan attempts to speak words in our minds, trying to make us think they are our thoughts. These are used like leaches to get us to succumb to those beliefs. Once we take ownership, they breed into sins of hatred, rebellion, jealousy, and vindictiveness. Spit these seeds out as quickly as they enter the mind. Reject the injector of deception.

> *But the LORD is with me as a dread warrior; therefore my persecutors will stumble; they will not overcome me. They will be greatly shamed, for they will not succeed. Their eternal dishonor will never be forgotten.*

> —Jeremiah 20:11

The Escape

> *Therefore let anyone who thinks that he stands take heed lest he fall. No temptation has overtaken you that is not common to man. God is faithful, and he will not let you be tempted beyond*

your ability, but with the temptation he will also provide the **way of escape**, *that you may be able to endure it.*

—1 Corinthians 10:12-13, emphasis added

What this is saying is that in this world there are troubles; we all have weak vulnerable areas. Men and women go through a lot of similar trials. The only one faithful in this mixed-up world is God Himself. The emphasis is not our ability. When an ordeal is beyond our scope to reason or handle, God makes an *escape* door through which we can flee so that we can endure whatever we're going through.

Not realizing then the entire scripture in context, I needed to discover more of the meaning of "escape." It can be defined as an escape from confinement or to get free, as in a Monopoly game. It even means to avoid a serious or unwanted outcome.[1]

Proverbs 19:5 tells us unmistakably, *"A false witness will not go unpunished, and he who breathes out lies will **not escape"*** (emphasis added). Whether we are in a public or private position, there should be a moratorium of all flagrant lies, as they render harm.

Escape is proposed to be derived from the Latin word *excappare*, with the prefix "ex-," which means, "out, out of," and the Latin word *cappa*—"head covering" or "cloak."[2] By combining these together, we get the idea of *"coming out of your covering."* The New Testament derivatives of *escape* speak of fleeing. That's like paralyzing our protection status in Christ.

But watch yourselves lest your hearts be weighed down with dissipation and drunkenness and cares of this life, and that day come upon you suddenly like a trap. For it will come upon all who dwell on the face of the whole earth. But stay awake at all times, praying that you may have strength to escape all these things that are going to take place, and to stand before the Son of Man.

—Luke 21:34-36

The ancient Roman culture tried to avoid capture by throwing off they're adorning capes when fleeing from their enemy in a battle. So this is where the word derived its emphasis and usage.

Going back to 1 Corinthians 10:12, it says, *"Therefore let anyone who thinks that he stands take heed lest he fall."* Pride makes us think we can stand on our own two feet, capable of some great feat as I had thought I was doing for my marriage. But it was crumbling all around me. Verse 14 tells us to flee from idolatry. We aren't to glorify anyone greater than God, and that includes ourselves.

> *How shall we **escape** if we neglect such a great salvation? It was declared at first by the Lord, and it was attested to us by those who heard.*

—Hebrews 2:3, emphasis added

Avoid Who?

There is a focused picture in 2 Timothy 2:23 of what we should avoid if we are seeking the Lord with a pure heart. We are told not to have anything to do with those who are foolish or craving controversies just for the sake of it. Are there familiar people around us who relish quarreling? Our society today seems on a rampage of argumentativeness. Quarreling starts to reproduce in like kind everywhere it finds expression. It's like a fire of venom spreading rapidly through every vein, right to the heart.

But the Lord's servant has a different character reference. We are to be known, not for quarreling, but by being kind to everyone, able to teach, patiently enduring evil, and correcting our opponents with gentleness (v. 24). This is a tall order for most people, but these fruits or character qualities distinguish us as partaker's of God's Spirit.

Verse 26 tells us why: *"They may come to their senses and* **escape** *the snare of the devil, after being captured by him to do his will"* (emphasis added). God wants our senses to function, so they need to be developed to avoid demonic control. Senses are of the faculties—sight, hearing, smell, taste, or touch—by which we perceive stimuli originating from outside or inside the body.[3] The Lord instructs us to see and perceive spiritually so He can perform His Word.

This is our witness to those not following these attributes, causing a righteous appetite within them. If we can exhibit these qualities, then it makes it a possibility for them too. This will cause an unbeliever to repent by coming to the truth they *see* in you. People are always watching, so give them something worth witnessing. Give the world an optical fusion transfer of light.

> *I appeal to you, brothers, to watch out for those who cause divisions and create obstacles contrary to the doctrine that you have been taught;* ***avoid*** *them.*
>
> —Romans 16:17, emphasis added

Escape from the Enemy

> *"Son of dust,"* he said, *"you live among rebels who could know the truth if they wanted to, but they don't want to; they could* ***hear me if they would listen,*** *but they won't, for they are rebels."*
>
> —Ezekiel 12:2-3, TLB, emphasis added

Metal Dragon Dream, 8.13.04

I dreamed I was in a school building with my son. It had been reported over the loud speaker that there was a dragon flying outside of the building.

My son and I went to take a closer look outside, using the back entryway door. The metal dragon was flying over the school parking lot area. It had come to spy on us!

It left the premises for awhile. I felt I needed to leave the school and go somewhere else for safety. So my son and I ran quickly and got inside my car. We drove down the street traveling from west to east (spiritual change) in direction.

We noticed a dull gray, mechanical-looking dragon coming from behind us, gaining speed. It got very close to my driver's side window as it skirted the side, causing me to almost swerve. The dragon had tough, strong plates on its anatomy, welded together much like a suit of armor. It appeared cold in its demeanor, clunky in its mobility and threatening. Its piercing eyes were a sickening, yellow color.

I decided to turn the car around and go back to the school for protection.

*Joseph remembered the dreams which he had about them, and said to them, "You **are spies**; you have come to look at the undefended parts of our land."*

—Genesis 42:9, NASB, emphasis added

It was satan's plan to spy out and find vulnerable, weak, and unprotected places in my life. I was trying to run away from the enemy, but my boundaries had already been established by God. My son and I needed to go back to school, as something important had not been learned yet. That was also our place of protection from the enemy.

The armor appeared to be made of iron, which is symbolic of stubbornness or self-will. Armor is a hard, protective covering worn defensively in a combat situation. Isaiah 48:4 says, "*I know how stubborn and obstinate you are. Your necks are as unbending as iron*" (NLT).

Yellow represents fear, cowardice, and intellectual pride. Flying is normally for spiritual giftedness or to rise above circumstances; but when not submitted to God, it is used for satanic purposes and intents. "*Now the Spirit expressly says that in later times some will depart from the faith by devoting themselves to deceitful spirits and teachings of demons*" (1 Timothy 4:1).

I believe this dream was intended to give me warning, protection, and some correction on how to handle the situation. We were right where God intended us to be. School was in session and we were not to change our course. More training was required!

> *The latter glory of this house shall be greater than the former, says the LORD of hosts. And in this place I will give peace, declares the LORD of hosts.*
>
> —Haggai 2:9

How Shall We Escape?

> *Then the LORD said, "Just as my servant Isaiah has gone stripped and barefoot for three years, as a sign and portent against Egypt and Cush, so the king of Assyria will lead away stripped and barefoot the Egyptian captives and Cushite exiles, young and old, with buttocks bared—to Egypt's shame. Those who trusted in Cush and boasted in Egypt will be dismayed and put to shame. In that day the people who live on this coast will say, 'See what has happened to those we relied*

*on, those we fled to for help and deliverance from the king of
Assyria! How then can we escape?'"*

—Isaiah 20:3-6, NIV

There is a significant amount of symbolism in this passage from
Isaiah 20, as a sign both to the Jews and the Egyptians. Their
nakedness has a meaning of uncovering, as Isaiah still wore
his simple tunic underneath (see John 21:7). "Buttocks bared"
refers to prisoners led into captivity. Stripping himself of his
outer layer signified that the Jews must strip themselves of their
dependence on other nations as their resource.

*But you will be cursed if you reject the commands of the LORD
your God and turn away from him and worship gods you have
not known before.*

—Deuteronomy 11:28, NLT

Sackcloth was made of a dark, course burlap type of material
used for storage. It was worn on certain occasions to show sorrow and shamefulness. Prophets dressed in it by fastening the
girdle to their waist. It implied a time of mourning for national
or personal disaster. It represented a time of repentance or
deliverance from bondage.

*Then David said to Joab and all those who were with him, "Tear
your clothes and put on sackcloth. Go into deep mourning for
Abner." And King David himself walked behind the procession
to the grave.*

—2 Samuel 3:31, NLT

The Jews have put their hopes and dreams in the land of Cush,
while the Egyptians were bragging about their abundance of
resources, never lacking anything. Anytime we put our hopes

and fortunes in a foreign substitute, there is a void. They ran to these nations for rescue from their distresses because they could see what these nations had to offer. They were running from the tyrannical Assyrian King.

What about God's unending covenant? *"They shall ask the way to Zion, with faces turned toward it, saying, 'Come, let us join ourselves to the LORD in an everlasting covenant that will never be forgotten'"* (Jeremiah 50:5).

Where did that leave their eternal source? God was warning them not to put their confidence in an alliance with nations that were not a part of Him. Now that these idolatrous nations are out of favor, they are left asking the question as a people group, "How shall we escape? Who's out there that can protect us now?"

> *For he himself is our peace, who has made us both one and has broken down in his flesh the dividing wall of hostility.*

> —Ephesians 2:14

Paul's Escape

> *I know your works, your toil and your patient endurance, and how you cannot bear with those who are evil.*

> —Revelation 2:2

Paul had his own kind of escape. Actually he spent a large part of his adult ministry escaping those who would try to kill him and his colleagues. However, in Acts 16 we find he's been put in prison with Silas making merry to the Lord in the midst of their turmoil behind bars (vv. 25). They had just been beaten with rods (v. 22). In verse 23 it says, *"When they had laid many stripes on them, they threw them into prison, commanding the jailer to keep them securely"* (NKJV).

Outside of Christ, I believe Paul endured more punishment, pain, and torture than any other figure of faith. He just kept on going like an Energizer Bunny. Yet, at midnight, it tells us in verse 25, *"Paul and Silas were praying and singing hymns to God, and the prisoners were listening to them"* (NKJV). Now that's a captive audience; everyone was a potential convert to Christ.

"Suddenly there was a great earthquake, so that the foundations of the prison were shaken; and immediately all the doors were opened and everyone's chains were loosed" (v. 26, NKJV). As Isaiah 9:4 reiterates, *"For God will break the chains that bind his people and the whip that scourges them"* (NLT).

This is a metaphor of what was about to happen spiritually on the inside of a heart. The doors of ignorance and chains of captivity were about to be broken. As the prison guard awoke from an obvious sound sleep, he knew the consequences for an escaped prisoner was his own death (v. 27).

Paul loudly yells out to the guard not to slit his throat for presumed escaped prisoners; they were all safely in their jail cells (v. 28). The jailer goes searching for a "light" to see the truth, and he gets more than he bargained for. The impossibility of the situation brings fear and trembling to his heart as he asks Paul how to be saved (vv. 29-30).

Verse 31 gives a great witness and promise to all: *"Believe on the Lord Jesus Christ, and you will be saved, you and your household"* (NKJV). This is the first time salvation is extended to the entire family as the Holy Spirit moves in that capacity. The jailer then takes them home to wash and cleanse their stripes, *"and immediately he and all his family were baptized"* after *"having believed in God with all his household"* (vv. 32-34).

They were broken off because of their unbelief, but you stand fast through faith. So do not become proud, but fear.

—Romans 11:20

His Voiceprint

As long as you did what you felt like doing, ignoring God, you didn't have to bother with right thinking or right living, or right anything for that matter. But do you call that a free life? What did you get out of it? Nothing you're proud of now. Where did it get you? A dead end. But now that you've found you don't have to listen to sin tell you what to do, and have discovered the delight of listening to God telling you, what a surprise! A whole, healed, put-together life right now, with more and more of life on the way! Work hard for sin your whole life and your pension is death. But God's gift is real life, eternal life, delivered by Jesus, our Master.

—Romans 6:20-23, MSG

Your life depends on hearing the voice of God without excuses. His voice sounds like His Word. Even without the credentials of a three-letter title like PHD, CPA, etc., we can know the voice of the One who loves us. He designed us to know His voice, just like we can recognize the voice of each family member. There is no mistake, because it's always been there for us. We need only listen for His voiceprint imbedded on the inside of each one of us. Turn up the frequency, but listen for it.

Genesis 22:16-18 tells the unbelievable story of Abraham who had believed for his only son, his promise that took 100 years of his life to conceive:

By myself I have sworn, declares the LORD, because you have done this and have not withheld your son, your only son, I will surely bless you, and I will surely multiply your offspring as the stars of heaven and as the sand that is on the seashore. And your offspring shall possess the gate of his enemies, and in your offspring shall all the nations of the earth be blessed, because you have obeyed my voice.

This was an incredible promise given to Abraham that also included us. As his offspring, all the nations were given God's blessing. What were the criteria for such an extensive blessing? To hear and obey God's voice. So it is determined here we can unequivocally hear Him so we can obey Him.

Anyone who chooses to do the will of God will find out whether my teaching comes from God or whether I speak on my own. Whoever speaks on their own does so to gain personal glory, but he who seeks the glory of the one who sent him is a man of truth; there is nothing false about him.

—John 7:17-18, NIV

A simple prayer for those choosing to hear God's voice clearly:

As Your child, Lord, You know me inside and out. Let me hear Your voice DISTINCTLY, CLEARLY, AND UNAVOIDABLY! Remove all noise pollution of the world, the enemy's lies, and my own clouded sounds of reverberations that are not undeniably of Your wavelength. I yearn to hear Your tender words, thoughts, and instruction on anything You choose to say. Let nothing come between Your voice and my ears. Remove any resentments or unforgiveness that clogs up my heart's "ear" pathway. I absolutely acknowledge knowing Your clear-cut, recognizable words, tones, and sounds. I thank You, Lord, that Your voice and presence are always near me.

Be teachable to hear *His voice*, getting rid of any confusion. The more we read God's Word, the more attuned to His voice we become: "My sheep hear my voice" (John 10:27, emphasis added).

Escape the End

You, therefore, have no excuse, you who pass judgment on someone else, for at whatever point you judge another, you are condemning yourself, because you who pass judgment do the same things. Now we know that God's judgment against those who do such things is based on truth. So when you, a mere human being, pass judgment on them and yet do the same things, do you think you will escape God's judgment? Or do you show contempt for the riches of his kindness, forbearance and patience, not realizing that God's kindness is intended to lead you to repentance?

—Romans 2:1-4, NIV

Paul's letter above is directed to believers. Those who should know better are NO better. We can't justify ourselves in any area. We can't do anything apart from Christ because He is our way of redemption. Those who look at others to condemn them are showing off their weakness of guilt. This builds within us a place of captivity to pride and false righteousness.

These roots of rebellion are hiding about in our own soil. When we realize how undeserving we are of God's grace, I believe looking upon others' soiled faces will no longer faze us. We have authority to judge our own sin, but none of us are good enough to save ourselves. It's beyond our human ability; there is no dignity in sin. We all have darkness lurking within.

God is eminently gracious with patient enduring love that allows a significant duration of time to turn away from what's killing us. Sin is decay; it rots inside us. There is nothing we can pay or earn to receive His relief from grief. None of us can audaciously presume to order God around in His just judgments. Take His fortifiable love which is beyond comprehension. Turn to Him to bring change from challenges. Trust in Christ who gives us eternal life.

If we put ourselves in a place of privilege that we think others are not acceptable enough to receive, then we are the ones penalized by judgments. Being a score keeper of right and wrong makes us of no greater standing to escape God's confrontations. God doesn't punish us by pushing us away, He draws us to Himself. Repentance is not punishment; it's an opportunity for openness and wholeness in Christ. Receive Jesus' forgiveness; it's the only way.

God Himself has been holding back a weight of judgment upon those who have gone over the edge of His graces. Boundaries have limits within which we participate. The playing field has been leveled. We must chose which way we will go and which god we will serve. There is no escaping His declaration for future visitations. Pretending a false escape has no fire escape; we will get burned back down the alley way. To be found, we must get lost in Him.

We must seek to know God's will in our life and situations. Use these thoughts and inclinations to pray to that end. Ask the Lord to remove any rigid resistant places, to pierce all impenetrable stubbornness of pride and the inflexible unrepentant heart. Desire the Holy Spirit's liquid solvent to dissolve the hard ground we've allowed. Ask for God's miracle of deliverance. Give Him every misguided piece, as He's the puzzle Master making us complete.

Romans 2:5-11 (NIV)

But because of your stubbornness and your unrepentant heart, you are storing up wrath against yourself for the day of God's wrath, when his righteous judgment will be revealed. God "will repay each person according to what they have done." To those who by persistence in doing good seek glory, honor and immortality, he will give eternal life. But for those who are self-seeking and who reject the truth and follow evil, there will be wrath and anger. There will be trouble and distress for every human being who does evil: first for the Jew, then for the Gentile; but glory, honor and peace for everyone who does good: first for the Jew, then for the Gentile. For God does not show favoritism.

CHAPTER FIVE

Shame Hides

Not only that, but we rejoice in our sufferings, knowing that suffering produces endurance, and endurance produces character, and character produces hope, and hope does not put us to shame, because God's love has been poured into our hearts through the Holy Spirit who has been given to us.

—Romans 5:3-5

Un-Shame It

*"Fear not, for you will not be ashamed; be not confounded, for you will not be disgraced; for you will **forget the shame** of your youth, and the reproach of your widowhood you will remember no more. For your Maker is your husband, the LORD of hosts is his name; and the Holy One of Israel is your Redeemer, the God of the whole earth he is called. For the LORD has called you like a wife deserted and grieved in spirit, like a wife of youth when she is cast off, says your God. For a brief moment I deserted you, but with great compassion I will gather you. In overflowing anger for a moment I hid my face*

from you, but with everlasting love I will have compassion on you," Says the LORD your Redeemer.

—Isaiah 54:4-8, emphasis added

The dictionary tells us the word *shame* elicits a painful emotion of condemnation or a strong sense of guilt, embarrassment, unworthiness, and disgrace.[1] The biting sting of shame never produces fruits of purity, sanctification, or righteousness. I have seen this used in the Body of Christ, the workplace, and elsewhere. Shame will sabotage our forward thinking every time. It generates a defeatist mentality, like we're stuck in the mud. It is a tangible source of negativity swaying us backwards.

In Greek the word translated "reproach" means shame, blame, etc. When Jesus took our reproach inside His body, that included all the malicious opposition this world can thrust upon us.

He deprived the enemy from wielding this weapon against us, unless we accept that lie. When others accuse us wrongfully, we must allow the Lord alone to vindicate us and not become self fixers. We need to allow the Holy Spirit to deal with those trying to put a black tarp upon our head. He gives us righteous light to repent. Let us shake out the old; fortify ourselves anew.

*In you, O LORD, do I take refuge; let me **never be put to shame**; in your righteousness deliver me!*

—Psalm 31:1, emphasis added

A few people tried to condemn me over my divorce because of what they were standing for in their own marriage. It was never conceivable to me that I would experience a divorce. Mentally, it felt like *sabotage*. It's not just the loss of separation from a life partner. There was the continual barrage of grievances thrust my way that made me feel off-kilter.

According to Wikipedia, "*sabotage* is a deliberate action aimed at weakening an [entity] through subversion, obstruction, disruption, or destruction....One who engages in sabotage is a saboteur. Saboteurs typically try to **conceal their identities** because of the consequences of their actions"[2] (emphasis added).

Anyone concealing themselves is a threat to their true identity. If we can't be ourselves in Christ, then we are playing the devil's advocate game. Psalm 69:17-18 declares, "***Hide** not your face from your servant; for I am in distress; make haste to answer me. Draw near to my soul, redeem me; ransom me because of my enemies!*" (emphasis added).

I felt the center was falling out of my life. Everything seemed to be a target all at once. Life was shut off from me while I was trying to endure the conflicts. Don't allow self-pity to bind us to our failings. Those are behind us, so don't reflect on that mocking mirror. Jesus freedom comes to help us live in the present. Use self-pity stripper; like worn out paint, get rid of that deceiver.

> *Let not those who wait and hope and look for You, O Lord of hosts, be put to **shame** through me; let not those who seek and inquire for and require You [as their vital necessity] be brought to confusion and dishonor through me, O God of Israel.*

> —Psalm 69:6, AMP, emphasis added

Finances were a constant reminder of what I did not have nor could pay for. My babysitter quit because I did not have enough food supplies in our house. Shouldering this single responsibility alone was decidedly difficult with a new commission sales job. The only hope with cash flow was I knew exactly where my earnings would go. I had a strict budget with no frills. It was a do-or-die list of what had to be paid.

Creditors were constantly calling me about bills that my ex-husband and I had split up during our separation period. Most collection calls left me in despair with silent tears. After months of being harassed by a car loan company, I finally told them if they threatened me again I would quit paying my bill. They wanted me to pay for Fred's car note and mine together. They relented when I told them I barely had enough food to feed my children, but I was still making *my* car payment on time every month. I was determined to make it for my children's sake.

> *Do not let me be* **ashamed***, O LORD, for I have called upon You; let the wicked be ashamed; Let them be silent in the grave. Let the lying lips be put to silence, Which speak insolent things proudly and contemptuously against the righteous.*

—Psalm 31:17-18, NKJV, emphasis added

Cut Off

> *For evildoers shall be* **cut off***, but those who wait and hope and look for the Lord [in the end] shall inherit the earth.*

—Psalm 37:9, AMP, emphasis added

I expect there are a large number of people who experience the effect of being cut off from someone's life; I have experienced it many times myself. The term "cut off" means the same as being alienated from a group or activity. Condemnation is similar in that it leads to separation, while conviction brings a coming together by repentance allowing freedom to move forward.

Fred cut me off using several divisive tactics. Family can quit responding for extended periods of time for all the wrong reasons. Confrontation of another's mortality, spiritual condition, or bitter embroiled relationships needing forgiveness can effectively obstruct communication. Usually the person doing it is the one that is hurting the most, whether they realize it or not.

Introspection, self-focus, and scrutiny will cut off the power of God by presenting a blockage in the flow of the Spirit. When we get beyond the fear of man and put all our focus on His Kingdom, we lose self-consciousness. The freest place to be is in full surrender of focus on what the Lord wants for us instead of what others think.

Human expectation and soulish power are manipulations of legalism. When we contrive our own wand of magic as a spell upon others, we have ventured out in another field of darkness. It's contriving to produce some spectacle of power that is not anointed of the Holy Spirit. It becomes the witchcraft of rebellion. Cut it off!

Trying to cover up grievous acts escalates us to a place of increased defiance. It will alienate our communion with God. Protection can be abated as conditions are exacerbated. Without our relationship in place, all connections and revelations can be erased. Attempted endeavors will fail; we'll have nothing to hail from the devil's wimpy throne.

> For rebellion is as the sin of divination, and presumption is as iniquity and idolatry. Because you have rejected the word of the LORD, he has also rejected you from being king.

> —1 Samuel 15:23

Presumption, according to the dictionary, is a behavior or attitude that is boldly arrogant or offensive. It's based on partial evidence, being incomplete in its knowledge or conclusion.[3] The Holy Spirit doesn't lead us to partial truths or error. This can be caused by ignoring the will of God in a situation instead of asking for His guidance or confirmation in the Word of God.

Numbers 14:43-45 tells the story of defeat by presumption. Moses was warning the Israelites who had refused to follow the Lord's instructions and then recanted and decided to follow through in their own strength. Moses said,

> *"For there the Amalekites and the Canaanites are facing you, and you shall fall by the sword. Because you have turned back from following the LORD, the LORD will not be with you." But they **presumed** to go up to the heights of the hill country, although neither the ark of the covenant of the LORD nor Moses departed out of the camp. Then the Amalekites and the Canaanites who lived in that hill country came down and defeated them and pursued them, even to Hormah.*

> —Numbers 14:43-45, emphasis added

Paul knew what it felt to be cut off by others. In his personal remarks to Timothy, he says, "*At my first defense no one came to stand by me, but all deserted me. May it not be charged against them*" (2 Timothy 4:16). This sounds identical to how Christ prayed for those who hated him even while dying for them on His wooden cross. (Wood is symbolic for humility.) Total betrayal; no one vouched for Paul in his trial, as everyone left him standing alone—abandoned.

> *In panic I cried out, "I am **cut off** from the LORD!" But you heard my cry for mercy and answered my call for help.*

> —Psalm 31:22, NLT, emphasis added

When people terminate communication in a permanent way, they are actually cutting off the need or want to be in relationship any longer. Healthy relationships communicate honestly. We could take their detachments personally and feel betrayed. The best response I know is to pray while committing to love them through it and wait for the Lord to work on their hearts and minds. If we don't feel love for them, we must ask the Lord to give us His.

> *Thus says the LORD, the Holy One of Israel, and the one who formed him: "**Ask me** of things to come; will you command me concerning my children and the work of my hands?"*

—Isaiah 45:11, emphasis added

Cut Off My Enemies Dream

I saw a room full of chickens (representing fear). There was an altar containing an interim pastor sitting on the throne. There were three men lavishing and pampering the man on the throne. They were determined to see that all his needs were met. This pastor was in the form of a turkey (think: gobble, gobble) as he had a spirit of greed.

Next, the turkey was grazing in a field that had very little green grass. His feathers were all spread out strutting proudly in all his glory. The turkey noticed me and came charging after me angrily as if to attack me. Before it reached me, a man's hand appeared with a hand full of corn (God's sustenance). Corn grows in "ears," covered in husks. The distraction of food changed his course, forgetting about me. Immediately, the turkey's' head was **cut off**!

I saw a disappointed, humiliated, and disgraced turkey with all his feathers tucked underneath and a suitcase in his hand. He was going home. His authority (Christ as the head) was gone. Later, I saw the foolish turkey had died. He was roasting in a pan for a Thanksgiving dinner. After much intercession, the chicken's heads were also cut off.

The spirit of fear and intimidation was broken over them in this community. Behaviors are transferable! Don't be diminished by poor perception. Look for God's evidence of revealed light exposing motives. Be comprehensive with those who influence you; don't be easily taken in by sightless, gawking appearances. Don't blindly screen yourself out of the Holy Spirit's insight. Ask the Holy Spirit to disclose everything that's necessary.

> *"Ah, stubborn children," declares the LORD, "who carry out a plan, but not mine, and who make an alliance, but not of my Spirit, that they may add sin to sin; who set out to go down to Egypt, without asking for my direction, to take refuge in the protection of Pharaoh and to seek shelter in the shadow of Egypt! Therefore shall the protection of Pharaoh turn to your **shame**, and the shelter in the shadow of Egypt to your humiliation."*
>
> —Isaiah 30:1-3, emphasis added

As hurtful as a broken relationship may be, the one we never want to be without is a heavenly one. The most important advocate we have is the Lord who promises us an eternal pathway. Don't ever be cursed by the isolation of not maintaining a lifeline with Him. We must cut off all false gods, idols, and arrogant pursuits in the world. These will carry us the wrong direction, then mislead and numb us from our reality in Christ. Don't allow the enemy to drain us dry; *cut him off!*

> *For those blessed by Him shall inherit the earth, But those cursed by Him shall be **cut off**.*
>
> —Psalm 37:22, NKJV, emphasis added

Secret Guilt

Then you will seek Me, inquire for, and require Me [as a vital necessity] and find Me when you search for Me with all your heart.

—Jeremiah 29:13, AMP

There are two kinds of guilt. One is what we reap from a criminal offense, deserving blame for a reprehensible act or a purposeful error or a violation of one's values. It is a deep conviction of wrongdoing. The other kind of guilt is one bestowed upon us for no valid reason; being forced into a false guilt trip because of a belief perpetuated skilled conniver. I call that manipulation by deception. Has anyone said, "You should be ashamed of yourself"? Our guilt (or fear) response tries to figure it out: "Am I?"

Guilt is a natural response to things against our God-given conscience. It is a self-corrector of remorse, regret, or conflict. If not dealt with, guilt leads to emotions of unworthiness, inferiority, despair, or inadequacy. If we've met someone who couldn't receive a compliment or praise, this may be the reason. Left unchallenged it could harden one's heart to never be dealt with again. Some try to avoid guilt by blame shifting, self-justification, pity, or making excuses.

If we keep looking at the past places of disapproval, we're living in guilt. It will stifle us and keep us from embracing Christ's Kingdom with confidence. It causes a breach in our relationship with Him. We must take captive these defeatist thoughts, as 2 Corinthians 10:4-5 says, *"For the weapons of our warfare are not of the flesh but have divine power to destroy strongholds. We destroy arguments and every lofty opinion raised against the knowledge of God, and take every thought captive to obey Christ."*

There is also a guilt kept hidden by secret pleasures, which has a way of changing us. Others feel those changes and are affected by them. Perhaps a wife, for instance, is unaware of her husband's addiction to pornography, but his addiction leads to the guilty pleasure of secretiveness changing his attitude toward her as his sexual partner.

It can potentially distort his perception of women and God's image for her as his companion by covenant. She perceives that change and speculates on the possible cause—he finds her unattractive, he doesn't love her any more, or he's having an affair. While none of these conjectures are factual, the consequences of his "private" perverted habit are potentially devastating to her, their marriage, and their family. This is evident if his secret is not discovered. Guilt and sin both separate us!

> For the wages of sin is death, but the free gift of God is eternal life in Christ Jesus our Lord.
>
> —Romans 6:23

Our value is not based on the precedence of our worthiness. We are sandwiched in Christ's virtues, not our own. It's in His righteousness that we are righteous as our inheritance. Build everything on Him, and it will not fail permanently. Everything impinges on what Christ has, not what we can earn or do. What the Son has set free is free indeed (John 8:36). We shouldn't let anyone sabotage our relationship with Christ. He's the Master key to open doors for us.

> GOD, you smiled on your good earth! You brought good times back to Jacob! You lifted the cloud of guilt from your people, you put their sins far out of sight.
>
> —Psalm 85:1, MSG

The Holy Spirit will convict us of sin (John 16:8), while satan condemns. The adversary's job title is the accuser of the brethren (Revelation 12:10). Our enemy wants us in the bondage of false guilt to tie us in immobilizing knots that prevent healing. First John 1:9 tells us, *"If we confess our sins, He is faithful and just to forgive us our sins and to cleanse us from all unrighteousness"* (NKJV). We are INSIDE of Christ; we're as righteous as He is. His righteousness is our protective shield from every assault. We're free, so dislodge all false disgrace and regret. Always move forward in life.

> *By entering through faith into what God has always wanted to do for us—set us right with him, make us fit for him—we have it all together with God because of our Master Jesus. And that's not all: We throw open our doors to God and discover at the same moment that he has already thrown open his door to us. We find ourselves standing where we always hoped we might stand—out in the wide open spaces of God's grace and glory, standing tall and shouting our praise.*
>
> —Romans 5:1, MSG

The Wicked Scheme

> *When the righteous triumph, there is great glory, but when the wicked rise, people **hide** themselves. Whoever conceals his transgressions will not prosper, but he who confesses and forsakes them will obtain mercy.*
>
> —Proverbs 28:12-13, emphasis added

The famous story of Mordecai and Queen Esther in the Book of Esther hones in on goodness as it contrasts to evil. Those in authority are in positions to devastate and undermine a nation and its people or to bestow decency and honor to the land. People perish beneath the thought patterns of those against God's precepts and designed order; diminishing in displayed lack of integrity. But the righteous ones can take an undeniably dominant stand unto Christ's overwhelming might.

What happened to the implementation of Haman's wicked scheme for the detriment of Esther's people? (Esther 6-9). Observing Queen Esther's view, let's determine what Psalm 35 says about such an individual or group pursuing the demise of God's children.

> Let them be put to shame and dishonor who seek after my life! Let them be turned back and disappointed who devise evil against me! Let them be like chaff before the wind, with the angel of the LORD driving them away! Let their way be dark and slippery, with the angel of the LORD pursuing them! For without cause they **hid** their net for me; without cause they dug a pit for my life. Let destruction come upon him when he does not know it! And let the net that he **hid** ensnare him; let him fall into it—to his destruction! Then my soul will rejoice in the LORD, exulting in his salvation.

—Psalm 35:4-9, emphasis added

Proverbs and Psalms say similar things about those that hide their evil ways. First it says they will not prosper, and then destruction is their reward. Whatever is sent against another will be recompensed. The one who plots harm will reap a consequence of his own demise. Our intentions determine our outcome—evil for evil or good for better. We will fall into whatever it is we are building. Quicksand will sink those who enter; so build on the solid rock of Jesus Christ, the stabilizer of our soul.

Oh that my ways may be steadfast in keeping your statutes! Then I shall not be put to shame, having my eyes fixed on all your commandments.

—Psalm 119:5-6

Boulder Dream: Unburden It

*And they were saying to one another, "Who will roll away the stone for us from the entrance of the tomb?" And looking up, they saw that **the stone** had been rolled back—it was **very large**.*

—Mark 16:3-4, emphasis added

I was tenaciously trying to pivot a large, heavy boulder towards the Lord. I was sizing it up at a standstill being larger in stature than myself. The Lord came toward me, reached out for the boulder with His hands, as it instantly became a large, lightweight plastic beach ball. The Lord twirled it around his waist *twice* in a rotating circular motion.

When the Lord does something twice it is doubly significant. It means to pay attention, *"that the thing is fixed by God, and God will shortly bring it about"* (Genesis 41:32). Now that's my kind of God! He amends the matter swiftly, carrying it out without unnecessary delay.

As the plastic ball moved around the Lord's waist the first time, I noticed the ball became smaller in diameter. By the second rotation the ball became the size of a marble, which turned into a small speck of sand. It then swiftly navigated to the tip of His index finger. It landed rolling into the Lord's left palm.

The left side of something in this dream conveys God's ability in the midst of my own incapability. I was striving to get something accomplished in my own effort. It became too difficult for me to handle. The use of hands relates to direction and relationship.

"My grace is all you need. My power works best in weakness."
So now I am glad to boast about my weaknesses, so that the
power of Christ can work through me.

—2 Corinthians 12:9, NLT

An index finger in dreams regards the prophetic realm. God took my boulder of problems and reduced them to a tiny grain of sand centered at the end of His protective covering. It had become insignificant to behold, something easily disposed of. Prophesy His possibilities to any clogged blockages; pray for discernment, while looking to the future for momentum.

A *blockage* is an entity that stops something (such as blood) from moving through something (such as a blood vessel).[4] Satan wants to stop us on every level. The blood of Christ is something satan did not possess; it's a mystery the devil can't trespass. We have the power in Jesus' name to use our voice, commanding all obstructions that get in our line of fire be abolished from our family.

A finger is something used *to grasp*. It is used as an analogy of God's Spirit, power, and dominion over all creation. The finger is tied to the blood in many scriptures such as Leviticus 4:17: "*And the priest shall dip his **finger** in the blood and sprinkle it seven times before the LORD in front of the veil*" (emphasis added). Let Christ's blood set us free from all burdens, unveil all travails.

Psalm 8:3-4 reflects,

When I consider your heavens, the work of your fingers, the
moon and the stars, which you have set in place, what is

mankind that you are mindful of them, human beings that you care for them?

—Psalm 8:3-4

Our every vain effort is negligible in contrast to the effortless acts of the Lord's fingertips which can move mountains.

I heard the words "nori laden" one morning, which made no sense to me. It rolled around in my head until I found out what these two words meant. Nori is dried "laver seaweed" pressed into sheets used for wrapping sushi.[5] Laden means burdened, as loaded down.[6]

The use of laver seaweed is striking because a laver was used in the Jewish tabernacle for the cleansing of the priests' hands and feet. It was considered a sacred copper water bowl. It was constructed from the remnants of metal mirrors the women brought out of Egypt. They took something from their time of captivity and used it as a sacrifice unto God.

We read of this in Exodus 38:8: "*They made the bronze basin and its bronze stand from the mirrors of the women who served at the entrance to the tent of meeting*" (NIV). Instead of using the mirrors to reflect their past image or mindset, they became instruments to reflect Christ as the laver held water.

The Holy Spirit cleverly gave me a new visual on how to view undesired, mind-breaking burdens. We are to wrap up all oppressive burdens and roll these over to the Lord. This will remove the entanglements of falsely perceived failure as He meshes His loving impressions for us. God wants us to achieve our future inheritance as we flourish and thrive today.

Roll your works upon the Lord [commit and trust them wholly to Him; He will cause your thoughts to become agreeable to His will, and] so shall your plans be established and succeed.

—Proverbs 16:3, AMP

Toils and Trials

Hear me, O God, as I voice my complaint; protect my life from the threat of the enemy. **Hide** *me from the conspiracy of the wicked, from that noisy crowd of evildoers. They sharpen their tongues like swords and aim their words like deadly arrows. They shoot from ambush at the innocent; they shoot suddenly, without fear. They encourage each other in evil plans, they talk about **hiding** their snares; they say, "Who will see it?" They plot injustice and say, "We have devised a perfect plan!" Surely the human mind and heart are cunning. But God will shoot them with his arrows; they will suddenly be struck down. He will turn their own tongues against them and bring them to ruin; all who see them will shake their heads in scorn. All mankind will fear; they will proclaim the works of God and ponder what he has done. Let the righteous rejoice in the LORD and take refuge in him; all the upright in heart glory in him!*

—Psalm 64, NIV, emphasis added

For those going thru trials, legal matters, or tribulations, the Word says to expect it. It's not something to be considered weird. We have not been singled out for abuse. James 1:2-4 tells us to "*consider it all joy, my brethren, when you encounter various trials, knowing that the testing of your faith produces endurance. And let endurance have its perfect result, so that you may be perfect and complete, lacking in nothing*" (NASB).

Blessed is the man who remains steadfast under trial, for when he has stood the test he will receive the crown of life, which God has promised to those who love him.

—James 1:12

After my divorce and eventual redemptive remarriage to a wonderful man I have called my own for many years, there was a succession of legal matters with which we seemed to always be involved. I was never the pursuant; in other words, I did not initiate a legal custody case. The only time I retained my attorney for legal attention was to make a joint custody agreement with Fred on already agreed mutual terms. My attorney drew up the necessary paperwork so the judge could sign off on it.

You shall not be partial in judgment. You shall hear the small and the great alike. You shall not be intimidated by anyone, for the judgment is God's. And the case that is too hard for you, you shall bring to me, and I will hear it.

—Deuteronomy 1:17

I posted a scripture on our refrigerator during that time, giving me the fortitude for the moment and the future: "*Return to the stronghold [of security and prosperity], you prisoners of hope; even today do I declare that I will restore double your former prosperity to you*" (Zechariah 9:12, AMP). We seemed to be prisoners of the legal processes, but I was declaring us prisoners of Christ's hope instead. *Hope* is a word to describe a future situation we are looking toward. It's an arrow pointing us toward something we believe will happen.

Mark 13:11 tells us, "*And when they bring you to trial and deliver you over, do not be anxious beforehand what you are to say, but say whatever is given you in that hour, for it is not you who speak, but the Holy Spirit."*

Hope was such a relevant and necessary theme to us. It was so important that we named a newly found rescue dog Hope and brought her home with us. We were calling out hope all the time in the form of a caramel-colored, mixed breed. At the time my new husband was having a custody case begin, and his sons moved out for the first time. It created a wretched brokenness in him. He cried many tears over the thought of their absence and the injustice he felt. God knew we needed a special friend to help us through, alongside the Holy Spirit. God made a way for companionship.

> *I've told you these things to prepare you for rough times ahead. They are going to throw you out of the meeting places. There will even come a time when anyone who kills you will think he's doing God a favor. They will do these things because they never really understood the Father. I've told you these things so that when the time comes and they start in on you, you'll be well-warned and ready for them.*
>
> —John 16:1-3, MSG

Position Legally and Spiritually

> *Don't be hotheaded and rush to court! You may start something you can't finish and go down before your neighbor in **shameful** defeat. So discuss the matter with him privately. Don't tell anyone else, lest he **accuse** you of slander and you can't withdraw what you said.*
>
> —Proverbs 25:8-10, TLB, emphasis added

Anyone who tells lies against the neighbors in court or on the street is a loose cannon.

—Proverbs 25:18, MSG

Does anyone believe God can use their dreams to help with litigation? Of course, He can use wisdom in any form to council us. He designed us for His usefulness and purposes. This can bring righteous leverage to turn matters around if we heed His voice.

They make many promises, take false oaths and make agreements; therefore lawsuits spring up like poisonous weeds in a plowed field.

—Hosea 10:4, NIV

Courtroom Dream

This dream was set in a large auditorium type building with a stage in front. It was packed with people from one end to the next. There was a male judge with a roll-taking clerk calling out all the people's names to be seen that day. There were about twenty to thirty rows of people sitting in individual desks with ten (journey/law) people in each row.

I was sitting in the first seat on the *third* row (Trinity) from the front on the right side (do what is right). The man calling the attendance called out my name first. He asked for my social security number. I proceeded to tell him the first *three* numbers, as the judge interrupted him. The judge wanted to know if there were other people expecting to be heard that day.

A lady stood up on the opposite side from my section and said she had hoped to be put on the docket that day. She stated that she could tell that our case would take all day and the judge agreed with her. This meant my case would take a substantial amount of time.

I noticed my Social Security number flashing on a large lit up screen over the stage. It showed the first *three* numbers I had spoken aloud before the group, followed by zeros behind it in white numbers in front of a black background. Sometimes these digits can be a scripture reference. We can take the first two numbers, followed by the last one and ask the Lord what verse in the Bible He is referring us to. It could also be the other way around—the first number, followed by the last.

The judge continued his conversation with what was most important to him. He spoke to us about the love of our children being of utmost precedent for any parent. That should be the main reason for any of us being in his courtroom. Our children should be the motivation for us and we should want their best!

This made my heart melt as I stood up from my desk. I walked over to a woman sitting in the same room on the other side from us. I went up to a lady and bent over to whisper in her ear. I got so close to her face that I felt her brown hair against my face. I spoke about the love of our sons and said that should be our motivation. Then I asked her, "Why are you doing this?" She would not look at my face or turn her head toward mine to look directly at me. She only said, "I want a compromise."

My interpretation of this: I believe God is giving instruction on how to present ourselves before the judge. This was what the Lord wanted us to emphasize, our love for our children. It also showed the intent of the other party involved. It's what people *don't* say at times that will speak volumes. The woman did not speak of love or wanting the very best for the children involved.

The use of numbers in this dream was staggering to me, as well as relevant. The twenty and ten equaled the fullness of God's judgment. There were two zeros, followed by four zeros at the end of my social. Two plus four equals the number six, meaning man's way.

Color has significant meaning as, will be explained further in other sections. The only color that stood out was brown hair. Brown relates to humanity or sinful nature. The other color that is important to look out for is white, that is God's signature He is the dream Giver.

Compromise (noun) is a concession to something that is detrimental.[7] As a verb it means to expose or make liable to suspicion or disrepute.[8] We must never compromise our true self to anyone for any amount or to allow shame to cause us to back down for what we are believing for. What can mere man do?

> *If anyone attacks you, don't for a moment suppose that I sent them, And if any should attack, nothing will come of it. I create the blacksmith who fires up his forge and makes a weapon designed to kill. I also create the destroyer—but no weapon that can hurt you has ever been forged. Any accuser who takes you to court will be dismissed as a liar. This is what God's servants can expect. I'll see to it that everything works out for the best.*

> —Isaiah 54:15, MSG

I found this prayer in my journal:

> It's time for a change. Show us Your love for us. Release those that have been sent against us. My husband is a man after God's own heart. You put us together for a purpose. We have been through fire, but we will not be burned. We have an attorney, but God is the attorney at our side. We take Your presence with us. We will feel His electricity with us in the courtroom. Release God's "authority" in the courtroom.

> *When you pass through the waters, I will be with you; and through the rivers, they shall not overwhelm you; when you*

walk through fire you shall not be burned, and the flame shall
not consume you.

—Isaiah 43:2

Legal Advice

The eyes of the LORD are in every place, keeping watch on the
evil and the good.

—Proverbs 15:3

He does not slander with his tongue, Nor does evil to his neigh-
bor, Nor takes up a reproach against his friend.

—Psalm 15:3, NASB

God is saying to us to speak kindly of our neighbors; never to gossip or say anything to destroy another's reputation. We are not to hurt another person in any way or become a reproach to them. Reproach is to blame or discredit, disgrace or shame another.[9] We must pursue love at all times, even when we feel the opposite. Love is a priority to God's law being fulfilled.

Peter gives us wise advice to follow (1 Peter 5:6-9):
- Humble yourselves under the mighty hand of God so that at the proper time He may exalt you.
- Cast all your anxieties on Him, because He cares for you.
- Be sober-minded.
- Be watchful. Your adversary the devil prowls around like a roaring lion, seeking someone to devour.
- Resist the enemy.
- Be firm in your faith.

- Know that the same kinds of suffering are being experienced by your brotherhood throughout the world.

What God will give you for it:

And after you have suffered a little while, the God of grace, who has called you to his eternal glory in Christ, will Himself **restore, confirm, strengthen, and establish you.**

—I Peter 5:10, emphasis added

To me grace is like a trampoline of stretching strength. We can fall upon it in dire weakness with enough bounce in the strong, taut material and coiled springs to bring us back up on our feet again. God wants to transmit that grace into every fiber of our being. He is the repair fix-it kit for every bump we encounter. He is favor for the future and establishes us in all we are lacking. He gives us everything we need when called upon.

When we bristle up against grace, we break. God is teaching us to gracefully stretch through the periods of suffering. Grace shines forth love to the unloving, giving us what we don't deserve or can't possibly earn. It is the opposite of judgment, which desires punishment on others.

Do not speak evil against one another, brothers. The one who speaks against a brother or judges his brother, speaks evil against the law and judges the law. But if you judge the law, you are not a doer of the law but a judge. There is only one lawgiver and judge, he who is able to save and to destroy. But who are you to judge your neighbor?

—James 4:11-12

Grace can cause us to recover and uncover all that has been lost. The law requires a certain set standard of ardent, rigorous structured rules. Satan wants to capture our present matter and put us at a "standstill." The deceiver offers a plausibility of truth and reason, all a deceptive appearance. Christ validates truth with undeserved favor toward us.

The strongest advice I can recommend is to protect your heart during a time of legal proceedings. It's a stressful time, so use the Word of God as a counterintuitive shift. Put on the full armor of God as found in Ephesians 6:10-18 against the strategies of the devil. Remember, our battle is not flesh and blood. Walk in the Gospel of peace as this affects the mind and cover all thoughts with scripture, as this keeps that peace stable. Don't be overcome by the evil avenues people lay out; avoid them. Take a different path called Straight Street.

Beloved, never avenge yourselves, but leave it to the wrath of God, for it is written, "Vengeance is mine, I will repay, says the Lord." To the contrary, "if your enemy is hungry, feed him; if he is thirsty, give him something to drink; for by so doing you will heap burning coals on his head." Do not be overcome by evil, but overcome evil with good.

—Romans 12:19-21

Justice

*When you spread out your hands, **I will hide my eyes from you**; even though you make many prayers, I will **not listen**; your hands are full of blood. Wash yourselves; make yourselves clean; remove the evil of your deeds from **before my eyes**; cease to do evil, learn to do good; seek **justice**, correct oppression; bring **justice** to the fatherless, plead the widow's cause.*

—Isaiah 1:15-17, emphasis added

I cannot improve upon scripture for the ways of justice expressed biblically. I hope by reading some of the scriptures below that it becomes quite evident what our place should be in the courtroom of law. Stave off vindictiveness and all other negative emotions flying around during this time.

> *Therefore justice is far from us, and righteousness does not overtake us, we hope for light, and behold, darkness, and for brightness, but we walk in gloom.*

—Isaiah 59:9

It is also crucial while we pray for justice that our own heart is not embittered toward our opponent. Justice will not work while we are accusing and speaking evil. We are to bless our enemies despite the situation. God knows exactly how to weigh the heart and mind. This warning comes from personal experience. If we want justice, we must completely forgive in the midst of the battle. Don't be afraid to make errors; God will qualify us.

- Be discrete with information.
- Be as comfortable with the situation as possible.
- Don't disguise facts; fight facts with truth.
- Be firm and resist any temptation to retaliate.
- Let the Lord correct, instruct, and chastise with just measure (see Jeremiah 10:24).

Leviticus 19:15 instructs us: "*You shall do **no injustice** in court. You shall not be partial to the poor or defer to the great, but in righteousness shall you judge your neighbor*" (emphasis added).

Psalm 37:28 gives this encouragement: "*For the LORD loves justice And does not **forsake** His godly ones*" (NASB, emphasis added). I would think it to be imperative to stay in the Word of God during this season. Wrap your head around things that are positive, supportive, and good. Don't allow the dirty business at hand to put you under the bus. Get scriptures to reinforce the fortitude in which you will endure this. Read them daily, including the ones in this section, to sustain you.

I had a simple dream.

Ring Dream

A man I knew from my dream class came up close to me on his bike. A bike in dreams is an individual ministry or calling. He said he had a word from the Lord for me. He shared, "The Lord wants you to stop hiding behind a ring. He wants you to fully come out and be yourself."

A ring symbolizes covenant. I was hiding behind it as if under the law instead of being comfortable in His grace. Christ is our mediator who fulfills our relationship. God writes His love on our hearts as He opens the doors of opportunity. This was more validation not to hide behind anything!

*Behold my servant, whom I uphold, my chosen, in whom my soul delights; I have put my Spirit upon him; he will bring forth **justice** to the nations. He will not cry aloud or lift up his voice, or make it heard in the street; a bruised reed he will not break, and a faintly burning wick he will not quench; he will faithfully bring forth justice. He will not grow faint or be discouraged till he has established justice in the earth; and the coastlands wait for his law.*

—Isaiah 42:1-4, emphasis added

Stand Firm—Don't Pass Out

What are we doing with the grace of God to endure in 1 Peter 5:12 is to "**stand firm in it**" (emphasis added). Don't waiver or be moved by the craziness of the world. Stand up, stand out, and stand in duration. Just *stand*; don't fall out or collapse by some invisible force. Emotionally we get exhausted, but Jesus revives us as we soak in His words of renewal. It's like taking a nutritional supplement every day for new energy.

These are powerful instructions Peter has set for us to follow, so let's consider digging deeper in their application. To review it further, I have delved deeper into the scripture text we covered above—1 Peter 5.

Our stance begins with one of humility. If we make a line in the sand of pride, we will most definitely sink right into it. Go to the Father instead; acknowledging we don't know how to handle the situation. Ask Him for the decision-making power to know which way to go, what choices to make, and for Godly guidance. Start these beginnings off right, so we won't have to pay the repercussions later for those representing our case.

All fear and anxieties must be cast into the Father's lap, because no one cares more than Him. We must recognize Him first in the battles of life, which spin out of control rapidly. The duration of a battle can wear us out, so casting these depleting emotions on Him will be what sustains us as we feed ourselves on His Word and strengthen ourselves in His presence. We must remind ourselves daily that we are loved despite controversy.

Don't be deceived by every word spoken. Weigh the balance. The enemy of our soul will use anything to trip us up. He goes for the weakest points and looks for wounded ones. Let's get our wits about us. If someone is addressing a situation for the first time, stop and wait for a correct response. If uncertain, then wait to proceed. Get clarity on the options. Remain consistent to goals and beliefs.

Once a method or plan has been reached, then deal with the opposers. Don't flinch by their behaviors or accusations as they're thrown. Firm up what's believed in, get a plan of action.

Put faith to practice, because every bit of it will be needed. You haven't been isolated in this test. Many are suffering all over the world in one way or another. Some we can't identify with because the conditions are so severe. We are unified by one faith and can trust in the Lord to see us through.

Walk through the fire. I said *through*, not around. After we have suffered for some duration, God's grace will wrap itself around us. His promise of restoration, confirmation, and strength will make us more than we were to begin with. The final outcome is in His hands.

Finally, we must **stand** for all we're worth, because our worthiness is built upon Christ who paid the ultimate price for it. Stand in faith trusting God who knows all and has our back, regardless of how we perceive it. Even when the circumstances don't line up to our expectations, acknowledge that God knows best. Fight the good fight of faith. It doesn't say the bad fight; it is a GOOD fight, spiritually speaking.

> *If you are not **firm in faith**, you will not be **firm** at all.*

> —Isaiah 7:9, emphasis added

Secrets Misconstrued

> *Precept upon precept, Line upon line...That they might go and fall backward, and be broken And snared and caught.... For we have made lies our refuge, And under falsehood we have **hidden ourselves**.*

> —Isaiah 28:13, 15, NKJV, emphasis added

There was something that I used to think was a virtue found in Proverbs 11:13, which says, "*He who goes about as a talebearer reveals **secrets**, but he who is trustworthy and faithful in spirit* *keeps a matter **hidden***" (AMP, emphasis added). Alongside that add Proverbs 25:9: "*Argue your case with your neighbor himself, and do not reveal another's **secret***" (emphasis added).

Taken in context this makes for a great friend, client, or advocate in our life. But when we "act as undercover police" hiding information meticulously, this can be applied against all sound reason. We may revel in the fact that we're a remarkable confidant because we would never betray their private matters. God didn't make us to be containers of sewage from other's dirty wells. When we step over that safe partition line leaping towards a destructive one, there is a price to pay. Not being able to discern what should be kept secret and what shouldn't be disclosed gets messed up quickly.

Betraying a friend, associate, or family member will undermine your credibility. This will break down trust causing insurmountable pain. Slander is never a solution as a believer. Proverbs 18:6 recounts that a self-confident fool's lips bring contention and his mouth invites a beating. It's a cop-out for wanting our own *fan club* by degrading someone else to his or her detriment. We are instead taught in the Word to deal with a situation in love and wisdom. We need *both* to be able to discern the difference.

If we're unsure whether we have a circumstance that needs to be examined outside of our perimeter of experience, then seek council. Shame has no leverage on us; that can only be the enemy. "Shame-dom" is a false influential measurement. Get "Kingdom" advice from the Word of God, church, a Christian counseling source, or some other Godly organization that has extensive references available. We need to surround ourselves with those who believe in us. Choose confidants carefully. They will stand with us no matter what life throws our way.

The most effective tool in my life was seeking out scripture that specifically addressed the needs I had. I would write them, type them, or highlight them in a scripture book and read them every day as if my life depended on it. It did indeed! I needed to know that God's Word was taking an effect on my circumstances. The greatest benefit I evidenced was while I was in outside sales. I highlighted all the pertinent scripture dealing with the benefits of God's provision for me. I read them every morning before work, and even while driving to appointments. I was consistently in the top percentile list of sellers in our company. That was despite the gossip I'd overheard of how naïve I was.

> *Those who look to him are radiant, and their faces shall **never be ashamed**. This poor man cried, and the **LORD heard him** and saved him out of all his troubles.*

—Psalm 34:5-6, emphasis added

Erroneous Reality

> *My friends scorn me; my eye pours out tears to God.*

—Job 16:20

For years my hiding the truth created a susceptibility based on untruth. It was something I was ashamed of. I became an easily tormented target of the enemy. My sensitivity level was so high, I'd analyze anything to an almost finite end. My mind was at stake! I sought God's Word and promises with abandonment. I gradually became skilled at declaring and confessing the Word over my life's necessities on all levels. Repetition became my friend, finding targeted key verses that helped my various predicaments. I knew who I was in Christ. I had every confidence in

Him, my Liberator. When others fail me, My Rock and Fortress were in Christ alone.

I still had difficulty when others put me down, whether I agreed with it or not. I hadn't learned to separate myself from those types of spiritual attacks. I pursued that area tangibly, reading books and taking courses that helped me understand.

Eventually, I studied materials from Cleansing Stream Ministries that I was a part of for twelve years. They categorized shame, condemnation, and fear all together. I had to get a grasp on this area. I set my heart to be free of it permanently. It was a stronghold in my life, knocking me down time and again.

Shame arrested and unnerved me boldly. I had to be free of these false shackles. When I realized shame was a deformity in my shield of life, I became determined to pursue this deviant invader. What was it doing to me? How could it really not hound me anymore?

While in church I envisioned garlic being pressed by a garlic press, squeezing it to a pulp. It was an oozy, strong-smelling substance coming out by being forced through the **holes**. This vivid garlic had many layers of tough resiliency, but with enough pressure it conformed to the image of what it was being pressed through. Shame had to be squeezed out of me so the image of Christ could sustain me.

Revelation 12:10 explains that iniquity (from past generations in our bloodlines) must be cast out (AMP). It must be cast out before power comes. Oil and water don't mix, just like dark and light don't join together. They are separate entities. Light always overtakes darkness as the superior source.

Iniquities are passed down through our mothers and fathers and theirs before them. It is like a damaged apple or wounded extremity that doesn't heal. It creates a soft darkened crevice.

This weakness or bend goes against Christ's best. I recommend not waiting to get free of this. Deal with it now. Seek the freedom that is yours in Christ through the method God has for you to take. Use His authority in Jesus, so curses that run in a family are broken off for good.

This same method holds true in our lives if we submit to the living Creator who knows us through and through. As our lives are squeezed from daily pressures, we can conform to Christ's image or become a mushy mess. Is it any wonder some don't want to pay the price for Christ when in fact they are suffering relentlessly by not submitting their ways to Him?

Answers are in God's Word. We can fast and pray and speak His words of life defiantly against the enemy of our soul. The weakness can't stay if we determine that is the way it will be. Pursue right and true answers. God is on our side; He has spiritual ammunition available for us to use.

> *You will not have to fight this battle. Take up your positions; stand firm and see the deliverance the LORD will give you, Judah and Jerusalem. Do not be afraid; do not be discouraged. Go out to face them tomorrow, and the LORD will be with you.*

> —2 Chronicles 20:17, NIV

You are Christ's beloved child. You are never alone in the fight.

I think sometimes people want to see us for less than we are. When they are compared with others, they don't want to fall short. But we have to pay a price for where we are and where we want to be. We must decide where we are going for the Kingdom of joy. There is freedom and more freedom for those that want it.

Personally, shame sabotaged a ton of pleasure from my life and caused me to worry too much about what others thought of me, even those with real credentials to their name. Over thinking ourselves, self-analyzing, or narcissistic tendencies rob us of happiness instead of enjoying others. Being delivered of people's opinions set me free to love on another level.

> And have no fellowship with the unfruitful works of darkness, but rather expose them. For it is **shameful** even to speak of those things that are done by them in **secret**. But all things that are exposed are made manifest by the light, for whatever makes manifest is light.

> —Ephesians 5:11-13, NKJV, emphasis added

King David's Secret Shame

> But now I have written to you not to keep company with anyone named a brother, who is sexually immoral, or covetous, or an idolater, or a reviler, or a drunkard, or an extortion—not even to eat with such a person

> —1 Corinthians 5:11, NKJV

Second Samuel, chapter 11, recalls springtime for all good kings to go to battle. Of course we all know it's also the time for love to bloom! This is when Bathsheba's bath is viewed from King David's vantage point on his rooftop. All David's fighting men were out fighting the Ammonites in Rabbath, but David stayed at home. Instead of spearheading his Ammonite war, David was setting himself up for a fall right from the start of the season.

Samuel describes Bathsheba as very beautiful—irresistible in David's eyes. His next step is to inquire about her, finding out she is married to one of his loyal fighting men, Uriah the Hittite. What's the direction he takes from there? His own! David sent his messengers to take her—swift decision, bad consequences. The result is an un-royal pregnancy.

David contrives a plan to try and cover up this big mess. Again reactively, he conspires for Uriah to take a sabbatical from fighting so he will sleep with his wife. *"But Uriah slept at the door of the king's house with all the servants of his lord, and did not go down to his house"* (v. 9). Why did he not obey his king? He had too much character, humbling himself instead. He would not sleep with his own wife when other warriors like him were out in the battlefields where the ark of God was placed. He stayed consistent to his true military stance.

Out of desperation, David wrote a letter to Joab, his military leader, to put Uriah at the front of the worst battle zone and then abandon him there so he would be out of the picture permanently. The enemy position was so fierce that David's own servants were killed in the process and Uriah the Hittite also died.

Bathsheba finished her mourning period over Uriah's death. Not wasting a moment, King David had her brought to his house, took her as his wife, and she had his son. Seemed like a neat little package undetected by those in his kingdom. But in the next chapter we read how Nathan the prophet confronted David and asked, *"Why did you despise the word of the Lord by doing what is evil in his eyes?"* (2 Samuel 12:9, NIV).

Verses 1 through 5 tell how the Lord sent Nathan to speak with David using an illustration he could relate to that would expose his sin. The picture story grips David with burning emotion.

The story describes a rich man and a poor one. The rich man had everything his heart could desire, including flocks and herds. The poor man had a little female lamb raising it with tender care before his family like a pet; *"it was like a daughter to him"* (v. 3). How many of us have pet animals that we concern ourselves over just like one of our children? They are endeared to us.

The rich man has a visitor and is *"unwilling"* (v. 4) to prepare an animal from his own herds for a fine feast. Instead, he takes the poor man's lamb to dine on with this passing traveler.

David is furious with this rich man's egotistical actions. He is so moved he tells Nathan, *"As the LORD lives, the man who has done this deserves to die, and he shall restore the lamb fourfold, because he did this thing, and because he had no pity"* (vv. 5-6). David set himself up out of his own mouth!

Nathan tells David clearly, *"You are that rich man"* (v. 7, TLB). Then the Lord goes over the many blessings that have been bestowed on him—from being a king over all Israel, being delivered many times, having a mansion and many wives. The Lord goes so far as to tell him if what He had given him was so small, why didn't he ask Him for much more (v. 8)? Oh, this breaks my heart. Can you see Father God saying to us sorely, "Just ask Me. I'm here, ask Me. Ask ME"?

> *This is what the LORD says: "Out of your own household I am going to bring calamity on you.* **Before your very eyes** *I will take your wives and give them to one who is close to you, and he will sleep with your wives in broad daylight.* **You did it in secret, but I will do this thing in broad daylight before all Israel.**

—2 Samuel 12:11-12, NIV, emphasis added

Uriah's murder under the cloak of war would also plague David and his household from then on. To say David was a man of war is an understatement, as this is what he would reap from then on. What David cleverly devised against his own kinsman in the land would come to foretell his future.

David saves his own face, admitting to Nathan, "*I have sinned against the LORD*" (v. 13). He can no longer hide the truth when it is looking at him square in the face. His heart has been exposed out loud as conviction steeps inward to all that has been done. Because of the integrity of his heart and his repentant response, David's life is spared.

Verses 15 through 22 tell the rest of the story. After Nathan left David's household the child Uriah's wife bore to David became ill. David fasted, wept, and lay on the ground at night. After seven days, his newborn baby died. David washed and anointed himself changing into fresh clothes. His first act was to enter the house of the Lord and worship Him there. It was time for fresh beginnings, no more shame to mourn over. David repented entirely, now he could look to his future again clean faced.

> *"Whoever believes on Him **will not** be put to **shame**." For there is no distinction between Jew and Greek, for the same Lord over all is rich to all who call upon Him. For "whoever calls on the name of the LORD shall be saved."*

> —Romans 10:11-13, NKJV, emphasis added

Strength to Run

> *Therefore thus says the LORD, who redeemed Abraham, concerning the house of Jacob: "Jacob shall no more be **ashamed**, no more shall his face grow pale. For when he sees his children, the work of my hands, in his midst, they will sanctify my name; they will sanctify the Holy One of Jacob and will stand in awe of the God of Israel. And those who go astray in spirit will come to understanding, and those who murmur will accept instruction."*

> —Isaiah 29:22-24, emphasis added

There is a spiritual law of reciprocity or reaping what we've sewn beforehand. If we quit one relationship for selfish, spiteful reasons, they will reappear in another one. I am not speaking of malicious relationships that are brutal or physically harmful. Those should never be tolerated or endured. We mustn't hesitate to get help and remove ourselves from anyone whose treatment is life threatening.

Isaiah 30:17 says, *"There will be nothing left of you—a flagpole on a hill with no flag, a signpost on a roadside with the sign torn off"* (MSG). Tormented souls who try to torment others for the sake of it will have their life's message, even their voices, torn away. All types of advertising will not proliferate by unjust ways or methods.

If we are standing still, alone and undone, there is nothing left to show for our life. It's vanished into thin air. Our brave flag of valor and competence is gone. Spent! It's been torn right out from our frontal view on the road of decisions. Now it feels life is empty. What do we cling too? The One who's been waiting all along. He's right there holding out His big Father's hand for the taking. Grab and hold on for keeps.

Our enduring loving Father is not finished until He says so. In verse 18 of The Message, it tells how, even when He's disappointed with us, He is gathering strength. What does he want to give us? Mercy, continual mercy. God takes the time to do everything right—*everything*. Those who wait for Him are the ones storing up their own strength to run the race before them (Isaiah 40:31).

God is instructing us as the reading continues in Isaiah 30. It says, *"Our time of **tears** is over"* (v. 19, MSG, emphasis added). Why are our tears now gone? Psalm 31:12 reveals, *"I've cried my eyes out; I feel hollow inside. My life leaks away, groan by groan;*

my years fade out in sighs. My troubles have worn me out, turned my bones to powder" (MSG).

Then what are we to do? Psalm 31:14 gives the answer, *"Desperate, I throw myself on you; you are my God!"* (MSG). Declare it now:

> God, I throw my whole life's being on You alone, You can take care of me above all else.

The psalm continues: *"Hour by hour I place my days in your hand, safe from the hands out to get me. Warm me, your servant, with a smile; save me because you love me." Receive your warm smile right now"* (vv. 15-16, MSG).

> ***Cry for help*** *and you'll find it's grace and more grace.* ***The moment he hears, he'll answer.*** *Just as the Master kept you alive during the hard times, he'll keep your teacher alive and present among you. Your teacher will be right there, local and on the job, urging you on whenever you wander left or right: "This is the right road. Walk down this road." You'll scrap your expensive and fashionable god-images. You'll throw them in the trash as so much garbage, saying, "Good riddance!"*
>
> —Isaiah 30:20-22, MSG, emphasis added

Continuing a bit more, we read, *"God will provide rain for the seeds you sow. The grain that grows will be abundant"* (v. 23, MSG). Without seeds our future does not exist because there is no harvest. Seeds lead the way to progress, hopes, and dreams fulfilled. No seeds, no future.

In verse 26 it says, *"Better yet, on the Day God heals his people from the wounds and bruises during their times of punishment* [captivity], *moonlight will flare into sunlight, and sunlight, like a whole week of sunshine at once will flood the land"* (MSG). Many in the land of America today and elsewhere have an abundance of captivity, but God is saying that the sunlight is coming to pierce through the darkness because He is Light and He's coming closer to our plight to make us whole.

God brings healing from all our hurts and disappointments. The disillusionments of *dull gray* are turning full force into sunlight, flooding over our entire soul. That light remains with us as we remain in the Lord. God will give us double the blessing for the trouble of our shame!

> There is therefore now **no condemnation** to those who are in Christ Jesus...who walk not according to the flesh but according to the Spirit.
>
> —Romans 8:1, 4, emphasis added

I Am Not Ashamed

> In you our fathers trusted; they trusted, and you delivered them. To you **they cried and were rescued**; in you they trusted and were not put to shame.
>
> —Psalm 22:4-5, emphasis added

Most of us have heard this before, but it's true: God doesn't make junk! He knows and accepts us exactly the way we are. He loves His children, even through our weaknesses and frailties. He says we are but dust, yet He treats us with dignity. "*The Lord knows the days of the upright and blameless, and their heritage will abide forever. They shall not be put to shame in the time of evil; and in the days of famine they shall be satisfied*" (Psalm 37:18-19, AMP, emphasis added).

Don't let the enemy convince us we are less than what God made us to be. We are valuable and highly favored in God's sight. We are more important than silver and gold. We are God breathed and inspired. He knew us before we were created in the womb. He is intimately aware of our thoughts and feelings. We are highly prized by the Lord Almighty.

> *I am not ashamed of the gospel, because it is the power of God that brings salvation to everyone who believes: first to the Jew, then to the Gentile.*

> Romans 1:16, NIV

Marionette Vision

A man at church came up to me with a vision he had of me as a marionette being held by a hidden puppeteer. Normally I would not consider this a good thing if a man were holding me on strings. I realized the Lord was holding each string which was attached to a different body part. As He pulled the string to my feet, my foot would lift up.

I was allowing God to be in charge of my faculties as I was letting go of controlling factors. I was trusting the Lord in a new, confirmed way. I was letting the Lord direct all of my being—soul and body. The shackles of old rulership had fallen off. I was undergoing submission training in progression with the Lord.

Joel 2:25-27 (emphasis added)

> *I will restore to you the years that the swarming locust has eaten, the hopper, the destroyer, and the cutter, my great army, which I sent among you. You shall eat in plenty and be satisfied, and praise the name of the LORD your God, who has dealt wondrously with you. **And my people shall never again be put to shame.** You shall know that I am in the midst of Israel, and that I am the LORD your God and there is none else. And my people shall **never again** be put to shame.*

CHAPTER SIX

Cry Out

*And Jesus went away from there and withdrew to the district
of Tyre and Sidon. And behold, a Canaanite woman from that
region came out and was **crying**, "Have mercy on me, O Lord,
Son of David; my daughter is severely oppressed by a demon."
But he did not answer her a word. And his disciples came and
begged him, saying, "Send her away, for she is **crying out** after us." He answered, "I was sent only to the lost sheep of the
house of Israel." But she came and knelt before him, saying,
"Lord, help me." And he answered, "It is not right to take the
children's bread and throw it to the dogs." She said, "Yes, Lord,
yet even the dogs eat the crumbs that fall from their masters'
table." Then Jesus answered her, "O woman, great is your
faith! Be it done for you as you desire." And her daughter was
healed instantly.*

—Matthew 15:21-28, emphasis added

Faith to Cry Aloud

*I cried to him with my mouth, and high praise was on my
tongue. If I had cherished iniquity in my heart, the Lord would
not have listened. But truly God has listened; he has attended*

to the voice of my prayer. Blessed be God, because he has not rejected my prayer or removed his steadfast love from me!

—Psalm 66:17-20

In 1 Samuel 1 we read the story of Samuel's birth and early childhood. Elkanah was a man from Ephraim who had two wives: Peninnah who had children, and Hannah who had none. Every year this family traveled to Shiloh to give worship and sacrifice to the Lord. Elkanah gave portions for the sacrifice to Peninnah and their sons and daughters. Hannah was given a special double portion just because he loved her, even though the Lord had closed her womb.

Like a tithe, portions were given out to each family member, including children, with which to worship the Lord. But Elkanah did the opposite of what was the typically traditional practice. Peninnah should have received a double portion for all the children she bore to Elkanah. But he chose to not leave Hannah out of his good graces. He was inspired with devotion and captivating love for her, as Christ is for us. He did not exclude by giving her a barren, or lesser, portion! Hannah got the double portion.

Some may relate to the priests of the tribe of Levi, who had their rights of ownership taken away. They were given no portion of land to call their own. We can *cry out* instead, as in Lamentations 3:24: "*'The Lord is my portion,' says my soul.*" Our God gives new tender mercies every morning with unfailing compassion and faithfulness (vv. 22-23). We can proceed in hope, for a future inheritance is ours.

Put on sackcloth, my people, and roll in ashes; mourn with bitter wailing as for an only son, for suddenly the destroyer will come upon us.

—Jeremiah 6:26, NIV

Samuel's story continues. Peninnah provoked Hannah grievously as she taunted her because she carried no seed of pregnancy. This was considered a curse in those times, as it was important to leave a legacy with their lineage. Ruthless Peninnah would rub Hannah's infertility in her face every year so much so that Hannah refused to eat or drink in despair. Elkanah questioned why she fasted when he was so generous to her: "*And why is your heart sad? Am I not more to you than ten sons?*" (v. 8).

To be barren, *akarah* in Hebrew, gives a sense of being torn away or *cut off* from your family, as if uprooted. It denoted a desert place, closure, constraint, bereaved, and useless. Hannah was feeling these emotions of scorn and hopelessness as a childless woman. Rachel had similar emotions declared in Genesis 30:1: "*Give me children, or I shall die!*"

This particular year Hannah was in exceeding turmoil at the temple. She prayed to the Lord and "*wept bitterly*" (1 Samuel 1:10). Verse 11 says,

> *And she vowed a vow and said, "O LORD of hosts, if you will indeed look on the affliction of your servant and remember me and not forget your servant, but will give to your servant a son, then I will give him to the LORD all the days of his life, and no razor shall touch his head."*

In Lamentations 3:25 the Lord tells us He is good to those who wait and seek Him. Our only hope can come from the Lord. This waiting time was building something inside of Hannah. It wasn't about suffering; it was about searching out the Lord's will. All those years of pondering over her unnatural barrenness was building a lasting legacy of virtue.

> "*Sing, O barren one, who did not bear; break forth into singing and* **cry aloud**, *you who have not been in labor! For the*

children of the desolate one will be more than the children of her who is married," says the LORD. "Enlarge the place of your tent, and let the curtains of your habitations be stretched out; do not hold back; lengthen your cords and strengthen your stakes. For you will spread abroad to the right and to the left, and your offspring will possess the nations and will people the desolate cities. "Fear not, for you will not be ashamed; be not confounded, for you will not be disgraced; for you will forget the shame of your youth, and the reproach of your widowhood you will remember no more. For your Maker is your husband, the LORD of hosts is his name; and the Holy One of Israel is your Redeemer, the God of the whole earth he is called.

—Isaiah 54:1-17, emphasis added

Samuel continues: Eli was the priest at Shiloh who watched as Hannah's lips moved silently but no words came out while she prayed. He assumed that she was tipsy with alcohol. In 1 Samuel 1:15-16, Hannah answered Eli:

No, my lord, I am a woman troubled in spirit. I have drunk neither wine nor strong drink, but I have been pouring out my soul before the LORD. Do not regard your servant as a worthless woman, for all along I have been speaking out of my great anxiety and vexation.

Eli responded correctly by giving her his blessing that the Lord would *hear and answer* her prayer just as she had requested it. We read in verse 20: *"And in due time Hannah conceived and bore a son, and she called his name Samuel, for she said, 'I have asked for him from the LORD.'"* Her waiting seasons had produced a sovereign legacy of redemption.

We read more of the story in verses 22 through 24:

[Hannah said,] "As soon as the child is weaned, I will bring him, so that he may appear in the presence of the LORD and dwell there forever." Elkanah her husband said to her, "Do what seems best to you; wait until you have weaned him; only, may the LORD establish his word." So the woman remained and nursed her son until she weaned him. And when she had weaned him, she took him up with her, along with a three year-old bull, an ephah of flour, and a skin of wine, and she brought him to the house of the Lord at while she prayed Shiloh. And the child was young.

When the time was right, she lent him to the Lord. Hannah addressed Eli the priest again reminding him that it was she that had asked for a son, and now she was delivering him to Eli to keep her vow.

Then Hannah makes a declaration prayer. The following are the last two verses of that prayer:

*He will guard the feet of his faithful ones, but the wicked shall be cut off in darkness, for not by might shall a man prevail. The adversaries of the LORD shall be broken to pieces, against them he will thunder in heaven. The LORD will judge the ends of the earth; he will give strength to his **king** and exalt the horn of his anointed.*

—1 Samuel 2:9-10, emphasis added

Hannah uses the word *king* here regarding the Jehovah Christ Man who was to come to Earth as Ruler and Judge. This is considered the first reference to the coming Savior King from the Old Testament. Notice who will be cut off: not the righteous but the dying wicked who are deceived. We should rally to reach to those in darkness before it is too late for them.

I cry out to God Most High, to God, who fulfills his purpose for me.

—Psalm 57:2

Help Me Believe

*Immediately the father of the child **cried out** and said with **tears,** "Lord, I believe; help my unbelief!"*

—Mark 9:24, NKJV, emphasis added

Mark 9:14-29 tells the story of a boy being healed. There was a large crowd of people gathered with the disciples on one side and scribes on the other of an ensuing argument. The scribes were having a field day going on about why the disciplines failed to cast out an evil spirit from a young boy. Jesus addressed the scribes about the issue; but before they could answer, an anguished father from the crowd boldly spoke up to the Teacher.

This father had brought his son to get free but the disciples were unable to bring forth the requested deliverance. The young boy had been robbed of *his voice* since childhood. The demon would seize him and throw him to the ground, while he foamed at the mouth and even ground his teeth, living as a stick in the mud.

Jesus replied in verse 19, *"You unbelieving generation....How long shall I stay with you? How long shall I put up with you? Bring the boy to me."*

When the demon saw Jesus, it began to manifest in the boy's body with convulsions. The father continued to explain the boy's symptoms saying it was trying to kill his son. Then he spoke with one of those doubting "but" questions Jesus: *"But if you can do anything, take pity on us and help us"* (v. 22). He's only hoping for a little help; his faith had not kicked in gear yet.

Jesus reiterated the unbelieving lack of faith with *"if you can?"* (v. 23). I can only imagine His exasperation with the atmosphere of doubt and unbelief all around Him. But His compassion for the boy carried him forward saying; *"Everything is possible for one who believes"* (v. 23).

That's when the trigger got pulled and the father confidently responded in his new found belief. The crowds continued to grow now fully ripened for the witness. Jesus rebuked the evil spirit! *"Listen, you spirit that makes this boy **unable to hear and speak**,"* he said. *"I command you to come out of this child and never enter him again!"* (v. 25, NLT, emphasis added).

The spirit put on one last meager show as it screamed, leaving the boy for good. The crowd of people gazed over the boy's body, appearing as a corpse. But Jesus knew better as He took him by the hand with compassion, helping him to his feet.

> *Afterward, when Jesus was alone in the house with his disciples, they asked him, "Why couldn't we cast out that evil spirit?" Jesus replied, "This kind can be cast out only by prayer."*

> —Mark 9:28-29, NLT

Cry Out in Protest

> *Get up and go to Nineveh, that great city! Then **cry out in protest** against it, because their evil has come to my attention.*

> —Jonah 1:2, ISV, emphasis added

The story of Jonah has to be one of the most well versed children's Bible stories ever told. Jonah got up all right and ran straight in the wrong direction toward Joppa. He hooked a ship bound for the seacoast of Tarshish. God wasn't silent about the matter. He sent a great hurling wind over the seas, disturbing the waters as a storm broke out.

All the cargo got thrown overboard in order to lighten the load. The sailors cried out to their various gods who were asleep, just like Jonah. One crewmember got a bright idea to cast lots to see where it fell to. Jonah was the unlucky winner as they interrogated him. *"'I'm a Hebrew,' he replied, 'and I'm afraid of the LORD God of heaven, who made the sea—along with the dry land!'"* (Jonah 1:9, ISV).

As the sea became stormier, so did the crewmember's nerves. They asked Jonah what should be done to be safe. He instructed them to throw him overboard for the nuisance he's caused to them. The crew tried to avoid this by rowing all the harder but nothing worked. Disobedience had to be dealt with to survive.

Jonah 1:14-16, finally get to the point:

> *At last they cried out to the LORD, "Please, LORD, do not let us perish because of this man's life, and do not hold us responsible for innocent blood, because you, LORD, have done what pleased you." So they picked up Jonah and tossed him into the sea, and the sea stopped raging. Then the men feared the LORD greatly, offered a sacrifice to the LORD, and made vows.*

This misadventure wasn't a single purpose event. God used it for His glory, despite Jonah's refusal to obey. He feared man more than God, which left him in a downward spiral. God demonstrated to the crewmen whose God was to be feared. Once the rebel Jonah was cast overboard, peace came immediately.

There was an altar call on the boat that day due to supernatural evidence. When the men saw the results of obediently ridding themselves of sin, they got saved. They made a sacrifice of praise and thanksgiving, committing themselves to the one true God by a vow of consecration.

Jonah stayed in Whales Inn three days and nights (v. 17.). He came to his senses, praying out to God from inside that deep, nasty pit (Jonah 2:1-9). Jonah thought he'd been cast out of the Lord's sight; but that's impossible.

The one thing Jonah wanted to see again was God's holy temple. Instead, he saw seaweed wrapped around his head, the roots of mountains, and the Earth's bars while passing out. Then in the midst of all his disillusionment, he remembered the hope of God's steadfast love. Salvation alone belongs to his God.

The Lord spoke to whom? The fish! God commanded the fish to spit up Jonah on dry land (v. 10). Thankfully, this sea creature obeyed, unlike Jonah the first time. But the God of second chances put the same message back on Jonah (Jonah 3:1-2). So, Jonah arose, traveled, proclaimed, and cried out as Nineveh repented in humility. Nineveh called out to God and turned from their wickedness, departing from their hands of violence (v. 3-9).

God saw their reaction of utter remorse against their evil ways. The destruction of the city and all its people was averted because of God's mercies to them all (v. 10). Salvation came to all three groups who were spared and given back life again: the mariners, Jonah, and the entire city of Nineveh. It's time for the body of Christ to cry out!

*He said, "**I cried out** to the LORD in my great trouble, and he answered me. I called to you from the land of the dead, and LORD, you heard me!*

—Jonah 2:2, NLT, emphasis added

Outcry

> The sound of an **outcry** from Babylon, And of great destruction from the land of the Chaldeans!

—Jeremiah 51:54, NASB, emphasis added

An outcry is an angry voice of public protest against something that has great disapproval. Babylon had a powerful, protesting voice, which they used to worship false gods of idolatry and paganism. Their land has become defiled with drunkenness on every corner and beyond. Their position of influence in the Earth had them tagged as destroyers.

They were the mightiest and oldest of Old Testament cities, used by God many times to bring judgment on other nations. Babylon stood for the world's adamant voice against Elohim, their Creator and Judge. Jeremiah penned his chapter, describing prostitute Babylon, known for its repugnant voice of pride that influenced the nations against the church.

God called Babylon an arrogant one. In verse 32 of Jeremiah 50, He said, *"The arrogant one will stumble and fall and no one will help her up; I will kindle a fire in her towns that will consume all who are around her"* (NIV). Then in Jeremiah 51:53 He says, *"'Even if Babylon ascends to the heavens and fortifies her lofty stronghold, I will send destroyers against her,' declares the LORD"* (NIV).

Babylon exhibited a quality of defiance against God by first destroying Jerusalem and then capturing the citizens of Judah. But they had an enemy, too, that would crush them under God's providential command. God was about to shatter their image so it would not infect other lands in the future. A blast of judgment came to decimate Babylon for the wrongs they had done to Zion. No nation can posture itself against God's purposes.

For I am raising up an army of great nations from the north. They will join forces to attack Babylon, and she will be captured. The enemies' arrows will go straight to the mark; they will not miss!

—Jeremiah 50:9, NLT

God's people have been oppressed, suppressed, and tied down. The Lord declares in Jeremiah 51:24: "*Before your eyes I will repay Babylon and all who live in Babylonia for all the wrong they have done in Zion*" (NIV). In chapter 50, verse 34, speaking of the Lord and His beloved Zion, it says, "*He will vigorously defend their cause so that he may bring rest to their land, but unrest to those who live in Babylon*" (NIV).

Rest brings peaceful *shalom*. When God brings rest to the land and its people, they are able to do all that's required of them in Jehovah's providence. It's His strength that accomplishes the rest. If we stumble in striving or fret in frustrations, we are not resting. Give Him the works, and then trust Him in resting and abiding faith. His accomplishments can come through us, with His presence-soaking ability to thrust through the work with mighty agility.

The people of both Israel and Judah came together as *one* with talking tears to seek the Lord of their habitation. They were looking for the way to Zion, asking Him which way to get there. His people set their faces like flint turned straight to the Lord. They bound themselves in collective relationship to an everlasting and unforgotten covenant (see Jeremiah 50:4-5).

Announce and proclaim among the nations, lift up a banner and proclaim it; keep nothing back, but say, "Babylon will be captured; Bel will be put to shame, Marduk filled with

*terror. Her images will be put to shame and her idols filled
with terror."*

—Jeremiah 50:2, NIV

God will capture our personal Babylon and deliver us from our
captivity permanently. Babylon precipitated an outcry of desolation as they instigated their own crisis. God has His own weapons of vengeance against our enemies of death and defiance.
God silenced their resistant voice with a swift and final plunder.

*At the **sound** of the capture of Babylon the earth will tremble,
and her **cry** will resound among the nations.*

—Jeremiah 50:46, emphasis added

The Voice of a Lion

*And one of the elders said to me, "Weep no more; behold, the
Lion of the tribe of Judah, the Root of David, has conquered, so
that he can open the scroll and its seven seals.*

—Revelation 5:5

There is no time to weep in intimidation; it is time to gird our
loins like the Lion of Judah with a loud, triumphant ROAR! "*A
mighty angel...called out with a loud voice, like a lion roaring.
When he called out, the seven thunders sounded*" (Revelation
10:1, 3). As a unit of one, we must be heard. It is our day, time,
season, and chapter; for the victory is at hand. We are instructed
to use our voices as never before, from darkness to light. Cry
out! Now!

The terror of a king is like the growling of a lion.

—Proverbs 20:2

If we look around the world and society we may see only dark wretchedness. Sin proliferates, as history shows a proclivity for such particular predispositions. We see weakness, rage, and corruption because we need a Deliverer. He has already come, overcoming all wickedness as we sustain our cry out to Him. Our Redeemer triumphs as indestructible for the battles invoked in our life. Our reliance upon THE ONE Lion King prevails in the shadows of time.

> *Behold, like a lion coming up from the thicket of the Jordan against a perennial pasture, I will suddenly make them run away from her, and I will appoint over her whomever I choose. For who is like me? Who will summon me? What shepherd can stand before me?*
>
> —Jeremiah 50:44

Jeremiah is speaking of the inhabitants of Babylon as a sturdy, comfortable, and prosperous people who are running away suddenly. There is no one who is strong enough to stand before the Lord. Whatever we commit to the Lord, He is able to handle at once. Those who lay back and do nothing will reap complacent recompense.

We are called to influence our generation of people, neighbors, and friends. We were born in this time frame to reach those God has ordained we reach. We have a decision. Either we live only for comfortable pleasures or we strike a life that may cost us something in eternity. Who wants a drab, everyday existence? Be powerful like a magnificent lion!

Amos 3:4 asks, "*Does a lion roar in the forest, when he has no prey? Does a young lion* **cry out** *from his den, if he has taken nothing?*" (emphasis added). When a lion sees its prey in view, he begins to roar. His voice paralyzes the enemy so it can't move.

The prey is unable to escape by disappearing back to the land again. As the lion roars, he invites others to participate with him in the win. The swift lion accelerates his movements, as a prophet with a deliberate voice to yell out what he sees will be! They have a determined victory in sight. Even the young lions (*kephir*) are not without a voice, but they must use it. They can't leisurely wait and rely on the older lions, as they are quite capable of roaring. The young lions, too, must activate their voices.

> *They shall go after the LORD; he will roar like a lion; when he roars, his children shall come trembling from the west.*

> —Hosea 11:10

We live in a nation of defiance against rulers, authorities, and God's Word. People mock the Godly, condemn the righteous, and betray the ways of God's standard. It's thrown in our faces rampantly, viciously, and with full force. Are we timidly waiting for others to make a difference? One of the things that Solomon found stately was *"the lion, which is mightiest among beasts and does not turn back before any"* (Proverbs 30:30).

"What causes a wicked person to flee? *"The wicked flee when no one pursues, but the righteous are bold as a lion"* (Proverbs 28:1). Fear robs people of the lion's call. They should be running to God, not slithering away. They are trapped in their own weakness. He who covers his sin will not prosper nor prevail (v. 13). We are never to cower in the face of the enemy, but rather just laugh. We have God's authority and victory at hand. Don't stifle those Godly tools—use them.

Then there are the blatantly rebellious who fear no one, not even God. And at the beginning of their dwelling in the land, they did not fear the Lord, *"therefore the LORD sent lions among them, which killed some of them"* (2 Kings 17:25). The Lions had to pursue and overtake some of their enemies to the death. Why? *"Because you have not obeyed the **voice of the LORD**, behold, as soon as you have gone from me, a lion shall strike you down"* (1 Kings 20:36, emphasis added).

> *But the Lord stood by me and strengthened me, so that through me the message might be fully proclaimed and all the Gentiles might hear it. So I was rescued from the lion's mouth.*
>
> —2 Timothy 4:17

Lift Our Voices Together

> *The members of the council were amazed when they saw the boldness of Peter and John, for they could **see** that they were ordinary men with no special training in the Scriptures. They also recognized them as men who had been with Jesus. But since they could **see** the man who had been healed standing right there among them, there was nothing the council could say.*
>
> —Acts 4:13-14, NLT, emphasis added

The religious leaders were confounded when they saw the faith of Peter and John. They didn't know what to do with these followers of Jesus because the evidence was standing right in front of them. They were trying to find a way to suppress the truth of what had happened. But, all of Jerusalem knew of it, including 5,000 new converts to Christianity.

Peter, who was full of the Holy Spirit, knew exactly how to handle the situation as Matthew 10:19 exhorts us: *"When they deliver you over, do not be anxious how you are to speak or what you are to say, for what you are to say will be given to you in that hour."* Luke 12:11 says, *"Do not be anxious about how you should defend yourself."*

Peter spoke,

> *Rulers of the people and elders, if we are being examined to-day concerning a good deed done to a crippled man, by what means this man has been healed, let it be known to all of you and to all the people of Israel that by the name of Jesus Christ of Nazareth, whom you crucified, whom God raised from the dead—by him this man is standing before you well.*

—Acts 4:8-10

What was the one thing the high council wanted to shut down? They desired to remove their voice! Since no one could deny the healing of the crippled man, they wanted to cripple the message so it wouldn't spread any further. They were charged never to speak or teach at all in the name of Jesus. In Matthew 10:32 Jesus said, *"So everyone who acknowledges me before men, I also will acknowledge before my Father who is in heaven."*

Peter and John responded to the leaders in verses 19-20 of Acts 4: *"Do you think God wants us to obey you rather than him? We cannot stop telling about everything we have **seen and heard"*** (NLT, emphasis added). The council tried to threaten and intimidate them, but ended up releasing them so a riot wouldn't break out.

The people were exultantly expressing their joy, giving praises to God for the healing they had witnessed. The man who was once lame had been in that condition for forty years. There was no possibility it was a falsified mistake. An entire generation knew of his ailment and now they were rejoicing in his divine recovery.

When Peter and John reported back to their friends all that had transpired, there was great exaltation. In verses 24-26 we read,

> And when they heard it, **they lifted their voices together** to God and said, "Sovereign Lord, who made the heaven and the earth and the sea and everything in them, who through the mouth of our father David, your servant, said by the Holy Spirit, 'Why did the Gentiles rage, and the peoples plot in vain? The kings of the earth set themselves, and the rulers were gathered together, against the Lord and against his Anointed.'"

Acts 4: 24-26, emphasis added

The people began to ask the Lord to look upon the threats against them. They asked the Lord for the ability to continue to speak with all boldness, as He continued to stretch out His hands with the evidence of miracles, signs, and wonders. Verse 31 says, *"And when they had prayed, the place in which they were gathered together was shaken, and they were all filled with the Holy Spirit and continued to speak the word of God with boldness."*

> This Jesus is the stone that was rejected by you, the builders, which has become the cornerstone. And there is salvation in no one else, for there is no other name under heaven given among men by which we must be saved.

—Acts 4:11-12

Cry for Freedom

> During those many days the king of Egypt died, and the people of Israel groaned because of their slavery and **cried out** for help. Their cry for rescue from slavery came up to God. And God heard their groaning, and God remembered his **covenant**

with Abraham, with Isaac, and with Jacob. God saw the people of Israel—and God knew.

—Exodus 2:23-25, emphasis added

The conditions of the children of Israel in Egypt continued to digress and get worse, not better. The long-drawn-out duration of entrapments in their bondage left them without hope. They could see no way of escape from their predicament. Their voices gave way to internal groaning and sighing. It finally brought a depth of crying from intense desperate anguish. This strong, audible clamor made its way to Heaven.

They could no longer survive on their own possibility of fixing things. Their sources for help were all dried up. They were left with an oppressively vehement and bellowing cry. In God's perfect timing and with the soil of the people's hearts ready to listen by way of relief, God answered.

God is merciful and true to His promises. We read in Genesis 46:4 where He told Jacob: "*I will go down to Egypt with you, and I will surely bring you back again. And Joseph's own hand will close your eyes.*"

Let's recount the promises given and kept:
1. The Israelites became a great nation.
2. Jacob's descendants returned to Canaan.
3. Israel's slavery in Egypt was 400 years.
4. Israelites conquered Canaan, claiming their Promised Land.
5. Jacob left his home to a strange land, never returning.
6. Jacob received confirmation from God in Beersheba that he was to live in Egypt.
7. God promised to be with him and take care of him.
8. The promise of a new land went to his descendants.

9. Jacob was not alone when he died (close your eyes),
    as Joseph was right beside him.

Jacob followed the instructions of the Lord to move his entire
family to Goshen in Egypt. His son Joseph made preparations to
meet them. Genesis 46:29 tells us, *"As soon as Joseph appeared
before him, he threw his arms around his father and wept for a
long time"* (NIV).

Alligator Dream

This dream started in a house with ants, which are an irritant
in dreams. I went to get some ant killer spray. I sprayed inside
the house, then the garage and the front yard. (Our house is
our family, a garage repairs and stores, and the front yard is
our future.)

My son was three (meaning in God) and my daughter was
five (God's grace). My daughter would have been two years
older had she been born on earth but she passed into heav-
en before her earth birth. The age difference was appropriate
and comforting. We walked to the front yard together. There
was a full-size bed (a place of full rest) sitting in the center in
front of our home.

I walked to the right side of the bed to spray underneath
it. I saw a medium-size alligator concealed beneath, which is
a bossy spirit with a big mouth to influence. I drew my children back to defend them. I sprayed the alligator's face and
upper jaw with the ant spray (to neutralize the irritant) as
it became agitated and took a swift movement toward my
daughter chomping its mouth her direction. (My daughter
symbolized God's grace to me).

It came beside me so I pressed down on the alligator's
ferocious jaw and had my daughter jump over the alligator
as I motioned for my son to get to the right of it and out of its

way. The right side of something is the right way to go. I cried out, "Lord, You are on the throne of our home!"

An angry alligator sends shivers down most people's spine at the mention of its name. In a dream it is the launching of a verbal attack directed at the main person or dreamer. In this case, it was me and my children in a spiritual sense. This dangerous, predatory alligator was hiding underneath our resting place intending to disturb us by surprise. Since the bed was placed in the front yard, it was warning of a future, character-damaging event on the horizon. My confession to the Lord was a declaration of faith beforehand.

> In my anguish I **cried** to the LORD, and he answered by setting me **free**.
>
> —Psalm 118:5, NLT, emphasis added

Jesus Cried Out

> On the last day of the feast, the great day, **Jesus** stood up and **cried out,** "If anyone thirsts, let him come to me and drink. Whoever believes in me, as the Scripture has said, 'Out of his heart will flow rivers of living water.'" Now this he said about the Spirit, whom those who believed in him were to receive, for as yet the Spirit had not been given, because Jesus was not yet glorified.
>
> —John 7:37-39, emphasis added

This was the eighth and closing day of the festival. It was a solemn assembly because it was designated for the Jews only. There were traditional observances that included sacrifices being made for Israel. All laboring had ceased for this time. They might have poured water at the foot of the altar to symbolize a cleansing for the land and their souls.

There was great rejoicing, shouting, and the blowing of trumpets. The priest would ascend to the altar, turning his left hand toward the two silver basins—one filled with water and one with wine. He would mix these two elements together.

Some believe this ceremony came from a time of Moses at Mount Sinai in which there was a secret or mysterious thing revealing itself as the pouring forth of the Holy Ghost. Isaiah 12:3 says, "*With joy you will draw water from the wells of salvation.*"

Jesus stood up, unlike other times when He would normally sit. This was to reveal His bold authority in reference to water being the same as the Holy Spirit. Jesus is emphasizing to them that He is their living water. No one needs thirst again. He cries to a people to believe on Him that they may be partakers of His grace unto salvation. He cries to us today to take this life gift inside us. Like water, we must also give it out freely like golden water vessels.

> Then Jesus, **calling out with a loud voice**, said, "Father, into your hands I commit my spirit!" And having said this he breathed his last.
>
> —Luke 23:46, emphasis added

Non-Selective Hearing

> And you heard me! You listened to my pleading; you heard my weeping! Yes, you came at my despairing cry and told me **not to fear**.
>
> —Lamentations 3:56-57, TLB, emphasis added

God powerfully penetrates our situations and circumstances when we invite Him into them. He is never out of reach to touch our infirmities, trials, or tears. It is not a strain for Him to hear our cries. He doesn't get tired of us. There is no distance that separates us. There are no limits, boundaries, or expanse so vast that He is not centered in the midst of every conceivable thought and desire we have the capacity for.

God's engaged—ALWAYS! He doesn't have selective hearing. Satellites aren't required. Telephone lines are antiquated. Cell phones get lost. Power lines break, radio frequencies change intervals, transmissions get scrambled, and mail gets muddled, while TV signals get static. Let's not even talk about email spam and junk mail! God's divine lines of communication are open ENDLESSLY. He intensely yearns for our presence. He wants to capture our affection and longs to hear our heartbeat's desire. God adores us!

We were created from an articulate design that only God knew how to form in His image, which makes us legitimate. God doesn't have one illegitimate child! We are all desired equally. God loves us as indescribably significant, fashioned, and shaped from the same essences that the Creator uses to form life eternal. He's the Master of ceremonies.

We are not rubbish. We are the God stuff that can't be discarded, removed, or remanufactured. There is no reincarnation. That would mean we were not made masterfully the first time and that we could therefore be easily discarded. We are not an inferior by-product of disappointment in God's eye. That is mankind's miserable evolutionary explanation of the existence of itself. It comes from a morbidly defeatist perspective with no life reality. It's as if man alone is against the whole universe. How ludicrous that we could sustain ourselves for one day without God's existence to support the planets, stars, and air of sustenance to breathe.

We are the queen quintessence or kingly champion. We are the apple of God's eye—wonderfully and fearfully made in His image (Psalm 17:8; 139:14).

> But I call to God, and the LORD will save me. Evening and morning and at noon I utter my complaint and moan, and he **hears my voice**. He redeems my soul in safety from the battle that I wage, for many are arrayed against me.
>
> —Psalm 55:16-18, emphasis added

Distraction to Answers

> But you, O LORD, are a shield about me, my glory, and the lifter of my head. I **cried** aloud to the LORD, and **he answered me** from his holy hill.
>
> —Psalm 3:3-4, emphasis added

I have a funny story that a girlfriend told me. I remembered it because it reminded me of myself at the time. She spoke of how the only time she could hear from the Lord was while using the powder room. She finally asked the Lord one day why she only heard from Him during her potty breaks? The response she heard back was, "It's the only time I can get your attention." Anyone else been there?

Oh, those distractions that fowl up communication skills. There was one time the Lord asked me to stop getting French gel nails because they were consuming too much of my attention. It was actually interfering with my ability to meditate or focus on Him. That is not the case anymore, but at the time I had to obey. It was significant enough to keep my mind off Him when I needed responses He had for me. My ears became dull while my nails were so shiny!

Distractions muddle our sense of perception to the things of God. His intrinsic value in our life becomes placated by interruptions and stuff we must do, collect, or deal with. It's difficult to hear Him distinctly when our concerns are focused inward. When not giving God our astute attention, the relationship becomes desensitized and divisively crippled. His precise voice of instruction becomes murkily clouded by a list of operations that doesn't include Him.

We must keep God at the top of our *awareness* list and make sure we seek His face; look at Him! We must not duck and hide but be liberated from contrived controlling plans, oppressive executed ideas, and confining ways as we are released with Christ focus. His face has eyes that are ever looking upon our substantial beauty. His eyes pierce the darkness in our life and dispel it. So speak with Him and listen for His responses while relishing precious moments together. The deliberate answers we long for will follow and fortify our lives.

> *In the day when I cried out, **You answered me**, And made me bold with strength in my soul.*

> —Psalm 138:3, NKJV, emphasis added

Give Ear to My Voice

> *Now the word of the LORD came to me, saying, "Before I formed you in the womb I knew you, and before you were born I consecrated you; I appointed you a prophet to the nations." Then I said, "Ah, Lord GOD! Behold, I do not know how to speak, for I am only a youth." But the LORD said to me, "Do not say, 'I am only a youth'; for to all to whom I send you, you shall **go**, and*

*whatever I command you, you shall **speak**. Do not be afraid of them, for I am with you to deliver you, declares the LORD."*

—Jeremiah 1:4-8, emphasis added

Throw out the excuse syndrome. God is saying to us, "I've done everything in advance for your benefit." We've been thought of eons in advance, consecrated, appointed, delivered to Him, and given the specific words to speak.

*O LORD, I call upon you; hasten to me! Give **ear** to **my voice** when I call to you!*

—Psalm 141:1, emphasis added

Not even fear can hold us back from doing what God has called us to do. Our enemies are God's enemies, and He doesn't want them interfering in our destiny. Just like little David with a slingshot, who fired with perfect precision to just the right spot. His faith made the mark real. Believe that God will help us hit the targets in our life. It's by His strength and anointing.

Let's lift up our voice more brightly than ever! Let our voice raise us up to the heights of His glory. Allow it to clear the paths of shame and destruction behind. Advance a new cause of victory with a shrill voice that knocks down the fortresses of evil. Raise the heights for His Kingdom all around us. Shout it!

*The **voice** of the LORD is upon the waters; The God of glory thunders, The LORD is over many waters. The **voice** of the LORD is powerful, The **voice** of the Lord is majestic. The **voice** of the LORD breaks the cedars; Yes, the LORD breaks in pieces the cedars of Lebanon. He makes Lebanon skip like a calf, And Sirion like a young wild ox. The **voice** of the LORD hews out flames of fire. The **voice** of the LORD shakes the wilderness; The LORD shakes the wilderness of Kadesh. The **voice** of the*

LORD makes the deer to calve And strips the forests bare; And in His temple everything says, "Glory!"

—Psalm 29:3-9, NASB, emphasis added

Prayer Cry: Fast

Cry aloud; do not hold back; lift up your voice like a trumpet; declare to my people their transgression, to the house of Jacob their sins. Yet they seek me daily and delight to know my ways, as if they were a nation that did righteousness and did not forsake the judgment of their God; they ask of me righteous judgments; they delight to draw near to God. "Why have we fasted, and you see it not? Why have we humbled ourselves, and you take no knowledge of it?" Behold, in the day of your fast you seek your own pleasure, and oppress all your workers. Behold, you fast only to quarrel and to fight and to hit with a wicked fist. Fasting like yours this day will not make your voice to be heard on high. Is such the fast that I choose, a day for a person to humble himself? Is it to bow down his head like a reed, and to spread sackcloth and ashes under him? Will you call this a fast, and a day acceptable to the LORD?

—Isaiah 58:1-5, emphasis added

Fasting exercises our ability to lose self-focus and gain a God-focus. It opens our ears and eyes to spiritual needs and changes we need to address. It allows a time to seek the will of God in areas of life that have been lacking. It keeps us attuned to what the Spirit of God is saying without interference.

In the Old Testament, David fasted and mourned over Abner, Saul, and his own child. Esther fasted on behalf of her people. Daniel fasted over a mysterious vision God had given him.

*I lifted up my **eyes** and looked, and behold, a man clothed in linen, with a belt of fine gold from Uphaz around his waist. His body was like beryl, his face like the appearance of lightning, his eyes like flaming torches, his arms and legs like the gleam of burnished bronze, and the **sound of his words** like the sound of a multitude. And I, Daniel, alone saw the vision, for the men who were with me **did not see** the vision, but a great **trembling fell upon them, and they fled to hide themselves.***

—Daniel 10:5-7, emphasis added

Daniel had the keen discernment to hear "the sound of his words" as he fell prostrate on his face. All natural strength left him while a hand touched him. Daniel was commanded to stand upright. The angel spoke,

*Fear not, Daniel, for from the first day that you **set your heart to understand and humbled yourself** before your God, your **words have been heard**, and I have come **because of your words**. The prince of the kingdom of Persia withstood me twenty-one days, but Michael, one of the chief princes, came to help me, for I was left there with the kings of Persia.*

—Daniel 10:12-14, emphasis added

In the New Testament, Anna fasted for the redemption of Jerusalem. Jesus fasted forty days in the wilderness of temptation. Cornelius fasted while seeking God's plan of salvation. Paul fasted while aboard a sinking ship at sea.

Although no longer considered a command as in the Old Testament, fasting is still valid for today's living and intentions for change. Be guided by the Holy Spirit, while using wisdom and discernment on the content and length of the fast. Do it as unto the Lord and not man.

Joel 1:14 (emphasis added)

*Consecrate a fast; call a solemn assembly. Gather the elders and all the inhabitants of the land to the house of the LORD your God, and **cry out to the Lord**.*

CHAPTER SEVEN

Linen Girdle

Rebellion often hides behind misused truth.[1]
—Bill Johnson

Linen Cloth

In Jeremiah chapter 13 is the mysterious story of the linen girdle. The girdle is given another descriptive name of "waistcloth" in some versions. Typically, a linen cloth was light in color and used as a burial cloth. It covered the dead person's private areas. When Jesus arose from the dead, His burial cloth was left behind as evidence He was dead no longer, but He was alive. It was a sign for proof!

It's important to realize how securely the girdle held to the abdominal region. Nothing is meant to come between it and the loins it holds intimately, in an all-encompassing band around the waist. This symbolizes Christ's secure hold on us, unless we remove Him. When I think of this visually, it reminds me of a child reaching up and around a parent's body. Like holding on passionately to the one loved with cherished trust. Don't we all hold dearly to the ones we love? This symbolizes what our stance should be with our heavenly Father. This is what Israel's posture should have been unto the Lord.

In Mark 14:51 we read of a boy was found following Christ after His resurrection. He was wearing a loincloth around him and nothing else. It's possible that the resurrection power of Christ affected the entire region where Jesus had risen. The living Christ emanated resurrection power to such a degree that previously dead people were unraveling in their graves and coming alive as Christ had done!

> Do not marvel at this, for an hour is coming when all who are in the tombs will hear his voice.

> —John 5:28

Powerful effects of His recent resurrection power streamed all around that vicinity, rippling outwards into the rocks and fields. How do we explain the dressing of this young boy wearing only a linen cloth used as a burial garment? While young men saw the boy, they grabbed his undergarment but he ran off naked. He no longer needed a death shroud wrapped around his loins. He needed clothes for living life.

The Lord's instructions for Jeremiah were to "GO" and purchase the girdle then wear it around his loins. He was not to wash or clean it with water. Thus the garment remained stiff and rigid, just like the stiff-necked people of Israel. This would allow the garment enough time to get stained, soiled, and overall stinky.

Cleft in the Rock

> For many, of whom I have often told you and now tell you even with tears, walk as enemies of the cross of Christ.

> —Philippians 3:18

Jeremiah is given a second instruction while wearing his girdle. He was to get up and go the Euphrates River and *hide* the girdle in a cleft in the rock (Jeremiah 13:4). This crevice can also be termed a dark hole. During this time period, a hole was dug as a prison to confine a convicted Jew. The implication is that this generation was imprisoned to their false idols, arrogance, and corrupt acts with God-given privileges taken for granted.

The nation as a whole had lost its way into disparaging heathen worship. They responded to the allure of what they saw from pagans instead of forging into their soil of influence. Jehovah was no longer their intimate source. Psalm 10:4 says, "*In the pride of his face the wicked does not seek him; all his thoughts are, 'There is no God.'*"

However, Jeremiah did what he was instructed, regardless of it making sense or not.

In verse 6 of Jeremiah 13 we find many days have passed since Jeremiah buried the loin cloth as God had told him to do, and he is instructed to "*arise, go to the Euphrates, and take from there the girdle which I commanded you to* **hide there**" (emphasis added). To be "hidden" affirms their captivity in Babylon. In addition, considerable time had lapsed; referring to the seventy years of captivity they would endure.

The condition of the girdle is now decayed and destroyed. It is declared to be spoiled and good for nothing (v. 7). Due to Jeremiah's actions, the purpose of the garment had been severed, just like the apostate nation and God. It had, at one time, served its function and value; but could no longer be useful for what it was intended. The rough, rocky environment did not allow protection, exposing the linen garment to the elements of the terrain that held it in place.

Now, the fourth word of the Lord makes a statement in verse nine:

> *After this manner will I mar the pride of Judah and the great pride of Jerusalem. These evil people (God is speaking to his own children of Israel, not an enemy), who refuse to hear My words, who walk in the stubbornness of their own hearts and have gone after other gods to serve them and to worship them, shall even be like this girdle or waistcloth, which is profitable for nothing.*

—Jeremiah 13:9-10, AMP

The terrain of the hill country represented Israel's heart condition at that time. Their hearts had become rock hard with holes in it. This was not an area where plants or trees could grow easily. The environment had created crevice corrosion causing spaces, lacking soil contact in places. These gaps allowed further weakness, breaking it down then extending outward. The lack of ground cover washed out the soil leaving it unfertile for new growth.

When I looked up "crevice corrosion" in relation to stainless steel, it indicated a solution to the issue. It stated this, "This problem can often be overcome by paying attention to the design of the component."[2] In human terms, we must stay connected to our Designer God or the influences of the world will break us down with gaps, crevices, and corrosion to our soul.

Christian influence in America is losing the ground cover needed for growing trees of righteousness. It is extending itself outward throughout the land. Our united front has become a divided country, easily conquered if it is not fortified by the passageways to God. There is a time frame involved. We must move swiftly as a unit of one to fill in these gaping holes with the Word of God in place to defend us. Allow God's covenant to spread throughout the Earth.

Jeremiah's story goes on to describe the intentions of this girdle, which was meant to cling to the loins of a man, to illustrate our own lives as utterly dependent on our heavenly Father (v. 11). God wants the whole, not just part of a united house of both Israel and Judah to cling to Him, just like a child holds closely to his parent with unabated love. This is a jealous God wanting His most precious prize, you and me, to seek Him above all else. Why such a demand?

> *That they might be for Him **a people, a name, a praise, and a glory**!*
>
> —Jeremiah 13:11, emphasis added

Our common enemy knows that unity exercised in the Body of Christ is the finest and strongest weapon for our defense. When we are shattered and torn, woven in corruption and betrayal, we become divided. We set ourselves as easy prey for the enemy to capture. This is the irony; he is a stronghold that can and will hold us back from our forward position to change the world and ourselves.

Without this joint effort on their behalf, the Israelites became adrift, wasted, and wanting; purposeless, aimless, disjointed—a catastrophe in the making.

> *Lord, let my life count, let it not be worthless! Give me value to fulfill Your call and destiny for my life now and the future generations to come who I am are planting for.*

The sad conclusion is as God said it: "*But they did **not listen** or obey*" (Jeremiah 11:8, GNT, emphasis added).

And as the story goes and we know as any righteous parent, there are already consequences to be hurled. Isaiah 49:1 speaks of listening to Jesus, *"Listen, O coastlands, to Me, And take heed, you peoples from afar!"* (NKJV). What is significant here is that the audience has changed from only Jews to an all-inclusive group of Jews and Gentiles, as Jesus comes to us as the Servant to all people groups.

Who's Listening?

> *You stiff-necked people, uncircumcised in heart and **ears**, you always resist the Holy Spirit. As your fathers did, so do you.*
>
> —Acts 7:51, emphasis added

We must throw down our deafness; do not accept ownership of it. Pursuing only surface pleasures and pursuits has not fulfilled us long term. If we want sustaining change, we must HEAR the Lord! It is not an existence of "latent" survival by merely maintaining. God wants us thriving just the way He designed us and for our potential usefulness to Him. Some have turned a deaf ear to the Kingdom of God because they don't care. They don't know where they are going. People have been numbed to live only for today's titillating, momentary events.

"Latent" means we are "existing but not yet developed or manifest; hidden, concealed."[3] It is inactive or unseen capabilities that lay dormant—untapped, unused, undiscovered, invisible, undeveloped, unrealized, and unfulfilled potential. We will either live our lives fully for God or for nothing at all.

Why bother with God when we can determine our own wishes, actions, and desires right NOW? There's always a payday. The outcome we are planning for today will produce its self-destruction or benefits another day! This pattern can continue way past our lifetime, reaching to the future generations in our bloodline.

*But you belong to God, my dear children. You have already won a victory over those people, because the Spirit who lives in you is greater than the spirit who lives in the world. Those people belong to this world, so they speak from the world's viewpoint, and **the world listens to them**.*

—1 John 4:4-5, NLT, emphasis added

Some people can't hear the Lord because they are preprogrammed in their own thinking. They don't bother with the things that are above, but on carnal, day-to-day drudgery type thinking. Some are used to the way they think, full of complaining, blaming, and critical thoughts. They think that's just how they are. But like a computer, we can hit the refresh key anytime we want. It's the infinite inspiration of a God thought that renews our brain's capacity to His splendid thoughts of us.

But we belong to God, and those who know God listen to us. If they do not belong to God, they do not listen to us. That is how we know if someone has the Spirit of truth or the spirit of deception.

—1 John 4:6, NLT

Many of us just talk to God (or *at* Him) without worshipping who He is. We have taken our daily circumstances and conditions straight from the world. We bring them to the house of prayer and rehearse them by regurgitation. It's like dumping our "crap" on His lap without receiving real change. We are to deliver the word of change to our world—command circumstances to line up to the authority of God's words. Let's be life changers and re-arrangers as we use His greater power to perform through us. We must not allow our words to penalize us.

And he said to them, "I saw Satan fall like lightning from heaven. Behold, I have given you authority to tread on serpents and scorpions, and over all the power of the enemy, and nothing shall hurt you. Nevertheless, do not rejoice in this, that the spirits are subject to you, but rejoice that your names are written in heaven."

—Luke 10:18-20

We all have glitches in the way we think. Those glitches lead us to the ditches in our actions. A glitch can be described as a short-lived fault in a system.[4] It's like all these live wires short-circuiting our systems that go haywire. They aren't grounded into the eternal Host of Heaven, so we set off sparks all the time. These faulty thoughts don't lead to anything of value until we plug into the true Source of life, wisdom, and understanding. Then we reap the benefits of peace of mind, joy unspeakable, and Christ-like decision making ability.

How many people are really joyful? It doesn't mean we always have a smile plastered on our face. Nor does it say we never get upset or have issues! It's that quality that comes from below the surface that gives us an eternally secure perspective. We love people—all kinds of them—and desire the best for them. We look for good attributes not fault-finding ones. We desire to help others and go the extra mile even when it's inconvenient. We know we are loved and we want to love others.

I read that most people laugh forty to fifty times a day. But I know some people who don't seem to laugh, ever. We need to look for reasons to laugh, even if we need to purchase a DVD. Find a happy place in this life where there is so much unhappiness. Be the creator and instigator of giving someone a smile, or laugh, or hug, or God thought.

What can we accomplish singularly in our strivings versus what our Creator can do with and through us? If I had to stand on my own two feet rather than what God can do inside of me, I would fall flat on my face. I'll take God's way any day. I asked my aunt, who is hard of hearing, if she'd ever asked the Lord to help her hear His voice. She said she never thought to ask that before. I'm asking the Lord to open her fleshly ears while she's asking to hear from His listening ears. Ask, then listen; as God is eager to speak of the unsearchable riches He has for each of us.

*Simpletons! How long will you wallow in ignorance? Cynics! How long will you feed your cynicism? Idiots! How long will you refuse to learn? About face! I can revise your life. Look, I'm ready to pour out my spirit on you; I'm ready to tell you all I know. As it is, I've called, but you've turned a **deaf ear**; I've reached out to you, but you've ignored me.*

—Proverbs 1:22-24, MSG, emphasis added

Don't Monkey Around Dream, 8-31-2014

And your ears shall hear a word behind you, saying, "This is the way, walk in it," when you turn to the right or when you turn to the left.

—Isaiah 30:21

I was looking directly at the roofline of a familiar home. All edges of the roof, both front and back, were surrounded by writhing snakes. Most of them were smaller in size except for one very prominent, larger sized snake on the *left* side of the front roof.

My focus was raised to the top of the roof across the main beam that went horizontally across. On the far *right* side was an enormously large, stuffed monkey, like one might see at a circus. In its hands were brass clanging cymbals that it banged in order to disturb and bring confusion. It began to jump across the high beam from right to left and back again making an intended stomping sound.

My attention came back to the snakes again. The largest snake became angry and hissed at me when it realized that I could see it. This seemed to be the controlling snake captain, as its head reared up toward me, defying my presence.

In the Spirit, I called down a fireball from Heaven towards the snake's head. The effect completely incinerated its head and scorched its upper body. The smaller snakes cowered in response.

In Jesus' name, I commanded the deceitful monkey into a small jar with a closed lid. It could keep making noise, but no one would be able to hear its shenanigans any longer.

The mischievous, monkey business portrayed in this dream was sent to bang and clang unsettling noises to prevent the Spirit of God from being heard. Do not waste time and effort on erratic, reactive, and defiant monkeys.

The harassing snakes were there to spearhead accusations, lies, and distortions about anyone that they disliked. This would more specifically be targeted to those that serve God in Spirit and in truth.

An interesting fact about snakes is they do not depend on their sight or hearing like mammals. Instead, they rely on their natural, carnal senses like smell and touch.[5] Some species have pits between their eyes and nostril used to locate prey as they hide away inside hollow pits, waiting for their prey to venture into their domain.[6]

Monkeys are not shy primates, known to be quite loud. Some species, like the Howler monkey, can be heard from miles away[7] using their big voices to defend their turf.[8] They can demonstrate aggressiveness when protecting their food and territory.

They are pretty short-tempered beings and can get angry easily.[9] They are also known for their subversive trickery, being unpredictable, and given to tantrums.[10] That is why the monkey in my dream needed to be sealed up from its influence over the family. Its presence symbolized one of an intense, loud invader against the Holy Spirit's dealings. We are to be wise and not disguise what is true from false.

> *You quieted the raging oceans with their pounding waves and silenced the shouting of the nations.*
>
> —Psalm 65:7, NLT

Righteousness or Complacency

The entire chapter of Isaiah 32 speaks in contrast to a society that has become deaf and dumb. Its prior leadership had been righteousness conscious. When those in authority seek God's rulership, its citizen's are protected. It starts out:

> *Behold, a king will reign in righteousness, And princes will rule with justice. A man will be as a **hiding place** from the wind, And a **cover** from the tempest. As rivers of water in a dry place, As the shadow of a great rock in a weary land. The **eyes** of those who see will not be dim. And the **ears** of those who **hear will listen**.*
>
> —Isaiah 32:1-3, NKJV, emphasis added

Leadership has changed and promises have been broken while sin soars unabated. No one seems to notice while deficient man finds a way without Christ. There is no longer discernment to know right from wrong, good from evil. Brokenness has filled the land.

Isaiah 32:9 demonstrates the sunken condition of their nation: "**Rise up**, *you women who are at ease;* **Hear my voice;** *You complacent daughters,* **Give ear to my speech**" (NKJV, emphasis added).

Although speaking to daughters, it is inclusive of all genders. This is addressing a state of being: those who mindlessly conduct themselves, frivolously skating through life as if life were a rainbow. Their lives are a false existence as they waste their days carelessly feeling secure in themselves.

C'est la vie is a French term to express something less than ideal that has to be accepted because that's just the way life is; what will be, will be.[11] This distorts a Christ-centered lifestyle. It's a meaningless way to live, one eternally undesired.

But trouble is lurking around the corner because their sustenance is about to fail. Provisions had come so knowingly and easily; they were thankless of the Provider who gave it to them. They lived a lie of "no worries in the world."

> *Oh tremble, you indolent women. Get serious, you pampered dolls! Strip down and discard your silk fineries. Put on funeral clothes. Shed honest tears for the lost harvest, the failed vintage. Weep for my people's gardens and farms that* ***grow nothing*** *[barren]* ***but thistles and thornbushes***. *Cry tears, real tears, for the happy homes no longer happy, the merry city no longer merry.*
>
> —Isaiah 32:11-13, MSG, emphasis added

Watch the turn-around:

> *Yes,* ***weep and grieve*** *until the Spirit is poured down on us from above. And the badlands desert grows crops and the fertile fields become forests. Justice will move into the badlands desert. Right will build a home in the fertile field. And where*

there's Right, there'll be Peace and the progeny of Right: quiet lives and endless trust. My people will live in a peaceful neighborhood—in safe houses, in quiet gardens. The forest of your pride will be clear-cut; the city showing off your power leveled. **But you will enjoy a blessed life.**

—Isaiah 32:15-20, MSG, emphasis added

Be Strong in the Lord

On January 9, 2011, the Lord spoke to me in a dream to read the Book of Joshua for one full year. I was touched that the Lord compared me to Joshua in certain attributes, revealing that I was "caring" like Joshua was in his day. Joshua also embraced the Word of God as I crave it in my soul. I could not find exact words implying he was a caring man, but it is implied throughout the book. Ask the Lord what biblical character resemblance there is as your life virtue to encourage and validate your life. Those strong attributes will serve a purpose for your destiny to follow.

Allow me to share three consecutive promises from Joshua, chapter one (NKJV).

1. Verse 7: *"Only be strong and very courageous, that you may observe to do according to all the law which Moses My servant commanded you; do not turn from it to the right hand or to the left, that you may prosper wherever you go."*

2. Verse 8: *"This Book of the Law shall not depart from your mouth, but you shall meditate in it day and night, that you may observe to do according to all that is written in it. For then you will make your way prosperous, and then you will have good success."*

3. Verse 9: *"Have I not commanded you? Be strong and of good courage; do not be **afraid, nor be dismayed**, for the LORD your God is with you wherever you go"* (emphasis added).

All of these have been read, declared, and rehearsed in my life many times. They are what I call "life scriptures," as they have played such a strong and relevant role along life's pathway. They gave me strength even as a teenager, when I didn't know a lot of the Word yet. It was then that I put Joshua 1:9 on a paper index card and tacked it right below the light switch in my bedroom. At that time there were many fearful things in my life. This stirred up my courage knowing God was with me.

Kings Hide in Caves

Before discussing these fear-struck kings, let's find out what happened with Joshua in chapter 10. There is a battle between the Amorites and the men of Gibeon. Joshua is at the camp in Gilgal and word is sent to him saying, *"Don't abandon your servants now!" they pleaded. "Come at once! Save us! Help us! For all the Amorite kings who live in the hill country have joined forces to attack us"* (Joshua 10:6, NLT). The Lord spoke to Joshua, *"Do not fear them, for I have delivered them into your hand; not a man of them shall stand before you"* (v. 8, NKJV).

So with that promise, they proceed as the Lord directed them on the right route. There was a great slaughter to the point they were chasing them down the road and kept pursuing them a great distance. Then like icing on a cake, the Lord starts to throw large hailstones from Heaven upon those that remained, and they died. In verse 11 it says, *"There were more who died from the hailstones than the children of Israel killed with the sword"* (NKJV). Great God of hailstones—what a sight! Swords are flying, warriors are running wild, and God's throwing down huge hailstones from the sky!

As if that isn't enough, Joshua spoke to the Lord again, and said out loud, *"Sun, stand still over Gibeon; And Moon, in the Valley of Aijalon. So the sun stood still, And the moon stopped, Till the people had revenge upon their enemies"* (vv. 12-13, NKJV). We may wonder what the necessity of this was, as Joshua just won Jericho and Ai.

There were five Amorite kings remaining that refused to relent. Their intention was to stop the efforts of any further advancement, militarily and spiritually. These kings worshipped other gods. Joshua did not want the battle to end until he established full victory and the idolatrous enemies were extinguished. It was not enough that they relinquish themselves. Joshua exhibited complete tenacity to get his conquest completed. His forecast of faith touched God supremely; stopping the cycle of time from moving forward, based on Joshua speaking directly to the sun and moon with authority. The Lord heeded the voice of one man, Joshua.

It seemed the battle was done. We read in verses 16 through 19 how the five kings found a cave and hid themselves inside of this dark place at Makkedah. So, Joshua ordered large stones to be placed temporarily in front of the entrance with guards standing beside it. Joshua was not a man to stand still for a moment. He issued more orders to capture the remaining enemies on their *rear guard*. The objective was not to allow any stragglers to enter their own cities for rest and protection. Joshua again declares, *"The LORD your God has delivered them into your hand"* (v. 19, NKJV).

What we find in verse 21 is that *"no one moved his tongue against any of the children of Israel"* (NKJV). Are you kidding?

Who would speak against anyone no matter whose side they were on? It was a holy hush. They dare not speak a bad word unless the Almighty God got them thrust inwards.

The victory was the Lord's in the power of His might. The land had new ownership over this strategic area.

So what happened to the five kings? Joshua said, *"Open the mouth of the cave, and bring out those five kings to me from the cave"* (v. 22, NKJV). They were brought before him. Just to make a point, Joshua summoned all the men of Israel. He instructed all the captains to put their feet on the necks of the kings (v. 24). This was a custom in those days as a sign to all their enemies of a complete victory.

Joshua spoke to them all, *"Do not be afraid, nor be dismayed; be strong and of good courage, for thus the LORD will do to all your enemies against whom you fight"* (v. 25, NKJV).

This has become a lifetime scripture for me as I have used and claimed it so many times in my life over circumstances and my state of mind. I have been delivered of the spirit of fear.

Joshua killed each of them and then hung their bodies on five separate trees until evening (v. 26). The men were assigned to throw the dead bodies back into the caves, so that what had been a means of hiding was now their tomb (v. 27). In the fullness of the kings' iniquities, judgment had come against them. As we pursue the remnant of darkness, we then must command it to flee so that God's glory may fill us completely.

> *Joshua commanded, and they took them down from the trees and threw them into the cave where they had **hidden themselves**, and they set large stones against the mouth of the cave, which remain to this very day.*
>
> —Joshua 10:27, emphasis added

Rebel Children

In Isaiah 29 God spoke to the city of Ariel, which was being compared to Jerusalem—a city where David had set a camp. God is talking about a person's life there, as the years are adding up and the holidays, seasons, and cycles come and go.

Again we have an unblessed city with riotous sieges, driven to the ground and people mumbling words from the dirt. It says in verse 4:

> And you will be brought low; from the earth you shall speak, and from the dust your speech will be bowed down; your voice shall come from the ground like the voice of a ghost, and from the dust your speech shall whisper.

It's mesmerizing that, even at our very lowest, God still hears our faint whispers when we have almost given up all hope. He sees the unspoken breath that comes straight from the heart.

Then God shows up! The reverse may happen of what we might imagine. Our enemies are treated with what injury we have sustained before—beaten and blown away out of our midst. It says this mob of enemies came to (1) trouble, (2) hassle, and (3) torment. I love the analogy in verse 8 from The Message Bible comparing a thirsty woman dreaming she's drinking ice tea and wakes up thirsty as ever. We may have drunk so much tea before that all of a sudden we are craving water because the caffeine has run amuck while we run to the restroom. Only the water of the Holy Spirit can truly revive us while cleansing out all of yesterday's residue.

The rebel of our soul declares: "*Drug yourselves so you feel nothing. **Blind yourselves so you see nothing**. Get drunk, but not on wine. Black out, but not from whiskey. For GOD has rocked you into a deep, deep sleep*" (vv. 9-10, MSG, emphasis added).

Is this sounding like current television news? Of course! The Bible is relevant for all times and seasons. How do people hide their sorrows and problems today? People use drugs, glamour, drunkenness, and pornography to lull themselves and others into a deep, dark, secret place of deception and denial.

God calls them rebel children in Isaiah 30:1. Then He says, *"You make plans, but not mine. You make deals, but not in my Spirit. You pile sin on sin, one sin on top of another"* (MSG). It sounds like a deli sandwich filled with various layers stacked with a smorgasbord of sins. We might as well call it what God calls it. God says here are His people going off to places without even talking to Him about it; not the slightest inkling of a God thought of any avenue.

Are we running off to Pharaoh for protection? Where might we go for protection other than God, and will it last? Only our eternal Father has the capacity for that load of protection. The expectation is to "hide out" somewhere for relief. Big people are only as great as God allows them to be. But their stature is puny in God's sight, considering who is protecting them.

We don't have to stay in that place. It's a choice on either side of the coin. We choose what we will serve—darkness or light. Our Earth experience gives us that opportunity every day we live.

Following, Isaiah 30:4 says, *"They look big and important, true, with officials strategically established...but there's nothing to them. Anyone stupid enough to trust them will end up looking stupid—All show, no substance, an embarrassing farce"* (MSG).

God rebuked them in verse 15: *"Your strength will come from settling down in complete dependence on me—The very thing you've been unwilling to do"* (MSG). Those that won't will say, "No way!" and don't wait a moment to listen, will rush to do their own thing. But we can't get far enough away from God. How foolish to think that going on a vacation or moving to another city or finding another partner can get us better results. Things will either resemble the past scenarios or get more muddled if left up to our own devices.

There is a spiritual law of reciprocity or simply reaping what we've sewn beforehand. If we quit one relationship because of selfish ambitions, these will reappear in another one. I am not speaking of malicious relationships that are brutal and physically harmful.

When we're left standing still, alone and undone, with nothing left to show for our lives—seemingly vanished into thin air—the brave front of valor and competence is gone. Spent! It's been torn right off the road of decisions. Now life has become empty. What is there to cling to? The One who's been waiting for us all along; He's right there holding out His big Father's hand of love for us to take.

Our enduring, loving Father is not finished until He says so. In verse 18 it says He's gathering His own strength up, even when He's disappointed with us. What does He want to give us? Mercy; He wants to show us mercy. *"God takes the time to do everything right—**everything**"* (v. 18, MSG). Those who wait around for Him are the ones storing up their own strength to run the race before them.

> So the LORD must wait for you to come to him so he can show you his love and compassion. For the LORD is a faithful God. Blessed are those who wait for his help.
>
> —Isaiah 30:18, NLT

God is instructing us as the reading continues. It says, "Your time of **tears** is over" (v. 19, MSG, emphasis added). Why are our tears now gone? Psalm 31:9-10 reveals that: *"I've cried my eyes out; I feel hollow inside. My life leaks away, groan by groan; my years fade out in sighs. My troubles have worn me out, turned my bones to powder"* (MSG).

Then what are we to do? Psalm 31:14 says it: ***"Desperate, I throw myself on you; you are my God!"*** (MSG, emphasis added). Declare it now:

> God, I throw my whole life's being onto You alone. You can take care of me.

The psalm continues in verses 15 through 17: *"Hour by hour I place my days in your hand, safe from the hands out to get me. Warm me, your servant, with a smile; save me because you love me"* (MSG).

Turning to Isaiah 30 in verses 19-22 we get instruction for all generations. Take your victory here.

> *Cry for help and you'll find it's grace and more grace. The moment he hears, he'll answer. Just as the Master kept you alive during the hard times, he'll keep your teacher alive and present among you. Your teacher will be right there, local and on the job, urging you on whenever you wander left or right. "This is the right road. Walk down the road." You'll scrap our expensive and fashionable god-images. You'll throw them in the trash as so much garbage, saying, "Good Riddance!"*
>
> —Isaiah 30: 19-22, MSG

The Jewish people had secretly preserved the idol practices of serving other gods. But those vain metals were finally shred as shrapnel. Once we dispose of our disgraces there comes a new call to the races of humanity. The Light has shone forth to exonerate His people everywhere. There is a "now call" to prayer in which to unite ourselves by consecration.

Isaiah 30:23 tells us, *"Then the LORD will bless you with rain at planting time. There will be wonderful harvests!"* (NLT). Can you see this? God brings healing for all our hurt, pain, and disappointment. The real disillusionment of *dull gray* turns full force into sunlight, flooding rays throughout our soul. That light remains as we remain in the Lord.

> *Better yet, on the Day GOD heals his people from the wounds and bruises during their time of punishment, moonlight will flare into sunlight, and sunlight, like a whole week of sunshine at once, will flood the land.*

> —Isaiah 30:26, MSG

Iniquity Brother to Brother: Obadiah's Story

> *O how Esau will be ransacked, And his hidden treasures searched out!*

> —Obadiah 1:6, NASB

It started with Jacob and Esau back in Genesis 27 with the loss of Esau's inheritance due to selling out his birthright carelessly for a meal. Preferring the meal was an insignificant gesture of Esau's reckless condition. Hunger overrode the destiny of God's promise for Esau's lineage and the privilege of that inheritance. His wicked mindset referenced his apathetic relationship with His heavenly Father. He chose not to obey the instructions he was given by proving himself aloof to the meaning it would portray.

Generations down the road, Esau's kindred, the Edomites settled in high cliffs southeast of the Dead Sea, about 6,000 feet above sea level. This mountainous terrain imbedded presumptuous feelings of security and grandeur. As today, there was open defiance and warlike aggression to God's Law. They haughtily thought of themselves as untouchable. But, underneath God's watchful eye, unattainable they were not.

> *Every valley shall be lifted up, and every mountain and hill be made low; the uneven ground shall become level, and the rough places a plain.*

—Isaiah 40:4

The disdain, bitterness, and hardheartedness passed on to future generations and divided lands north and south between them. This was restoration in reverse, not seeking unity of the brethren. The Edomites would not allow the Israelites to pass through their land, turning them away (Numbers 20:21). No hope or future awaited this narrow-minded clan. They had made their mark! The line had been drawn in the rocks, rippling through their foundation causing it to crack underneath this deadly fortress.

The hostilities grew to such a point that the Edomites joined forces alongside the Israelites' foes, the Babylonians. There had been two previous invasions and another one was looming over the horizon. That is when Obadiah stepped up to the plate in a prophetic blast toward Edom's erroneous stand against their relatives, Judah. Obadiah 1, verse 15, says, "*For the day of the LORD is near upon all the heathen; as thou hast done, it shall be done unto thee: thy reward shall return upon thine own head*" (KJV).

Obadiah foretold Edom's sins, judgments, and permanent destruction of their fortress city. In verse 13 he speaks of "*the day of their calamity*" three times in the same verse. The theme is the same as chapter five, "Shame Hides." This group of people fell into pride and destructive behaviors.

The sounds of deliverance for the house of Jacob brought them back to their inheritance. They were able to repossess all the blessings God had for them. In God's Kingdom there are no boundaries of separation to divide us; we are in the same class. Our true function is to move forward as one people serving one God.

That is when we can employ His authority by our actions and our voice. We are equipped to declare with His authority as Jesus Christ commands. Remember the childhood chant that said, "I don't care what you say, I'm gonna do it anyway?" That is a rebel stance to complete ruin. We must care what Jesus says so our lives don't suffer virulent effects.

Some people have made an idol of our freedoms and rights. Freedom isn't a perverted demand of immorality; it's a weighted privilege.

> *During the reigns of those kings, the God of heaven will **set up a kingdom** that will never be destroyed or conquered. It will crush all these kingdoms into nothingness, and it will stand forever.*
>
> —Daniel 2:44, NLT, emphasis added

The last thing spoken by Obadiah in this short story is the punch line, "***And the kingdom will be the LORD's***" (Obadiah 1:21, emphasis added). When people believe they are singular gods unto themselves, they will fail, fruitlessly abandoned. Avoid the darkness of this age; cling to the Light that never goes out.

Isaiah 49:11, NLT

And I will make my mountains into level paths for them. The highways will be raised above the valleys.

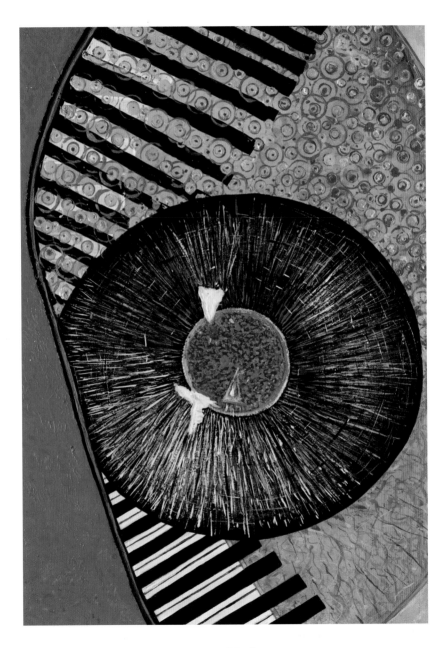

Eye of God
by Karen Wright

CHAPTER EIGHT

The Black Veil

I can never escape from your Spirit! I can never get away from your presence! If I go up to heaven, you are there; if I go down to the grave, you are there. If I ride the wings of the morning, if I dwell by the farthest oceans, even there your hand will guide me, and your strength will support me. I could ask the darkness to hide me and the light around me to become night—but even in darkness I cannot hide from you. To you the night shines as bright as day. ***Darkness and light are the same to you***.

—Psalm 139:7-12, NLT, emphasis added

The Black Veil

If the Good News we preach is hidden behind a veil, it is hidden only from people who are perishing. Satan, who is the god of this world, has blinded the minds of those who don't believe. They are **unable** *to* **see** *the glorious light of the Good News. They don't understand this message about the glory of Christ, who is the exact likeness of God.*

—2 Corinthians 4:3-4, NLT, emphasis added

I had a dream in October 2012 that I titled

The Black Veil

In my dream there was a festival in our area that my husband and I visited. We parked close to the entrance, while the canopy of green foliage and tall, large trees above us entranced me. This was an open area setting with other activities extending beyond our scope.

We were joined with a small group of people near the entrance as if taking a tour of the facilities. We began to follow a path around the western side of a large rectangular white tent. It reminded me of the huge circus tents we might see at a carnival. Of our group, my husband and I were with others I did not recognize, but we spoke on friendly terms. The canopy of the tent was closed around its sides, while we curved toward the southern corridor following the outlined paved pathway.

It felt mysterious and strange as if on a search. I observed a boy or young teen sitting on the ground unattended at the end of the back pathway. He was leaning up against a massive tall and long black veiled curtain. The pathway turned a sharp right past the boy, continuing on southward then out of sight.

I wanted to see the boy up close, as he specifically struck my attention. I felt from a distance that there was something not right. He appeared to be in agony. I led our group closer to him, stepping up to a faster pace. I noticed the boy's mouth was wide open with vertical, contorted movements that kept changing and moving spontaneously. His eyes were glazed over and he appeared possessed. Right before I could reach him, his body was suddenly snatched from underneath the black veil by an unseen force. He vanished, never seeing him again.

Ecclesiastes 9:12 tell us, *"For man does not know his time. Like fish that are taken in an evil net, and like birds that are caught in a snare, so the **children of man** are **snared** at an evil time, when it suddenly falls upon them"* (emphasis added). A snare means to lure, entice, trap, or snared by bait,[1] figuratively meaning the devices of the wicked.

> I asked the Holy Spirit about the young boy. What did he represent? I heard this, "These are the spiritual orphans that were aborted." Then it was like seeing a roadside sign with a flashing arrow pointing out a name. He was like the Moses's that were sent down the waterway, the byways, and highways. But they (as there are *many*) were never received or picked up (abandoned in their calling) by those leaders that would train and nurture them to spiritual health. Isaiah 8:15 reiterates this, *"And **many** shall stumble on it. They shall fall and be broken; they shall be **snared** and taken"* (emphasis added).
>
> Their spiritual parents did not come to receive and rescue them. They neglected their future call in the Body of Christ to heal the dying. They have not fulfilled the "search and find" rescue effort of their spiritual sons and daughters. Their assigned mission was terminated. These spiritual sons were abandoned in an infinite moment, never to be found again.

> *He lies in wait near the villages; from ambush he murders the innocent. His eyes watch in secret for his victims.*
>
> —Psalm 10:8, NIV

The young boy was left to the devices of an evil system. He was easy prey, a victim of the ways of mankind left to their own demise. Second Timothy 2:26 explains that we must come to our senses by escaping the snare of the devil if we have been captured by him to do his will.

Our youth think their own choices are involved as they succumb to the enemy's will through neglecting God's truth. In Ezekiel 18:32 we read how the Lord feels: *"I don't want you to die, says the Sovereign LORD. Turn back and live!"* (NLT). Where are the hearts and hands to receive these youth in need of a new spirit? Training must come from spiritually minded people who put action to their words while there is still time to overcome this veiled, distorted anarchy.

> *Justice is turned back, And righteousness stands far away; For truth has stumbled in the street, And uprightness cannot enter. Yes, truth is lacking; And he who turns aside from evil makes himself a **prey**. Now the LORD saw, And it was displeasing in His sight that there was no justice.*

—Isaiah 59:14-15, NASB, emphasis added

I looked further down the path paved to my right following alongside a heavy, dense, black veiled curtain to look for an opening. I finally found a slit that ran up and down vertically as the folds of the veil overlaid one another. The folds of the curtain expanded to the right and left as I pulled them slowly apart. I sensed this was another dimension I was being allowed to view without being noticed.

I purposed to separate myself from inside the blacked veiled room, by continuing to stand on the pathway, which felt like the safe side (paths of righteousness). I looked inside the room waiting for my eyes to adjust to the darkness while taking in as much detail as I could. The first thing I noticed toward the northern backside was a dull, pinkish gray light source in the center of a stage type setting. For a moment, I'd thought the light was a normal "bright" light source. But, as I continued to hone in on the surroundings, it appeared more dim and muted. Artificial!

Suddenly there was movement from the center of this ominous room. A large black object expanding outward horizontally came into my view. Its head was focused on the dimly lit light source at center stage. As its body continued to gradually rise from the floor, it took on the shape of an enormous bird like beast with a wingspan that filled the room. I watched as the tips of each wing spread outward wall to wall. The creature's body continued to drift slowly upward like a plane suspended in midair, as if the light source was giving it that ability. It was completely fixated on the eerie light as if in a trance.

The profane image took on a form that was a combination between an eagle and a dragon. It focused entirely upon the light source causing enhanced feelings of self-exaltation and empowerment.

Hebrews 4:13 says, "*Nothing in all creation is hidden from God's sight. Everything is **uncovered** and **laid bare** before the eyes of him to whom we must give account*" (NIV, emphasis added). By being laid bare, or "open" as some texts read, there is a meaning of being overthrown. In the Greek it renders a message of "bending back the neck" as in wrestling.

The seductive dragon tried to cloak itself deceptively as an eagle, but that was an illusion. There is no escaping the magnificent, eye-detecting exposure of God. Every secretively devised plan, whether conscious or unconscious, is perceived by Almighty God. Psalm 19:12 reiterates this again by saying, "*Clear me from **hidden [and unconscious]** faults*" (AMP, emphasis added).

Satan is referred to in Ezekiel 28:17-19: "*Your heart was proud because of your beauty; you corrupted your wisdom for the sake of your splendor. I cast you to the ground; I exposed you before kings, to feast their **eyes** on you*" (v. 17, emphasis added).

In verse 17 of the King James Version it states, "*Thine heart was lifted up* [the dragon bird], *because of thy beauty* [lust of the eye], *thou hast corrupted thy wisdom by reason of thy brightness* [eerie pink light]. The prideful King Tyre thought himself equal to the heavenly throne, thinking his power alone could protect his earthly kingdom.

Arrogance caused a corrupt flip from wisdom by the false brightness. The radiant glistening light blinded satan's eyes so that he could not see the one true Light. He obstinately turned away from the Word of God. Like satan, Adam and King Tyre saw themselves as superior perfection; they were void of sense, unable to see their error.

On the opposite side of the room from where I was standing, the wall was covered in a thin black veil. I mention "thin" for a purpose. The curtain material on this section of the room was semitransparent in nature, like fine mesh.

Isaiah 40:22 describes it this way, "*It is He who...stretches out the heavens a like* [gauze] *curtain, And spreads them out like a tent to dwell in.*" The layer of covering closest to the window of heaven was the finer, thin veil material.

The word translated "tent" in Hebrew is one's covering, dwelling place, home, or tabernacle. In this case, it's the adversary's counterfeit secret lair or hideout dungeon. Psalm 69:25 tells us this about the enemy's place of hiding: "*Let their habitation and their encampment be a desolation; **let no one dwell in their tents**"* (AMP, emphasis added).

Actually, all the outside establishments at this festival were white canopied tents of varying sizes except for this one. Ephesians speaks of the vast and glorious temple where the Spirit of God dwells. Today, that spiritual temple lives inside of every believer. Jesus is our permanent tent in which to dwell.

In him the whole structure is joined together and grows into a holy temple in the Lord; in whom you also are built together spiritually into a dwelling place for God.

—Ephesians 2:21-22, NRSV

My focal point went further down to the far right of the outside tent wall where I found a large rectangular window without any covering or glass. God is always on the right side of any situation, and that explains the window's placement. This opening revealed the glory of God's presence between this dark occupancy and the Lord's open window. I could see blue sky everywhere.

Appearing out of nowhere, or as Matthew 6:6 says, out of the "secret place" (NKJV), was an enormous, single eye. This grand eye had moved upward and horizontally across the window. Isaiah 40:22 describes the vastness of God: "*It is God Who sits above the circle (the horizon) of the earth, and its inhabitants are like grasshoppers*" (AMP). This would be like someone flying in a plane observing the tiny people below after takeoff, seeing from afar off.

This single eye was so expansive I merely saw a portion of the top half of it. The black eyelashes were perfectly straight and spaced evenly all the way across the eyelid just like piano keys. Each eyelash was the exact same length, seeming to be six feet long each. Everything about it was flawlessly exquisite, total perfection! God's all seeing eye is on His Holy temple, not allowing a foreign substitute to invade it.

*The LORD is in his holy temple; the LORD's throne is in heaven; his eyes see, his **eyelids** test the children of man.*

—Psalm 11:4, emphasis added

While thinking upon on the preciseness of God's eyelashes, I was reminded of the scripture on the width, length, depth, and height of Christ. Following through with this thought brought a whole new revelation in correlation to our eyesight.

That scripture is found in Ephesians 3:16-19:

> *That He would grant you, according to the riches of His glory, to be strengthened with might through His Spirit in the inner man, that Christ may dwell in your hearts through faith; that you, being rooted and grounded in love, may be able to comprehend with all the saints what is the* **width and length and depth and height**—*to know the love of Christ which passes knowledge; that you may be filled with all the fullness of God.*

—Ephesians 3:16-19, NKJV, emphasis added

Let's expound on each adjective from the scripture above:
- Width of Christ—God's love extends out universally, reaching without limits.
- Length of Christ—He is infinite, expansive, omnipresent, and omnipotent.
- Depth of Christ—His unfathomable grace is in this world and the one to come. The depths of hell could not hold Him, nor can evil touch Him.
- Height of Christ—God has the all seeing eye. He can come from any dimension of Heaven He chooses. He lifts us up and makes us to sit together in heavenly places in Christ Jesus.

For comparison, Deuteronomy 25:15-16 says, "*You must have accurate and honest weights and measures, so that you may live long in the land the LORD your God is giving you. For the LORD your God detests anyone who does these things, anyone who deals dishonestly*" (NIV).

It was stunning to behold this sight as I had a bird's-eye view. As God's eye pupil became centrally focused in the middle of the window; it fixated upon what was inside.

Jeremiah 16:17 reveals to us, *"For My eyes are on their ways; they are not **hidden** from My face, neither is their iniquity concealed from My eyes"* (NASB, emphasis added). God is about to turn everything inside the "demonic tent" upside down. Iniquity cannot be contained before El Shaddai, our Almighty God. He marks us all eternally.

Instantaneously, came forth a bolting blast from within the room. The huge dragon bird exploded outward, along with everything else that was contained inside the black veil. The magnificent force expanded outward in every direction. Nothing of substance remained hidden inside the devil's foggy fortress.

By your many sins and dishonest trade you have desecrated your sanctuaries. So I made a fire come out from you, and it consumed you, and I reduced you to ashes [represents final judgment and death] *on the ground in the sight of all who were watching. All the nations who knew you are appalled at you, you have come to a **horrible end and will be no more**.*

—Ezekiel 28:18-19, NIV, emphasis added

The wisdom of satan is foolishness to God. For it is written, *"He catches the wise in their **craftiness**"* (1 Corinthians 3:19, emphasis added). The word *craftiness* here means cunning trickery. It's the use of false arguments that sound correct but intentionally mislead, as told in Job 5:12-13: *"He frustrates the schemes of the **crafty** so that they achieve no success. He traps the wise in their **craftiness** so that the plans of the deceptive are* *quickly brought to an end"* (HCSB, emphasis added). Craftiness represents the seductive serpent's hidden agenda, which is exposed by God's visibility to see with an everlasting imprint.

Strong's says a*lam* is **to veil** from sight. It is a word for concealing or to blind from sight. It is an attempt to hide oneself from the Almighty God in a secret matter. In Greek it means to deny, unfavorably; to lurk, lay up, keep secret. This distinctly conveys the meaning of a*lam* as to veil from sight. Generally, it means to conceal something of evil intent or desire from sight. A majority of sin comes out of things hidden in the night.

Ultimately, the enemy's foreboding future is revealed. It will be horribly bitter, but it will finally END. The dragon bird was destroyed from its secret lair!

> *How you are fallen from heaven, O Day Star, son of Dawn! How you are **cut down** to the ground, you who laid the nations low! You said in your heart, "I will ascend to heaven; above the stars of God. I will set my throne on high; I will sit on the mount of assembly in the far reaches of the north; I will ascend above the heights of the clouds; I will make myself like the Most High." But you are brought down to Sheol, to the far reaches of the pit.*

> —Isaiah 14:12-15, emphasis added

The Carnival

According to Wikipedia, a "carnival typically involves a public celebration or parade combining some elements of a circus, [wearing] **masks** and a public street party."[2] Circus is a Latin word meaning ring or circular line, such as the Roman circuses named for their circular arenas for performances (e.g., the Circus Maximus).[3] It comes from the Greek word *kirkos*, root word *kirk*, from which we get the word *church*,[4] pertaining to or belonging to the Lord's house. Interesting how early church revivals and circuses were both held inside of a large tent. Let's hope church never becomes a myriad of circus acts.

Historically, there were carnival celebrations of indulgent merrymaking before the denials of Lent.[5] It has some semblance to Lupercalia, a fertility festival held each February in ancient Rome.[6] Today, Mardi Gras meaning "Fat Tuesday" came from Shrove Tuesday, the day before Lent begins.[7]

Some scholars believe the pagan practice of "weeping for Tammuz" that Ezekiel denounced has origins from these times.[8] Ezekiel 8:14, *"Then he brought me to the entrance of the north gate of the house of the LORD, and behold, there sat women weeping for Tammuz."* The pagan god Tammuz was associated with death and rebirth in nature.

Carnival people called carnies run the booths, food stands, games, or rides at these festival events which can be around boardwalks or amusement parks. They can also be held at playgrounds, rodeos, and civic event areas.

Carnival balls were when people dressed up in elaborate masquerade outfits during these celebrations. Like any rite of passage as in a sweet sixteen party, *bat mitzvah*, or Quinceañera, they mark an overturning of daily life. It's a time of celebratory family gatherings in a public arena marked by tradition and pomp.

> *Don't be teamed with those who do not love the Lord, for what do the people of God have in common with the people of sin? How can light live with darkness? And what harmony can there be between Christ and the devil? How can a Christian be a partner with one who doesn't believe? And what union can there be between God's temple and idols? For you are God's temple, the home of the living God, and God has said of you, "I*

will live in them and walk among them, and I will be their God and they shall be my people." That is why the Lord has said, "Leave them; separate yourselves from them; don't touch their filthy things, and I will welcome you and be a Father to you, and you will be my sons and daughters."

—2 Corinthians 6:14-18, TLB

Mask

Since God has so generously let us in on what he is doing, we're not about to throw up our hands and walk off the job just because we run into occasional hard times. We refuse to wear **masks** *and play games. We don't maneuver and manipulate behind the scenes. And we don't twist God's Word to suit ourselves. Rather, we keep everything we do and say out in the open, the whole truth on display, so that those who want to can see and judge for themselves in the presence of God.*

—2 Corinthians 4:1-2, MSG, emphasis added

It is no coincidence this carnival setting used these type of elements. The typical function of a mask is to cover and conceal one's true identity. This is exactly the function that satan covets most, to disguise his evil exploits of prideful prowess. People might paint their faces false appearances of pretense, wear elaborate costumes of deception, or scheme about in a wishful merry charade.

A disguise serves the purpose of concealing one's true identity or misleading others. It's a camouflage in order to prevent recognition by means of altering one's features. It's used by those seeking to avoid identification. Disguise means "to *conceal* or cover up the truth or actual character of by a counterfeit form or appearance; misrepresent: *'to disguise one's intentions.'"*[9]

Uzziah in 2 Chronicles 26 *"did what was right in the **eyes of
the LORD**"* (v. 4, emphasis added) as a young King. God helped
him defeat his enemies as his fame spread, while building cities
and towers in the land. His head swelled in arrogant pride from
what he considered his own milestones and accomplishments,
even though it was God alone who gave him these abilities
of victory.

> *But when he was strong, he grew proud, to his destruction. For
> he was unfaithful to the LORD his God and entered the temple
> of the LORD to burn incense on the altar of incense.*
>
> —2 Chronicles 26:16

When Uzziah entered the temple acting the part of a priest, the
real priest, Azariah, and eighty other men of valor blocked his
way. His mask of pride marred his heart, causing him to forget
his placement in God's house. God alone reigns supreme in
Heaven and Earth.

> *They withstood King Uzziah and said to him, "It is not for you,
> Uzziah to burn incense to the LORD....Go out of the sanctuary,
> for you have done wrong, and it will bring you no honor from
> the LORD God." Then Uzziah was angry. Now he had a censer
> in his hand to burn incense, and when he became angry with
> the priests, leprosy broke out on his forehead in the presence
> of the priests in the house of the LORD, by the altar of incense.*
>
> —2 Chronicles 26:18-19

Uzziah's reaction was one of angry rage at the denial of entrance
to the temple. This choleric response caused an immediate
breaking out of leprosy all over his forehead. Our foreheads are
like a billboard of character. Verse 21 says he was excluded from

the house of the Lord the rest of his life as the sin of leprosy stayed with him until his death.

The Hebrew word sometimes translated *hide* means to seek, causatively to conceal oneself or *mask-change* disguise self. If we have found ourselves imitating a phony life inside of a mask, then it's time to unmask. Trying to be someone we are not or don't want to be says our identity is not what it should be. It's time to get grounded on the truth of our true identity in Christ. Wipe off the false paint and remove a fake smile by starting life's true journey with honest humility.

In Matthew 12:23, the Pharisees, after observing a man's healing, go out to conspire against Jesus calling Him a *"prince of demons"* (NIV). Their intention was to destroy Jesus, the Man, because they were jealous of His ministry. But the people were amazed at Him.

> *Put on the whole armor of God, that you may be able to stand against the schemes of the devil.*
>
> —Ephesians 6:11

It's Inside the Leaven

In scripture leaven is compared to hypocrisy. We find that in Luke 12:1: *"Beware of the leaven of the Pharisees, which is hypocrisy."* It's an act people display in order to be seen or noticed for all their achievements or notoriety. They do things in order to impress upon others how important they are. They lavish accolades and adorn people with awards and metals bestowed upon their title. As the Old Testament verifies, they are lovers of rules, doctrines, and manners performed; whereas God looks upon heart matters.

The purpose of leaven is to enlarge something from small to grand in scale. A pinch of leaven added to a flour mixture expands it from something miniscule to a puffy, swollen overgrown mass. The leaven *influences* the entire batter. It's just like the pride of hypocrites that swells their opinion of themselves. Leaven is hard to distinguish as it hides inside the flour mixture dramatically growing it into a large loaf.

> *Then Pharisees and scribes came to Jesus from Jerusalem and said, "Why do your disciples break the tradition of the elders? For they do not wash their hands when they eat." [Jesus] answered them, "And why do you break the commandment of God for the sake of your tradition? For God commanded, 'Honor your father and your mother,' and, 'Whoever reviles father or mother must surely die.' But you say, 'If anyone tells his father or his mother, "What you would have gained from me is given to God," he need not honor his father.' So for the sake of your tradition you have made void the word of God. You hypocrites! Well did Isaiah prophesy of you, when he said: 'This people honors me with their lips, but their heart is far from me; in vain do they worship me, teaching as doctrines the commandments of men.'"*

> —Matthew 15:1-9

A hypocrite is one devoid of a love for people or God. As it tells us in Matthew 15, a hypocrite is one who uses spiritual language hidden behind dark motives that benefit himself to convey his tricky message.

Hypocrites try to put people into the bondage of captivity because they never measure up to the standards they have set, when in fact they have a different false measure for themselves. So, beware when people try to hook you up into unloving, contradictory chains. Ask the Holy Spirit for discernment when unsure about someone's predesignated influences that pull life down and out. Jesus came to set the captives free and give us the freedom of a new life.

Remember, Jesus is in the beautiful building business. He always builds up the Body of Christ; whereas the deceiver is in the dysfunctional demolition business of destroying, devouring, and trashing people. The devil maintains the lowest rank on Earth to maliciously bring down a person to the same level as himself—to the ground. The serpent in Eden lost his legs when demoted to eat dust the rest of his days. Let him eat dirt balls; we have been inspired to aspire to new heights and destinations.

Our example is Christ, as He quoted Isaiah's prophecy concerning Himself:

> *Behold, my servant whom I have chosen, my beloved with whom my soul is well pleased. I will put my Spirit upon him, and he will proclaim justice to the Gentiles. He will not quarrel or cry aloud, nor will anyone hear his voice in the streets; a bruised reed he will not break, and a smoldering wick he will not quench until he brings justice to victory; and in his name the Gentiles will hope.*

> —Matthew 12:18-21

Significant Veil

Initially, many elements in this dream were indiscernible to me. Several months later, the Holy Spirit began to reveal scriptures to me about the significance of this dream from God. The first scripture correlating to it was Job 12:22. Before I share it, I'm going to relay the use of numbers in dreams based upon John Paul Jackson's dream card.[10] In Job 12:22, the twelve stands for government and order, and twenty-two relates to a light source. Both of these correspond to "The Black Veil" dream.

In Job 12:22 it states: *"He reveals the deep things of darkness, and brings deep shadows into the light"* (NET). My entire dream reflected on contrasts of darkness and light from Earth's enemy versus a righteous God. The dragon acted the part of an artificial, sub-standard light source, but it was from without. The Lord's light source is from within, extending outwards beyond all boundaries.

The government is upon Christ's shoulders, as it tells us in Isaiah 9:6: *"For to us a child is born, to us a son is given; and the government shall be upon his shoulder, and his name shall be called Wonderful, Counselor, Mighty God, Everlasting Father, Prince of Peace."* All nations were set up according to God's divine plan and purpose so that they might **hear His voice**.

A removed veil in scriptures is a symbol of revelation or revealed truth. The black veil was a darkened quarantine guarding against the revelation of God's glory. Darkness cannot overcome darkness. Hardness brings darkness. But the light of Christ overcomes it instantly.

> *But when one turns to the Lord, the veil is removed. Now the Lord is the Spirit, and where the Spirit of the Lord is, there is freedom.*
>
> —2 Corinthians 3:16-17

In Christ's glory is a thin veil between Heaven and Earth. The black, heavy veil in the dream required moving it aside to reveal truth coming in through a window, although the entire atmosphere seemed contained by the enemy, much like a cocoon. The one true Light chose to invade it by penetrating and shattering the darkness. Believing in Christ is the only way the veil can be eliminated.

Ephesians 5:14 tells us, *"For anything that becomes visible is light. Therefore it says, 'Awake, O sleeper, and arise from the dead, and Christ will shine on you.'"*

Find Your Tent

*For he will hide me in his shelter in the day of trouble; he will conceal me under the cover of his **tent**; he will lift me high upon a rock. And now my head shall be lifted up above my enemies all around me, and I will offer in his **tent** sacrifices with shouts of joy; I will sing and make melody to the LORD. Hear, O LORD, when **I cry aloud**; be gracious to me and answer me! You have said, "Seek my face." My heart says to you, "Your face, LORD, do I seek." **Hide not** your face from me. Turn not your servant away in anger, O you who have been my help. Cast me not off; forsake me not, O God of my salvation! For my father and my mother have forsaken me, but the LORD will take me in. Teach me your way, O LORD, and lead me on a level path because of my enemies. Give me not up to the will of my adversaries; for false witnesses have risen against me, and they breathe out violence. I believe that I shall look upon the goodness of the LORD in the land of the living! Wait for the LORD; be strong, and let your heart take courage; wait for the LORD!*

—Psalm 27:5-14, emphasis added

Here in Psalm 27 is a passionate verse about the tent of God— that sanctified sanctuary of our Father's house where His revealing light emanates throughout. This is a true hiding place of refuge from the voracious storms that arrive without warning.

It is here in His holy presence we can reside for strengthening, peace of mind, and assurance of heart. He is the lifter of our head (Psalm 3:3) in order to propel us upward upon the sturdy rock of Christ. We are to be there with Him in Christ, not separately weakened. We are reminded to seek His face, as we are not forsaken! In that secure position we will not be swayed by our adversities, anxieties, or the various enemy entrapments.

The LORD wraps himself in light as with a garment; he stretches out the heavens like a tent.

—Psalm 104:2, NIV

Abraham saw the triune God outside of his tent as told in Genesis 18:1-2:

*And the LORD appeared to him by the oaks of Mamre, as he sat at the door of his tent in the heat of the day. He **lifted up his eyes** and looked, and behold, three men were standing in front of him. When he saw them, he ran from the tent door to meet them and bowed himself to the earth.*

—Genesis 18:1-2, emphasis added

According to the Ancient Hebrew Research Center, the door of the tent was like the "throne of a king" as the ruler of his family.[11] In Abraham's culture he held the fullest authority over the family. All family matters of importance were done at the tent door. He watched over his household and all those that came close to his tent.

Originally tents were used in nomadic times in the Middle East where people dwelt in these movable fortresses of temporary shelter. These cloth tents were woven material typically made from black goat's hair as illustrated in our story above. The typical shape used was rectangular with flaps raised to catch the breezes. Ropes were used to tie them to tent pegs driven in the ground.[12]

In Numbers 14:10 we read: "*But the glory of the LORD appeared at the **tent of meeting** to all the people of Israel*" (emphasis added). It was also called the Tabernacle of Moses when he carried the Ten Commandments inside the tent. Another English translation is *tabernacle*. The Hebrew word is *mishkan*, meaning residence or dwelling place. It was built as a place of worship, transportable from the bondage in Egypt to the Promised Land of Canaan.

Luke 16:9 refers to the tent as a home of *eternal dwelling*. The apostle Paul in 2 Corinthians 5:1 says it this way: "*For we know that if the earthly tent we live in is destroyed, we have a building from God, an eternal house in heaven, not built by human hands*" (NIV). We presently carry around our heavenly tent with us. It lives on the inside of us, afresh and anew. When we go to Heaven, our tents will permanently reside with us.

For those experiencing neglect, painful suffering, or abandonment, let's confidently find the tabernacle of God and remain there. This is not a place to escape from trepidations and life's trials; it is rather a rebuilding depot for the stalwart endurance to focus our navigation and then proceed again. John 16:33 reminds us that in this world we will have tribulations, which means "pressure" in the original Greek; but Jesus declares to all He has already overcome the world.

It can be a time for examining our next move with God's enhanced, discerning voice echoing in our ears. It's not a situation to hide our emotions or feelings in shameful legalistic condemnation. It's time to pitch our stakes deeply in the fertile soil of God's presence drawing ever closer.

> *I will set My dwelling in and among you, and My soul shall not despise or reject or separate itself from you. And I will walk in and with and among you and will be your God, and you shall be My people.*
>
> —Leviticus 26:11-12, AMP

When you are hurting the most, get inside His safe tent; relish God's nourishment for endurance to run the race. We don't seek failure but opportunities, regardless of how it appears. We must set our mind on things that are above for an eternal perspective of our situation. If we try to inspect our issues microscopically; it's like envisioning a hollowed out tree standing in front of you. All we have is insufficiently empty and vain. A hollow tree can be ravished quickly with life's fiery trials. Christ fills every form of decay and emptiness by His Holy Spirit's penetrating fire. Then He refills us with His newness like a dawning rain. Make an abiding place for Him in your spiritual home.

Send out your light and your truth; let them lead me; let them bring me to your holy hill and to your dwelling!

—Psalm 43:3

Tent into God's presence. Worship Him through the pressures of life. Sometimes it's just the act of getting still, then allowing Jesus to penetrate our focus. It's one of the best remedies I know for peace of mind. Allow Him to console, build, and strengthen the life you are allowed to live. Quiet the soul and find moments to cherish the Lord, as He is your best friend. Talk to Him as He is walking right beside your soul. There will be a time shortly to help others in the same way.

Like the tent in the black veil, Job 11:14 says to put far away from us the iniquity that is in our hand and allow no evil or injustice to dwell in our tent. This is saying to not allow sin in our actions or in our heart. It's all or nothing; so we give Him all so something great can happen that we can't do alone. All that darkness inside must flee in Christ's name!

LORD, who may dwell in your sanctuary? Who may live on your holy hill? He whose walk is blameless and who does what is righteous, who speaks the truth from his heart and has no slander on his tongue, who does his neighbor no wrong and casts no slur on his fellowman, who despises a vile man but honors those who fear the LORD, who keeps his oath even when it hurts, who lends his money without usury and does not accept a bribe against the innocent. He who does these things will never be shaken.

—Psalm 15, NIV

Evil Eyes

But the eyes of the wicked will fail, and escape will elude them; their hope will become a dying gasp.

—Job 11:20, NIV

Has anyone seen the eyes of a rock-hardened criminal? There is no light emanating from the eyes. It seems overshadowed in dull darkness around their entire eye socket. There is just something eerie about their countenance. It's not their eye color or other facial features, except for a possible grimacing frown. It's the expression in and around their eyes that tell it all, without a word.

We are mirrors in our expression. The thing people read the most is the look in our eyes. Many can tell the truth from a lie, joy from sadness. Psalm 101:3 says, *"I will not set before my eyes anything that is worthless. I hate the work of those who fall away; it shall not cling to me."*

Proverbs 28:22 refers to a stingy man. In Matthew it speaks of a man whose *eye is evil* (6:23, KJV). A worthless person is considered a wicked man, who is known by four gestures: he *"goes about with crooked speech, winks with his eyes, signals with his feet, and points with his finger"* (Proverbs 6:12-13). I get a glimpse of Scrooge when I read this passage.

In the Amplified Bible, reading Matthew 20:15, it says, *"Am I not permitted to do what I choose with what is mine? [Or do you begrudge my being generous?] Is your **eye evil** because I am good?"* (emphasis added). The heathen took from the generosity of the righteous. Just like Judas who horded the money bag, stealing from the generous, which ended in his own demise.

> *Your eye is the lamp of your body. When your eye is healthy, your whole body is full of light, but when it is bad, your body is full of darkness.*
>
> —Luke 11:34

Eye Color

> *And God said, "Let there be light," and there was light.*
>
> —Genesis 1:3

Like a palette of varying paint colors, scripture phrases conjure up word images, like the "rose of Sharon" or the manifold, multi-color seven layer rainbow God made as a sign of His covenant. The twelve tribes of Israel were each described by a colored gemstone in the priest's symbolic breastplate (Exodus 28:17-19). The Earth itself is a vast array of various spectrums of shades for all of His children to enjoy.

When we think of color conceptually in scripture, it even revolved around a priestly examination of leprosy. Leviticus 13:55 says, *"Then the priest must examine the object again. If he finds that the contaminated area has not changed **color** after being washed, even if it did not spread, the object is defiled. It* *must be completely burned up, whether the contaminated spot is on the inside or outside"* (NLT, emphasis added).

After the suspect garment was considered contaminated of leprosy by a priest, it was required to be washed. Upon a second inspection, if the color of the spot had not changed color like from red to green or remained just as it was during the first observation, nor faded, it was still considered defiled which required burning. Even if the leprosy had not spread through-out the garment, it was still defiled just by the observation of its color.

Ephesians 3:10 says, *"To the intent that now unto the prin-cipalities and powers in heavenly places might be known by the church the manifold wisdom of God"* (KJV). The word translated "Manifold" means **many colored**, giving the church age *revealed secrets* in how to rule and reign in the infinite wisdom of God to operate in the Heavenly realm.

> *According to the eternal purpose which he purposed in Christ Jesus our Lord: In whom we have boldness and access with confidence by the faith of him.*
>
> —Ephesians 3:11-12, KJV

Genesis 37:3 says, *"Now Israel loved Joseph more than any other of his sons, because he was the son of his old age. And he made him a robe of many colors."* The Hebrew phrase for the translation "coat of many colors" is *kethoneth passim*. The word *passim* can be translated as "colorful." It can suggest the intricate patterns woven on coats. It may even indicate favor in a relationship. The message of redemption is woven colorfully through the church, calling forth the glory of the Lord and revealing it to all His creation.

The striped semicircle rainbow of covenant was given to us as a sign of promise (Genesis 9:13). The world would never be put in an underworld waterlogged condition again. This was God's sign for new beginnings for His children and promises of good things to come. The prophet Ezekiel, in a vision, saw a rainbow above the throne of God as a form of the glory (Ezekiel 1:28).

The Jewish Encyclopedia notes that Biblical Hebrew contains no specific term to describe *color*, but it is indicated by the Hebrew letter *ayin*, meaning "the eye."[13] Strong's Concordance; confirms this. Our eyes are the interpreters of color and light. It's a comparative word for material. Colors can hold significant symbolism. All colors in dream interpretation have a valid use in meaning, including the background, people, and objects. For instance, if they sky is turbulent with swirling grays and black, then this could indicate a foreboding situation.

> *Come now, let us reason together, says the LORD: though your sins are like* **scarlet**, *they shall be as* **white** *as snow; though they are* **red like crimson**, *they shall become like wool.*
>
> —Isaiah 1:18, emphasis added

The Eye of God

> *Am I a God at hand, declares the LORD, and not a God far away? Can a man hide himself in secret places so that I cannot see him? declares the LORD. Do I not fill heaven and earth? declares the LORD.*
>
> —Jeremiah 23:23-24

I don't know what someone might think about a dream like mine, but I was initially struck with bewilderment. I wrote it in my journal understanding it was some kind of warfare dream.

One day it became simple. Even the sinister darkness of satan himself cannot hide inside the tents, corridors, and institutions of mankind. Our all-knowing God finds him out every time and strikes him down precisely and imminently.

Pastor Bill Johnson said in a sermon, "The devil got caught up in his own beauty, and was booted out of Heaven because he couldn't handle the measure of glory he was designed for."[14] God's glory is immeasurable! The enemy would not submit to the very thing he was created for. He chose to use the reflection of his image as a deflection of vain falseness.

Psalm 32:8 (KJV) tells us, "*I will instruct thee and teach thee in the way which thou shalt go: I will guide thee with mine eye.*" This scripture assures us we have divine guidance with the very eye of God. He dictates to us right movements to take. His eyes shine forth our instructions in how to put things together so they make sense. There is no wasted time in false starts or status.

When we are lost or confused on which way to turn, the Lord teaches us as a student in our turnings and decisions. All we need for the task is ask and listen for the proper instructions.

> *For My eyes are on all their ways; they are not hidden from My face, nor is their iniquity concealed from My eyes.*
>
> —Jeremiah 16:17, NASB

Clear Eyes

> *The light of the body is the eye: if therefore thine eye be single, thy whole body shall be full of light.*
>
> —Matthew 6:22, KJV

The light of God is for many purposes. As Kim Clement has said in several teachings and books, it is designed for sight, insight, and foresight. Sight is for vision so we do not stumble. Insight is for wisdom in making right decisions, and foresight helps us to prepare with discernment our future goals, situations, and needs.

Our eyes reveal what is on the inside of us. They are the transparency and vulnerability that people view us with at first glance. They have been called the gateway to the soul and pathway to the heart. People in love have been said to have dove's eyes (Song of Solomon 1:15; 4:1, NKJV).

Strong says the use of the word *single* in Matthew 6:22 is from the Greek *haplous*, meaning *as part of a union* properly folded together. Figuratively it means clear. In the glory of God, we see clearly. We are to be inside of Christ's glorious union, interwoven with Him.

Our eyes can examine and decide discretions of wisdom as in Proverbs 20:8: "*A king who sits on the throne of judgment Scatters all evil with his eyes*" (NKJV). This gives me the impression that the light within us can penetrate out to our environment dispelling all crooked deceptions.

> For your steadfast love is before my eyes, and I walk in your faithfulness.

> —Psalm 26:3

Fish Eye

> And immediately something like scales fell from his eyes, and he regained his sight. Then he rose and was baptized.

> —Acts 9:18

When the Lord speaks to me on a subject, theme, or just a single word, He will confirm it many times with an object lesson. On a day I was focusing on the word *eye*, my dog Hope was given her favorite treat: a fish from our bay waters.

After a time of feasting, I came to see what remained of the devoured fish. I looked over the ground and saw a soft, whitish shiny round object the size of a small marble. I rolled it around in my hand finding it had a front position, a single fish eyeball. Yuck! Then I had to laugh inside; the Lord's sense of humor. Today's object lesson was, of course, the eye.

Let's reflect on the functions of the eye area, which are by far the most susceptible to harm. The bone structure around this delicate area is created as a hollowed out cavity just for its protective placement. The eyelids, eye brows, and eyelashes all protect this precious creation of vision from the elements. The eyelid itself is designed just like windshield wipers, to clean and adjust clarity to the viewing area.

To explain how sensitive an area it is, I remember as a teenager wearing hard contacts daily, which somehow scratched my cornea one time. That night I woke up with excruciating pain. I remember running over to where my mother slept, begging her to take me to the hospital to "take my eye out." Yikes, that's a painful wish. Of course, only soothing drops and a patch were required for the pain as the cornea healed. My overly dramatic request was not granted.

Thy neck is as a tower of ivory; thine eyes like the fishpools in Heshbon.

—Song of Solomon 7:4, KJV

Later the same day that I observed the fish eye, I also chanced on watching a show on health issues that I'd never seen before. It was called "Eye to Eye." This wasn't coincidence; it was an exhilarating confirmation of the message. Proverbs 22:9 tell us,

"*Whoever has a bountiful eye will be blessed.*" A thief's eyes are not blessed, always craving for things to steal that are not his own. A curse is on his whole being. Stay in God's covenant with your eyes to keep your entire being whole.

> *Then those who feared the LORD spoke with one another. The LORD paid attention and **heard them**, and a book of remembrance was written before him of those who feared the LORD and esteemed his name.*

> —Malachi 3:16, emphasis added

A Hardened Heart

In 2 Chronicles 16:7-12 is a story of Hanani the seer and Asa the king of Judah who was delivered many times by the hand of the Lord because Asa had relied on the Lord. But now Asa had **hardened** his heart. Hanani's message from the Lord is: "*For the **eyes** of the Lord run to and fro throughout the whole earth to show Himself strong in behalf of those whose hearts are blameless toward Him. You have done foolishly in this; therefore, from now on you shall have wars*" (AMP, emphasis added).

What a delight to know reliance on the Lord provides us protection, safety, and deliverance from potential wars and evil encounters! Even wise Solomon lost his way with a thousand wives and their multi-gagging gods. His life was shortened considerably even though he didn't encounter the treacherous wars like his father, King David.

As recorded in 1 Kings 11, we find that Solomon no longer relied on the Lord even though he had a visitation from Him twice to warn him of his ungodly ways. He succumbed to the confusion of dark vanity. His visual lust for women bore upon him so hard that he tried to win them by granting their wishes to worship strange gods. It sabotaged his integrity, kingdom, and his vision for the future.

The foolish end of their lives tarnished both King Asa and Solomon, who once served God earnestly in their early years. To be called a fool is one of the lowest benchmarks of existence we can acquire. People can lose all truthful wisdom if they become disconnected from the Source. We can separate ourselves, become bewildered without a sound mind of purpose and direction, and then lose everything.

> Whoever conceals his transgressions will not prosper, but he who confesses and forsakes them will obtain mercy.

> —Proverbs 28:13

Out of Bondage

Ezra shows us the way out of bondage:

> And now, for a brief moment, grace has been shown us by the Lord our God. Who has left us a remnant to escape and has given us a secure hold in His holy place, that our God may **brighten our eyes** and give us a little reviving in our bondage. For we are bondmen: yet our God has **not forsaken** us in our bondage, but has extended mercy and steadfast love to us before the kings of Persia, to give us some reviving to set up the house of God, to repair its ruins, and to give us a wall [of protection] in Judah and Jerusalem.

> —Ezra 9:8-9, AMP, emphasis added

The dragon had been hiding under a barricade of walls and curtains in the veil of deluded darkness. While deceiving himself into thinking he was concealed from the manifold presence of God, Satan lured himself into a false sense of security. We also must make sure we are not deceived into destructive ways of thinking. Walls have always been built for protection; even the enemy in this dream had walls to insulate it momentarily.

But not even thick fortified walls keep God out, thankfully. It only took trumpet blasts to blow down the guarded walls of Jericho. They did not preserve the people as they thought. God rules and reigns throughout all His structures, manmade or not. Remember, there is always a window nearby, even if invisible to us.

Romans 6 explains it this way:

> That means you must not give sin a vote in the way you conduct your lives. Don't give it the time of day. Don't even run little errands that are connected with that old way of life. Throw yourselves wholeheartedly and full-time—remember, you've been raised from the dead!—into God's way of doing things. Sin can't tell you how to live. After all, you're not living under that old tyranny any longer; you're living in the freedom of God.
>
> —Romans 6:12-14, MSG

Romans 5:19 sums up our position. Referring to Adam first, then Christ, Paul said, "*One man said no to God and put many people in the wrong; one man said yes to God and put many in the right*" (MSG). Christ made the only decision that counted and redeemed us forever from the stipulations of sinfulness. Make a determination to do what is right. It counts!

Think of the beautiful benefits of choosing right today. Romans 5:17 says, "*Can you imagine the breathtaking recovery life makes, sovereign life, in those who grasp with both hands this wildly extravagant life-gift, this grand setting—everything—right, that the one man Jesus Christ provides?*" (MSG).

Those at the bottom of the nasty now and now, there is a place to look. If anyone gets into the bottom of a dark well, look up. Sometimes stars can be seen, even in the middle of the day. This is as true naturally as spiritually. Always know there is a place to look up to. Our heavenly Father is positioned in the stars day or night. He can see through every adversity we face. Look upon His face for His fortress is there to behold.

> *Do you not say, "There are yet four months, then comes the harvest"? Look, I tell you,* **lift up your eyes***, and see that the fields are white for harvest.*

—John 4:35, emphasis added

A City of Vision

Relating my vision above to one in Isaiah 22, a mournful inspired prediction, where is this place? It's in the Valley of Vision. Once again, the imagery of eyesight becomes harmonious. What kind of city is this? They are shouting, "A tumultuous city, and a joyous and exultant city." (v. 2, AMP). Where? Jerusalem. The warriors have fled this town without protection. They threw away their bows, acting the coward, huddled together in a faraway place.

In verse 5 Isaiah says, "*It's a day of discomfiture and of tumult, of treading down, of confusion and perplexity from the Lord*" (AMP). It was "a day of breaking down the walls and of *crying* to the mountains" (AMP). As in "The Black Veil" vision, there are two extremely different perspectives here, one from the inside and one from the outside. The people are without perspective, losing sight of their Lord God. The people are celebrating when it is a time of mourning.

Following in verse 8, we read how God "*removed the protective covering of Judah*" (AMP). As in the previous vision, God exposes satan's secret haven of allure. Verse 9 tells us there are many breaches in the wall (the citadel of Zion), broken places of insecurity. So wrecked is the damage that homes are broken into for materials to preserve the walls (v. 10).

The existing water supply had been poisoned. Verse 11 tells us they were making a reservoir inside the city to hold drinking water for the people between the two walls—the source was the Lower Pool. The people did not recognize their preserver of the drinking water was providential provision by the Lord.

The people are being called to a time of weeping and mourning and shaving of their heads and wearing sackcloth (v. 12), which was a symbol of submission, surrender, and humility. They are defeated and oppressed and don't even know it.

In hopelessness, the people decide to party all night, as their only purpose from it is death, *"for tomorrow we die"* (v. 13). Repentance brings life, but they are choosing the opposite consequence. People give up so easy when they think it's on their shoulders to figure stuff out. They just quit, knowing how little they have to offer.

I cherish how verse 14 says, *"The LORD of hosts revealed Himself **in my ears**"* (emphasis added), as God is ever present to speak as we listen. But a solemn declaration of this un-atoned sin will not be purged from the people until they are punished; and that punishment is death.

The palace's head governor and treasurer was Shebna. In Hebrew the name Shebna is from an unused root word meaning to grow; growth or vigor. Strong's says it refers to his master's house. Shebna was to be a steward of God's house. He is considered presumptuous by building unto himself (for his own glory) a tomb to be built among the greatest, the kings.

Isaiah is being sent to challenge Shebna's cause and reason for doing such a thing. In verse 16, Isaiah says, *"He hews out a sepulcher for himself on the height!"* (AMP). Sound familiar? Self-exaltation centered on him alone; he was oblivious to what was going on around him. *"He carves out a dwelling for himself in the rock!"* (v. 16, AMP). What rock is this? It's the rock of Jesus that found no place in him.

Continuing in verse 17, we read, *"Behold, the Lord will hurl you away violently, O you strong man; yes, He will take tight hold of you and He will surely cover you with* shame" (AMP). Sounds just like satan's demise taken from his comfort zone. The strong man is a mocking overture to what position he really takes with the Lord. Instead of his desired praise, he received the status of shame.

Getting more graphic in verses 18-19, it says,

> *He will surely roll you up in a bundle [Shebna] and toss you like a ball into a large country; there you will die and there will be your splendid chariots, your disgrace to your master's house! And I will thrust you from your office, and from your station will you be pulled down.*

> —Isaiah 22:18-19, AMP

Destiny: DOOM!

Who does God have waiting in the wings? Eliakim, son of Hilkiah is chosen (v. 20). God always has a plan, and it's not "plan B." As a divine transfer of power, Eliakim is clothed in what was Shebna's robe; He's instructed to *"bind your girdle"* while committing his authority into Eliakim hand's (v. 21, AMP). *"The key of the house of David I will lay upon his shoulder; he shall open and no one shall shut, he shall shut and no one shall open"* (v. 22, AMP).

Verse 23 goes on to say, *"And I will fasten him like a peg or nail in a firm place; and he will become a throne of honor and glory to his father's house*" (AMP). Eliakim is honored because he will not hold the glory to his own, knowing that God and His Kingdom receive all the glory.

Eliakim, whose name means "God will establish," is given the full responsibility of the entire house, from the smallest to the biggest matter. He has been found trustworthy and faithful in his Father's business. Psalm 86:11 reiterates this, "*Teach me your way, O LORD, that I may walk in your truth; unite my heart to fear your name.*"

> *How blessed is the one whose rebellious acts are forgiven, whose sin is pardoned! How blessed is the one whose wrongdoing the LORD does not punish, in whose spirit there is no deceit. When I refused to confess my sin, my whole body wasted away, while I groaned in pain all day long. For day and night you tormented me; you tried to destroy me in the intense heat of summer. (Selah) Then I confessed my sin; I no longer **covered up** my wrongdoing. I said, "I will confess my rebellious acts to the LORD." And then you forgave my sins. (Selah) For this reason every one of your faithful followers should pray to you while there is a **window of opportunity**. Certainly when the surging water rises, it will not reach them. You are my hiding place; you protect me from distress. You surround me with shouts of joy from those celebrating deliverance. (Selah) I will instruct and teach you about how you should live. I will advise you as I look **you in the eye.** Do not be like an unintelligent horse or mule, which will not obey you unless they are controlled by a bridle and bit. An evil person suffers much pain, but the LORD's faithfulness overwhelms the one who trusts in him. Rejoice in the LORD and be happy, you who are godly! Shout for joy, all you who are morally upright!*

> —Psalm 32:1-11, NET, emphasis added

His Eyes See

How long will the land mourn and the grass of every field wither? Because of the evil of its residence, animals and birds have been swept away, for the people have said, "He cannot **see** *what our end will be."*

—Jeremiah 12:4, HCSB, emphasis added

In this passage, false voices have been calling to the people through phony prophets lulling them into false securities. Now the land is proving that they were listening to the wrong ones. The winds of change obey His voice as they come up before Him. The Lord is calling forth a judgment of His own design against those who think Him a novice of detection.

Some might be toiling in the winds of adversity in their life, succumbing to the fears and pressures around you. Give this fight to the Lord for all the resources needed. He wants more for us than relegating to only survival skills. He came to give us a full supply of life. It is a life of plentitude, where there is more than plenty for all that come to Him.

God sees our testing and trials, our victories and triumphs, our thoughts from afar, our tears, and our tomorrows. His eyes are upon our ways, comings, and goings. He sees and knows all things perfectly. Psalm 33:13 tells us, *"The LORD looks down from heaven; he sees all the children of man."* We count to the Lord; He counts each of us as one of His who is eternally loved.

*For the **eyes of the LORD run to and fro throughout the whole earth,** to give **strong support** to those whose heart is blameless toward him.*

—2 Chronicles 16:9, emphasis added

Let the "Son" Shine Out

The eye is the lamp of the body. So, if your eye is healthy, your whole body will be full of light, but if your eye is bad, your whole body will be full of darkness. If then the light in you is darkness, how great is the darkness!

—Matthew 6:22-23

Again, the shift from darkness to light comes into play. We read in Matthew 12:22 how "*a demon-oppressed man who was blind and mute was brought to him, and he healed him, so that the man spoke and saw.*" His faith had come alive!"

When we are held in bondage to satan, we see nothing but darkness. Our words of unbelief are held captive. Christians are not to live in compromising shadows but in the light of day. We are told to open our eyes so we can see what is real and what's not.

This incident blew the lid off the Pharisees. The Kingdom of God had come to the man's aid and made it clear that devils can't cast out devils. It is a contradiction to itself. Doubt robs people of their miracle. It's nothing we can do; it's totally built on what Christ does presently, in the NOW. We only need believe Him.

*As they were going away, behold, a demon-oppressed man who was mute was brought to him. And when the demon had been cast out, the mute man spoke. And the crowds marveled, saying, "Never was anything like this **seen** in Israel."*

—Matthew 9:32-33, emphasis added

When Christ opens our lips to speak, it's to glorify His majesty. It's for the purpose of spreading the Gospel to all who will listen. Let penetrating lips and hearts be sanctified by the Lord so we can let the Lord shine out of us to everyone God allows in our life. We can be His minister right where we live. We need to be faithful to those God gives us to touch in this lifetime.

John 1:9

The true light, which gives light to everyone, was coming into the world.

1 Thessalonians 5:5-8 (MSG, emphasis added)

*But friends, you're not in the dark, so how could you be taken off guard by any of this? You're sons of Light, daughters of Day. We live under wide open skies and know where we stand. So let's not sleepwalk through life like those others. Let's keep our eyes open and be smart. People sleep at night and get drunk at night. But not us! Since we're **creatures** of Day, let's act like it. Walk out into the daylight sober, dressed up in faith, love, and the hope of salvation.*

CHAPTER NINE

Investigate My Life

*GOD, investigate my life; get all the facts firsthand. I'm an open book to you; even from a distance, you know what I'm thinking. You know when I leave and when I get back, I'm never out of your **sight**. You know everything I'm going to say before I start the first sentence. I look behind me and you're there, then up ahead and you're there too—your reassuring presence, coming and going. This is too much, too wonderful—I can't take it all in!*

—Psalm 139:1-6, MSG, emphasis added

Examine My Heart

God means what he says. What he says goes. His powerful Word is sharp as a surgeon's scalpel, cutting through everything, whether doubt or defense, laying us open to listen and obey. Nothing and no one is impervious to God's Word. We can't get away from it—no matter what.

—Hebrews 4:12-13, MSG

I'm sure we've all heard the expression, "Cut the crap." It may sound crass; but it is the truth people want, not phony baloney.

People today have been exposed to so much rhetoric, puffed up advertising, over-the-top drama, and diva behavior that it makes us out to be some unnatural subhuman.

God wants the real from us! We must cut through everything else if we want a real relationship. If anyone has doubts, ask for more faith. If we are on the fence with defensiveness, we need to ask God to be our safeguard. Most defensive behaviors are derived from insecurity or guilt. Let us allow Christ be our justification. Just lay it out before Him like it really is.

Don't hide your loneliness, if that is what you feel. How else are you going to get a real answer from God? Pretending only makes it worse. Avoidance delays the answer we desire. Denial strips us of reality. Blaming others removes the responsibility we deserve.

If you want the desires of your heart answered, then listen and obey, doing what your feet, heart, and hands lead you to. In John 5:30, Jesus said, "*I can do nothing on my own. As I **hear**, I judge, and my judgment is just, because I seek not my own will but the will of him who sent me*" (emphasis added).

> But be doers of the word, and not hearers only, deceiving yourselves.
>
> —James 1:22

Intentions Revealed

> Cleanse me from secret faults.
>
> —Psalm 19:12, NKJV

In Matthew, the second chapter, is a familiar story of Jesus' birth being pronounced, drawing attention to Herod and his "secret coven meeting" with the scholars from the East (notice I used "coven" not "covenant"). The intention of this private rendez-vous was to do harm in guise of good. As with most secrets, important information was withheld. Heinous Herod had a snake up his sleeve. By the very nature of a snake, they tell "tall tales" because it's in their natural DNA, being equipped with "long tails of lies."

Herod sought the information he desired on the whereabouts of baby Jesus. These famous mystics from the East were following their instincts to check out the sky and see what it disclosed. They were sign seekers. Just like a billboard sign today might direct us to a store location, the bright star was the most significant signal to follow. The great divide showed them the path that brought them to the right place at the right time.

God used a "warning dream," redirecting them, so they did not report back to sinister Herod. They chose a covert diversion to the backside of their own country via another route. Their dream must have been conveyed to more than one magus, because scripture says, "*They were warned*" (v. 12, MSG). I can imagine the exponential factor of that experience, which they heeded wisely on another route to follow. Wisdom instructed them to avoid Herod's evil intentions.

Listed are a few more examples of what can't be hidden from God:

> *For there is nothing hidden that will not be disclosed, and nothing concealed that will not be known or brought out into the open.*

> —Luke 8:17, NIV

For everything that is hidden will eventually be brought into the open, and every secret will be brought to light.

—Mark 4:22, NLT

A woman came to meet him, dressed like a prostitute, having a hidden agenda. She is loud and defiant; her feet do not stay at home.

—Proverbs 7:10, HCSB

We can't hide anything in our heart (spirit) from God, because He made our delicate hearts. He knows what's going on inside and outside us all the time. What God is empowering us with in the Book of Proverbs is the power to forgive, so bitterness does not take root thereby smothering our love walk.

Staying free from the inception of offensiveness is one of the most freeing places for us as believers. Those who aren't easily offended walk in the greatest level of love.

Search me, O God, and know my heart! Try me and know my thoughts! And see if there be any grievous way in me, and lead me in the way everlasting!

—Psalm 139:23-24

Sheep Sense the Shepherd

Know that the LORD, he is God! It is he who made us, and we are his; we are his people, and the sheep of his pasture.

—Psalm 100:3

We are compared to sheep throughout scripture, but I wanted to delve into the rationale behind this comparison to human beings as His. In John 6:70 Jesus says, "*Did I not choose you, the*

Twelve?" Even Jesus compared Himself to a shepherd in John 10:11: *"I am the good shepherd. The good shepherd lays down his life for the sheep."*

> Sheep are mentioned in the Bible more than 500 times, more than any other animal. The prominence of sheep in the bible grows out of two realities. Sheep were important to the nomads and agricultural life of the Hebrews and similar peoples. Secondly, sheep are used throughout the bible to symbolically refer to God's people.[1]

Sheep have developed senses in facial distinctions, voice recognition, and smell discrimination. They seem to have the same auditory perceptions as humans.[2] Contrary to popular misconception, sheep are extremely intelligent animals capable of problem solving.[3] "They are said to have good memory power and can map their surroundings."[4] *"My sheep listen to my voice; I know them, and they follow me"* (John 10:27, NIV).

Sheep have a strong instinct to follow the leader. When one sheep decides to go somewhere, the rest of the flock usually follows, even if it is not a good decision. For example, if the lead sheep jumps over a cliff, the others are likely to follow.[5] Matthew 10:16 tells us: *"Behold, I am sending you out as sheep in the midst of wolves, so be wise as serpents and innocent as doves."*

Just like humans, sheep maintain a safe distance between themselves and others, and this flight distancing will increase if they feel danger.[6] But they can become distressed when isolated.[7] Matthew 9:36 speaks of Jesus: *"When he saw the crowds, he had compassion for them, because they were harassed and helpless, like sheep without a shepherd"* (NIV).

Sheep see in color. They are dependent on their wide peripheral visual field of vision of 270 degrees. They avoid shadows or harsh contrasts between light and dark yet will move towards the light.[8]

> *Lift up your eyes and see those who come from the north. Where is the flock that was given you, your beautiful flock?*
>
> —Jeremiah 13:20

When sheep face danger, they have a natural instinct to flee instead of fight. After they flee, they will form their group and face the predator. Their herding instinct leads them to band together for safety. If a sheep is alone, it is more vulnerable to attack.[9]

> *My people have been lost sheep. Their shepherds have led them astray, turning them away on the mountains. From mountain to hill they have gone. They have forgotten their fold.*
>
> —Jeremiah 50:6

Sheep have excellent hearing, with similar auditory sensitivity to humans. They are frightened by high pitched or loud sounds.[10] They would be frightened by a roaring predator, such as a lion; and yet they know, recognize, and follow the right sounds. *"Israel is a hunted sheep driven away by lions"* (Jeremiah 50:17).

Sheep make bleating sounds spelled "baa." If we turn this around in reverse it would sound like "Abba!" I'd like to think they are crying out to their Abba Shepherd, just as we do when needing our heavenly Father for assurance. Sheep "can instantly recognize the voice of a familiar trusted person."[11]

> *Truly, truly, I say to you, he who does not enter the sheepfold by the door but climbs in by another way, that man is a thief and a robber. But he who enters by the door is the shepherd of the sheep. To him the gatekeeper opens. The sheep hear his*

voice, and he calls his own sheep by name and leads them out. When he has brought out all his own, he goes before them, and the sheep follow him, for they know his voice. A stranger they will not follow, but they will flee from him, for they do not know the voice of strangers.

—John 10:1-5

The Bible describes close relationships between shepherds and their flocks. "The sheep recognize the voice of the shepherd. They follow him (or her). The shepherd protects his flock and would give his life for them."[12]

And I have other sheep that are not of this fold. I must bring them also, and they will listen to my voice. So there will be one flock, one shepherd.

John 10:16

Come Out in the Open

Proverbs 24:12 advises us, "*If you say, 'Behold, we did not know this,' does not he who weights the heart perceive it? Does not he who keeps watch over your soul know it, and will he not repay man according to his work?*"

In 1 Samuel 11 is the story of how Saul became King of Israel.

*Nahash the Ammonite marched against Jabesh Gilead. All the men of Jabesh Gilead said to Nahash, "Make a treaty with us and we will serve you." But Nahash the Ammonite said to them, "The only way I will make a treaty with you is if you let me gouge out the **right eye** of every one of you and in so doing humiliate all Israel!"*

—1 Samuel 11:1-2, NET, emphasis added

This eye business is all over the Bible. Not only would gouging out their eye extend their mark of shaming Israel, but it would also annihilate their vision for the future.

> The elders of Jabesh said to him, "Leave us alone for seven days so that we can send messengers throughout the territory of Israel. If there is no one who can deliver us, we will come out voluntarily to you." When the messengers went to Gibeah (where Saul lived) and informed the people of these matters, all the people **wept loudly**. Now Saul was walking behind the oxen as he came from the field. Saul asked, "What has happened to the people? Why are they weeping?" So they told him about the men of Jabesh. The Spirit of God rushed upon Saul when he heard these words, and he became very angry. He took a pair of oxen and cut them up. Then he sent the pieces throughout the territory of Israel by the hand of messengers, who said, "Whoever does not go out after Saul and after Samuel should expect this to be done to his oxen!" Then the terror of the Lord fell on the people, and they went out as **one army**. When Saul counted them at Bezek, the Israelites were 300,000 strong and the men of Judah numbered 30,000. They said to the messengers who had come, "Here's what you should say to the men of Jabesh Gilead: 'Tomorrow deliverance will come to you when the **sun** is fully up.'" When the messengers went and told the men of Jabesh Gilead, they were happy. The men of Jabesh said, "Tomorrow we will **come out** to you and you can do with us whatever you wish." The next day Saul placed the people in three groups. They went to the Ammonite camp during the morning watch and struck them down until the hottest part of the day. The survivors divided up; no two of them remained together.

—1 Samuel 11:3-11, NET, emphasis added

So they were scattered, because there was no shepherd, and they became food for all the wild beasts. My sheep were scattered; they wandered over all the mountains and on every high hill. My sheep were scattered over all the face of the earth, with none to search or seek for them. Therefore, you shepherds, hear the word of the LORD: As I live, declares the Lord GOD, surely because my sheep have become a prey, and my sheep have become food for all the wild beasts, since there was no shepherd, and because my shepherds have not searched for my sheep, but the shepherds have fed themselves, and have not fed my sheep, therefore, you shepherds, hear the word of the LORD: Thus says the Lord GOD, Behold, I am against the shepherds, and I will require my sheep at their hand and put a stop to their feeding the sheep. No longer shall the shepherds feed themselves. I will rescue my sheep from their mouths, that they may not be food for them.

—Ezekiel 34:5-10

His Ways Are Higher: Obedience

*Whether it is good or bad, we will **obey the voice** of the LORD our God to whom we are sending you, that it may be well with us when we **obey the voice** of the LORD our God.*

—Jeremiah 42:6, emphasis added

In general, the concept of obedience is hearing the voice of God. It comes by positioning ourselves in acknowledgement of our divine Creator God. He has the greater authority than we ourselves; as we live underneath His house in Heaven. Biblical obedience turns our distrust to trust, defiance to submission, and resistance to surrender in the Lord. God searches for those who will be faithful to Him.

For those thinking obedience is impossible to do, God says we can. Jeremiah had the same concern:

> "O Lord God," I said, "I can't do that! I'm far too young! I'm only a youth!" "Don't say that," He replied, "for you will go wherever I send you and speak whatever I tell you to. And don't be afraid of the people, for I, the Lord, will be with you and see you through."

—Jeremiah 1:6-7, TLB

What He says to do, *He empowers us* to do it.

The issue, therefore, is not in faithful obedience; it's in the listening. Proverbs 1:5 says, "*Let the wise hear and increase in learning, and the one who understands obtain guidance.*" Solomon was considered the wisest man alive in his time. He asked God for the most important thing, a hearing ear to perceive and recognize the wisdom of God.

People don't bother to ask for guidance from God if they don't plan on following through with it. If we desire the mind of God, we can simply ask for it. Our intentions may be the culprit, defaulting on our own will, motives, and interests. If we deflect on a whim, our course will end. Nothing will profit us without God being involved—and He is.

James tells us:

> If any of you lacks wisdom, let him ask God, who gives generously to all without reproach, and it will be given him. But let him ask in faith, with no doubting, for the one who doubts is like a wave of the sea that is driven and tossed by the wind. For that person must not suppose that he will receive anything from the Lord; he is a **double-minded man**, unstable in all his ways."

—James 1:5-8, emphasis added

The term *double-minded* is translated from the Greek word *dipsuchos*, meaning a person with two minds or souls. They're in a constant flux of restless frustrations. They double back and forth, as they doubt everything, undecidedly considering circumstances one way or another. It seems they're never quite sure which way to go, vacillating with uncertain confusion. That is why Acts 5:29 captures the truth, "**We must obey God rather than men**" (emphasis added). Choose the Rock that faces the right direction!

Where there is no peace there is only confusion. John 10:27 reiterates this again: "*My sheep hear my voice, and I know them, and they follow me.*" Be teachable to hear His voice, *getting rid of any confusion*. A large portion of scripture that addresses His voice is preceded by the word *obey*. Why would someone make a request of us if we weren't going to follow the instructions given? This is on-the-job training 101.

1 Thessalonians 5:17-22 (KJV) gives us short, key instructive verses:

> *17 Pray without ceasing.*
> *18 In every thing give thanks: for this is the will of God in Christ Jesus concerning you.*
> *19 Quench not the Spirit.*
> *20 Despise not prophesyings.*
> *21 Prove all things; hold fast that which is good.*
> *22 Abstain from all appearance of evil.*

In a brief nutshell this gives us our guide list for everyday purpose. If we put these on like clothing, we will never stop our prayer life, as we are too thankful not to pray. We won't interfere with the Holy Spirit's ways. We will receive all prophecies and people as we are focused on what is good in them. Evil will have no hold or desire on us as His set apart ones.

285

Listen to Him because He anticipates speaking to you, His treasured child. Remember to stay moldable, transparent, and be resilient to the Lord! Allow Him to use your life for what matters instead of for what doesn't. Don't waste your time on what will not lead you anywhere. As you listen to and obey the words He speaks, know it will be well for you.

*Now if you will obey me and keep my covenant, you will be my own **special treasure** from among all the peoples on earth; for all the earth belongs to me.*

—Exodus 19:5, NLT, emphasis added

It's Time to Hear

*Know this, my beloved brothers: let every person be quick to **hear**, slow to speak, slow to anger; for the anger of man does not produce the righteousness of God.*

—James 1:19-20, emphasis added

Jesus' Ear Dream, 8.24.96

In this dream I came to see Jesus for a visit. Mostly, I felt a strong need to sit on His lap, relax, and put my arms around His neck. As I looked up at Him, I saw His right ear had a big cork in it.

I wanted to talk to Him, but I desired to hug on Him first. I took the invasive plug out when a great wind burst from His ear. That ear began to take on a misshapen form, as if finger impressions were left from people pulling on it so long. It was stretched out of shape to the point it had become inflamed and enlarged.

I tried to consider the situation. As I did, I saw His body melt to the floor and slide away from me. It looked like a big puddle of wax with ripples throughout His melted body.

*Behold, the LORD's hand is not shortened, that it cannot save, or his ear dull, that it cannot hear; but your iniquities have made a separation between you and your God, and **your sins have hidden his face** from you so that **he does not hear.***

—Isaiah 59:1-2, emphasis added

People have turned away from listening to the Lord to such a degree that it has corked up the ears of Jesus. A cork is made of an impermeable, buoyant material. In botany it is "a non-living, water-resistant protective tissue that is formed on the outside of the cork cambium."[8] It's used to stop up, seal, and restrain.[13] Cork and wax are both insoluble in water; they don't mix together.

Once the cork was released, the Holy Spirit blew forth with a gush of wind. But the physical damage became apparent immediately. His ear was hurting in a dreadful, mutilating way. The reaction was traumatizing to see. *Inflammation* is the body's attempt at self-protection. It is "a localized reaction of tissue due to irritation, injury, or infection, characterized by pain, redness, swelling, and sometimes loss of function."[14]

Instead of listening, people are pulling on Christ's ears with their demoralizing, deadened demands. I see people using their fingernails as weapons; scratching at the soft tissue of His earlobes, clawing them until they droop down. This ravaged enlargement is caused by people's vulgar ultimatums. Finger mark impressions have left a branding iron effect.

People are yelling at Christ, "Hey, You listen to me, Son of God. I'm screaming at the top of my lungs. I'm dictating what I want

NOW. I insist You do it the way I say, on my time tables, on my terms. I don't need Your okay. I'm not asking for Your approval and I'm not repenting. I'm stipulating my demands for YOU. Expedite what I want done since You're in the blessing business." Our agenda's are nullified; coercive threats have voided our access to Jesus Christ. This is corrupt covenant; falsified.

People are using brute-force, hurting Jesus with their tactics of abuse to get His attention. They have taken their liberties by aiming their hot shots at Him. This antagonizing barrage of evil is an encumbrance to Christ's ability to know them, much less answer. Their lack of discernment in humility is hijacking a relationship of communion with compassion.

> *The mountains melt like wax before the LORD, before the Lord of all the earth.*
>
> —Psalm 97:5

What a role reversal, as I saw Christ's body (the Church) melted to the floor before the mountains of the Earth. The waxy ripples represent waves of plastic people who are creating contentious, self-seeking fleshly factions that divide and conquer.

> *When I shut up the heavens so that there is no rain, or command the locust to devour the land, or send pestilence among my people, if my people who are called by my name **humble themselves, and pray and seek my face and turn from their wicked ways,** then **I will hear from heaven** and will forgive their sin and heal their land. **Now my eyes will be open and my ears** attentive to the prayer that is made in this place.*
>
> —2 Chronicles 7:13-15, emphasis added

God is *not* referring to haters, but only those who act this way as His known children. The conditions are stated so well. Humility of heart is first. This will lead to the recognition of praying for others and not your own needs. Seek His face, not the preservation of self. Chose this day whom you will serve by relenting of those sins you've tucked away as a privilege of sorts. Destroy all idols or they will be your demise. Only then will God hear you.

Hebrews 4:7 says, "*Today, if you hear his voice, do not harden your hearts.*" Scripturally, "hardness of heart" is a persistent inner refusal to hear and obey the Word of God. Hardened hearts compare to the resistant glare in a person's eye. The dictionary describes hardness as "the cohesion of the particles on the *surface* of a mineral as determined by its capacity to *scratch another or be itself scratched*"[15] (emphasis added). These were the hard ones clawing at Jesus' ear.

We may have noticed a cold, steely look in someone's eyes. It should cause us to feel unnerved and to even want to look away. Something is wrong inside. God's tender mercies are missing. We need to become desperate to hear God's loving voice strings. Pray for that right now. Allow those frozen places to melt by the living fertilizer of warmth He bestows.

Recently I received an email relating to increased inclement weather patterns deterring effective mail service with delays. They wrote these conditions were disrupting shipments and hindering communications. I could not help but believe this is an outcome of our clouded ability to hear, causing disruptive communication relays with our heavenly Father.

> *Watch what God does, and then you do it, like children who learn proper behavior from their parents. Mostly what God does is love you. Keep company with him and learn a life of love. Observe how Christ loved us. His love was not cautious*

but extravagant. He didn't love in order to get something from
us but to give everything of himself to us. Love like that.

—Ephesians 5:2, MSG

Proverbs 8:32 tells us, "*Now therefore, listen to me, my children...*"
(NKJV), speaking as if a parent were talking. Actually this is the
voice of wisdom speaking to us to listen to her voice. Wisdom
is distinguished because it was present when creation began.
In verse 22 it reveals that the Lord possessed wisdom to begin
the works of old, even before Earth began. This is intriguing to
begin with the preestablished ways of infinite wisdom in God's
purpose for humanity.

In Jeremiah 13 we read where the Lord declares every bottle and jar should be filled with wine (v. 12). But these proud
people will most certainly say that they already know all that
stuff anyway. This is pure mockery of their God. Ever notice that
people just don't stop to think and ask why this type of information is being used on their behalf? Being reasonable is just not
reasonable to them.

The verdict being passed down is that drunkenness will take
over all those that live in this land, even the kings upon David's
throne (v. 13). No one is excluded from its course of actions.
Then the Lord says He will dash them one against another, even
the fathers and the sons together (v. 14). Do we not see this
today? It's rampant evil, the undermining of authority in our
home. The parental role is broken and undone with its closest
allies, the father-son or mother-daughter relationship. The relationships are broken wholly.

To sum up this story there will be no pity, sparing, or compassion given by a just God who waited until the utter end when all
hope is gone (v. 14). He will not hold back destruction on them.
There is a price to pay, good or evil.

What is the key that could release them from this condition, as stated in verse 15? Unlocking all pride! It has a self-destructive bend overstepping its boundaries, taking it further than it should. Human nature at times will take us to the point of no return. It's all or nothing; perverse or pure. Release all arrogance and accept His humility of mobility.

> *Humble yourselves before the Lord, and he will exalt you.*

> —James 4:10

Godly discernment is vital to understand what is best, even in the most obscure ways or remote places. It searches out what is not noticed, revealing what was hidden and making it clear. We're an open book to the Lord who knows what is in between our outer covers. Every bent page, coffee stain, earmark, ink mark, or crease is exposed to Him. As we allow Him to manifest Himself, He reveals more of His life inside us.

The God of the second chance says there is more than a gleam of hope, yet! It's giving our all to the glory of God. He is saying something very familiar to us today. It is that the slip sliding of a dark mountain slope, the shadow of death, and even thick tangible darkness or the light of Christ can be chosen.

Finally, the Lord concludes with His own broken heart: "*But if you will not hear and obey, I will* **weep** *in secret for your pride; my eyes will* **weep** *bitterly and run down with* **tears***, because the Lord's flock has been taken* **captive**" (v. 17, AMP, emphasis added).

I envision a Holy God crying warm, bitter, salty tears of sorrow. What else can He do but warn them? It is all on them and their unwillingness to allow God to direct and protect them. They will not listen, as if putting their index finger inside each ear adamantly refusing to hear His words; as in a contemptible tantrum fit of a rebellious child shutting out a parent's pleading. Obstinacy abounds everywhere. No remorse.

What they *should* do, they do not. The symbolic, humble, and securely held girdle is not regarded, just as the Lord's presence is disregarded. If we position ourselves lowly on purpose, we seat ourselves as a friend. We can throw down a righteous, beautiful crown for earthly leaves.

It goes back to the land and who owns it. In this case the cities of the South had been shut up, and there was no one to open them. All Judah has been carried away captive; it has been wholly taken captive being thrown into exile.

> *Therefore my people are gone into captivity, because they have no knowledge: and their honourable men are famished, and their multitude dried up with thirst.*

> —Isaiah 5:13, KJV

To be spiritually famished is starvation from the Word of God. Their reliance on the Lord is gone; moisture from the Holy Spirit's lead is lacking. In the last days we will need the presence of God every day to survive. Unity must come.

God said His people have gone into *captivity* because they have no knowledge. Light brings knowledge forth. Then Hosea says:

> *My people are destroyed for lack of knowledge: because thou hast rejected knowledge, I will also reject thee, that thou shalt be no priest to me: seeing thou hast forgotten the law of thy God, **I will also forget thy children**.*

> —Hosea 4:6, KJV, emphasis added

No one wants to hear his or her children are forgotten. What a tragedy! No good parent desires their child to be an unnoticed victim. To be *forgotten* refers to these little ones as if they never existed. A parent sees a future or an even better future for their children. That is their God-given legacy to follow them. A loss comes from no longer following God's ways, plans, and purposes. Where does that leave our children today when God's ways are abandoned?

This is a critical revelation. As parents, we're decreed to raise the standard of the next generation by utilizing God's mandates and precepts so our heritage has a name and purpose in the landscape of their lives. That is the permanent legacy seed we have deposited on Earth that will last forever.

"*My people,*" God is speaking of His special people, "*are destroyed for lack of knowledge.*" They refused to enter or seek the true knowledge of God. They purposed to rebel from it. They were critically comfortable with their evil ways.

> *For the LORD* **hears** *the needy And does not despise His who are prisoners.*
>
> —Psalm 69:33, NASB, emphasis added

Not Seen

> *Here's what I want you to do: Find a quiet, secluded place so you won't be tempted to role-play before God. Just be there as simply and honestly as you can manage. The focus will shift from you to God, and you will begin to sense his grace.*
>
> —Matthew 6:6, MSG

While reviewing Matthew 6, I found five illustrations how *not* to be *seen* or heard. These examples come across as warnings of attitudes in our lives that will not be rewarded or noticed by God.

The first example is practicing to be righteous before other people. I believe the key word here is "practicing," as real heart change doesn't need to practice how to live. We are living Christ in us, the hope of glory (Colossians 1:27). In verb form "practice" means to carry out or perform a particular activity habitually or regularly.[16] Boring!

Scripture tells us we are changed into His image because of His life flowing through us (2 Corinthians 3:18). We weren't intended to be mimickers of artificial life. Every day we become more like He is. We can't afford to stay the same. That's what suffocation is like, so keep breathing life changes inside. Take deep irrevocable, sacred breaths of His glory!

Next are people who give to the good cause of "giving to the needy." What? It's not the giving that is detrimental, but all the loud commotion they make in order to be praised by others. God says in Matthew 6:1 that will be the only reward they get; their trumpet blast of self-exaltation. "Notice me," "look at me," or "see me" flesh is a-la-cart "stinky." God's not even in this equation.

The Word says instead to not let our left hand know what our right hand is doing. Bravo! Take no notice in our giving to the impoverished or abused. We mustn't let this act even register on the radar screen as some great sacrifice on our part. It should be a part of our life to help others in need because Christ always gave and still does through us. That produces the gift of overflowing joy in our hearts.

We do extraordinary giving in secret, so our heavenly Father sees our focused motivation in serving Him. He can richly reward us in His way. We must remove our right to be known or noticed. If we crave man's affections, we have the fear of man and we're afraid of being rejected. It's time to turn the tables; choose to be free of man's opinions.

Another group recognized is the hypocrites who love to stand out. They want to be seen praying openly in front of people. This one-second spotlight will be their only reward in this life, and none to follow. We mustn't publicize our prayer life just so we can be heard by people. We can't impress God. Self-promotion is a lack of trusting God. We need to allow someone else to promote us for His sake.

God's example for us is go "shut the door" to the devil, find our prayer hanging out place, and pray to Him who is in secret (Matthew 6:6) because He's watching us on His private multi-dimensional viewing screen. Since our identity is built upon exalting Christ, we can keep our motives secret.

There is a group that believes the most cultural enticements will impress many. It's not the latest craze, flabbergasting lingo, or advertising that wins people over in the long haul. We are instructed not to be clones of the world. Our Father knows what we need before we even ask Him (v. 8). We need to keep our requests to the point.

> Do not be conformed to this world, but be transformed by the renewal of your mind, that by testing you may discern what is the will of God, what is good and acceptable and perfect.

> —Romans 12:2

In Matthew 6:16-17 we read how the gloom and doom group of fasters don't need to act ashen and sickly seeking the sympathy vote. We need not change our looks or wear the ugliest thing we can find. We need to stay focused, put on a real smile, and act normal. We can ask God for an extra measure of strength and grace while we fast.

Get revived on God's Word and drink plenty of water. We should allow God alone to see our actions of removing extra calories (weights) from our menu. We can cast it over on Him when it gets tough. This is a treasured time, which receives a heavenly treasure.

Every description above comes with a caution, NOT TO BE SEEN BY OTHERS. But our Father who *sees in secret* has His full focus on what we're doing, why, and for what purpose. Our Father God has rewards to give us that will last for eternity. He anticipates rewarding those whose hearts are turned to Him privately.

> *Whatever you do, work heartily, as for the Lord and not for men, knowing that from the Lord you will receive the inheritance as your reward. You are serving the Lord Christ.*

> —Colossians 3:23-24

Our Reward's at Stake

> *You can never please God without faith, without depending on him. Anyone who wants to come to God must believe that there is a God and that he rewards those who sincerely look for him.*

> —Hebrews 11:6, TLB

In context this sounds so simple. God wants us to trust *Him* for our needs, not ourselves. Our Creator made everything. We didn't make God, Jesus, or the Holy Spirit. They existed before time began. Think about that statement—Selah! He is the ultimate lasting source for all of our lives. The only real requirement, it seems, is to believe in Him and look for Him with our whole hearts.

The world can't fix very much, at least not anything lasting. Systems eventually fail along with our temporary bodies, which wear out. The special thing is having a doting Father who loves for us to speak by making requests known to Him.

There are courtrooms all over America and abroad with standing judges. That's the idea Jesus is steering us to consider. Jesus is the ultimate righteous Judge, knowing truth from a lie. He will judge the entire world. The day for this has already been pre-appointed. It is determinedly fixed by Heaven.

Our assurance for a final judgment is the value of resurrection, when Christ blew open a grave door and went right through it. No obstacles can hold Him back from our lives. This resurrection power overcame anything that stood in His way. Matthew 5:12 is true: *"Rejoice and be glad, for your reward is great in heaven."*

Most people strive for a life full of riches, abundance, and provisions. They desire to be considered in the highest regarded esteem with vibrant, vivacious health. That is exactly what Christ wants for us as well. Proverbs 22:4 tells us the reward for humility and fear of the Lord is *riches and honor and life*!

Two elements make a shade of difference: a stance of humility to sieve all things through with the fear of our Almighty God. Faith leads us the way there. We are the benefactors by taking hold of what is truly life and rejecting all that is not life.

1 Timothy 6:17-19

As for the rich in this present age, charge them not to be haughty, nor to set their hopes on the uncertainty of riches, but on God, who richly provides us with everything to enjoy. They are to do good, to be rich in good works, to be generous and ready to share, thus storing up treasure for themselves as a good foundation for the future, so that they may take hold of that which is truly life.

CHAPTER TEN

God's Revealed Secrets

*Come near, you nations, and listen; pay attention, you peoples!
Let the earth hear, and all that is in it, the world, and all that
comes out of it!*

—Isaiah 34:1, NIV

Blue Whale Vision, 3.20.04

*It was by faith that the people of Israel marched around
Jericho for seven days, and **the walls** came crashing down.*

—Hebrews 11:30, NLT, emphasis added

My vision began during a time of church-wide prayer. It opened to an aerial view of a high stature, cement dam enclosed to block what was on the other side. It contained water full to the brim on the north side (take your inheritance) of the seemingly impenetrable, walled fortress.

The goal was to get through the barrier wall or collapse it entirely so the water could get to the other side. Close to the bottom of the wall, a hole appeared. It had been drilled out with a large commercial device with the majority of its apparatus looking like a gigantic screw head.

This hole allowed a small stream of water to come through the containment, but it was not enough. Urgently, a larger device was implemented in this unanimous effort. The new equipment had top and bottom rows of teeth, which were set in pairs. Each pair operated together to allow for deep trench digging.

The implemented device was actively "set in motion" as it was being directed toward the soil underneath the fortified structure. As the operation began at the lowest depth, the foundation broke through underneath the obstruction.

The barrier wall collapsed entirely, starting from top to bottom. As the restraining wall started to crack from above, the apparatus came out from below. It was followed by a huge whale as the waters allowed it to flow through from one side to the other.

The whale appeared to be a deep, slate blue color with black and white stripes beneath its belly.

The blue whale is considered to be the largest existing of all animals. It moves fast, traveling up to thirty miles an hour.[1] "The *call* of the mighty blue whale is the loudest on Earth, registering a whopping 188 decibels."[2] This deep, almost deafening sound can be heard 620 miles away according to the American Museum of Natural History.[3]

I spoke to my dream coach about this vision. He told me that the blue whale is the largest of all whales. It implies a monumental movement, which has arrived and is intended for a grand scale volume of people. It will be for ALL to receive when the visible wall comes crashing down. It will take an enormous, unified cooperation in the Body of Christ to deliver the blue whale.

The northward position of the water is very telling. In Deuteronomy 2:3 the Lord tells the children of Israel, "*You have been wandering around in this hill country long enough; turn to the north*" (NLT). We need to retrieve the promotion of the Holy

Spirit so it can be released in one massive momentum to the remaining unsaved Earth.

The manmade wall is a prideful form of restrictive withholding. It represents a defeatist power of bloated unbelief, combative religion, and greedy whoredom against the fresh wine of the Spirit. Proverbs 18:11 confirms this: *"The rich man's wealth is his strong city, and as a high protecting wall in his own imagination and conceit"* (AMP).

The Objective: A pouring forth of deep intimacy, as more things of the spirit are set free from confinement. Some are aware and some are not. Revelation and wisdom are buried under the wall and it must be RELEASED for the shift to come full force. The machinery had teeth (an ability to comprehend and understand) set in pairs (cooperation). I believe many denominations will work together as black and white join in a unanimous effort for the Kingdom's expansion. The equipment used to destroy the dividing wall were tools, as we go to the foundation (word of God). Just like rescue workers use the "jaws of life" tool to extricate, collapse, and cut trapped victims free from confinement; the jaws of this movement will bring life to the whole Earth.

Blue is the color for intimacy, revelation, communion, and prophecy. This is a building alignment season for a monumental motion of revelation. Many factors in society are accelerating, affecting exploration and knowledge in healing and energy, with other revolutionary secret finds. Things never known before are being unfolded before us exponentially for the benefit and preservation of mankind.

Gather the people, consecrate the assembly; bring together the elders, gather the children, those nursing at the breast. Let the bridegroom leave his room and the bride her chamber.

—Joel 2:16, NIV

I believe there are two efforts underway that will permanently destroy the enemy's domain as we take back the land the enemy has stolen. We will have the opportunities to bequeath these lands to help ministries that need further advancement of Kingdom vision. Joel 2:21 says, *"Fear not, O land; be glad and rejoice, for the LORD has done great things!"*

And all who believed were together and had all things in common. And they were selling their possessions and belongings and distributing the proceeds to all, as any had need. And day by day, attending the temple together and breaking bread in their homes, they received their food with glad and generous hearts, praising God and having favor with all the people. And the Lord added to their number day by day those who were being saved.

—Acts 2:44-47

I can see mixed generations of men and women, arms raised, standing shoulder to shoulder interlocked as woven together with a cumulative succession of advancements forward. Jonah's whale in the Bible came to preserve his life. He was sent to save a captive people and the *second time he obeyed*, just as the second device used prevailed in this vision. A gigantic movement is swiftly being ushered in with a voluminous voice of impact.

John 3:8 informs us, *"The wind blows wherever it pleases. You hear its sound, but you cannot tell where it comes from or where it is going. So it is with everyone born of the Spirit"* (NIV).

This Holy Spirit propagated movement will become more widespread, visible, outreaching, and persuasive. It will encompass all domains, levels, cities, and governments.

In the Book of Acts people were called out in pairs by the Holy Spirit. Acts 13:4 tells us that two were sent out in order to achieve more than they would separately. The two witnesses in Revelation 11:3-4 are symbolic of two olive trees or two lampstands. In Mark 6:7 the Apostles were sent out in pairs with Jesus' authority. In Luke 10:1 Jesus *"sent them ahead in pairs to all the towns and places he planned to visit"* (NLT). Many things of significance functioned in pairs throughout the Bible. The design of a partnership builds unified working relationships.

> *Two people are better off than one, for they can help each other succeed.*
>
> —Ecclesiastes 4:9, NLT

Building strong, intimate relationships is the turnkey for the move of God in motion. Twosomes will relate better to one another, and cooperation with the Holy Spirit will deepen a relationship with God. It will bring down any attack of the enemy to thwart them. This revelation is coming to the forefront of a new generation; but all ages will operate jointly for the truths of New Testament living.

> *For where two or three are gathered together in my name, there am I in the middle of them.*
>
> —Matthew 18:20, AKJV

God Exposes Secrets

> *For the Lord GOD does nothing without revealing his **secret** to his servants the prophets. The lion has roared; who will not fear? The Lord GOD has spoken; who can but prophesy?*

—Amos 3:7-8, emphasis added

God is using prophets more! Today as ever, prophecy is a lion's voice to the nations and its people. God knows our whereabouts. God has things to say, and we must hear it in a new way. It's not about elaboration and adornments. There are matters to be disclosed so we don't dissolve into dust by the enemy's pursuit. The prophet sounds the alarm, using a loud trumpet sound to expose what is undercover.

> *When a **trumpet** sounds in a city, do not the people tremble? When disaster comes to a city, has not the LORD caused it?*

—Amos 3:6, NIV, emphasis added

The term *reveal* means to uncover, disclose, strip away, and unveil.[4] God is openly disclosing His secret plans to the prophet for His people's inspiration and elevation. This is where much revelation comes from. It is a revealing of inspired truths through communion with our divine God. "*Do not think that I have come to abolish the Law or the Prophets; I have not come to abolish them but to fulfill them*" (Matthew 5:17).

People who clamp down like a clam, not allowing openness, seeking staleness over oxygen, get spiritual hypoxia. Some symptoms of this problem are confusion, restlessness, and visual impairment.[5] There isn't enough saturation of oxygen in the blood.[6] Oxygen nourishes our cells, tissues, and organs. We die without enough oxygen in the blood.

It's the same way without light in our world and in all living things. People who go into hiding lose their light and oxygen vital for living. They disjoin from God's blessings, positioning themselves back into silent captivity. They would remove themselves from God's glory: *"The glory has departed from Israel!"* (1 Samuel 4:21).

God is not an unremitting brute. He warns us of impending dangers unless we continually ignore those warnings, fruitlessly. His admonitions are His mercies extended to us. God doesn't want us ignorant. He wants us informed, allowing us to be reformed with the endurance to overtake a lifestyle change of power. He doesn't mix evil with good.

He is all about family connections. We are His people as He is our God. It's the unbroken covenant standard—do or die. Israel has been His beloved jewel from the beginning. We have much to comprehend to avoid their cataclysmic struggles, as we *are* connected.

> *The secret things belong to the LORD our God, but the things that are revealed belong to us and to our children forever, that we may do all the words of this law.*
>
> —Deuteronomy 29:29

This inheritance allows us responsibility and advantageous benefits. God gave Israel many warnings concerning their sins. God's motivation is love; His divine judgments keep them in balance. We would die on a diet of only sweets. It is time to rise to new heights of maturity. There is a significance our children must have to hold onto to propel them in the future.

We are all on equal footing in God's house. Everyone is treated with the same integrity of God's Word. God knows each of us just the same. He doesn't give in to tantrums. He sets the standards high and never lowers them. It's time to come up to the level of Christ's achievements for us all. Otherwise, the precipice of our lives will be too steep and hazardous to navigate.

God doesn't flagrantly react in shock when we go outside His will. God's not deaf and dumb! He deals with us, sometimes tenderly while other times firmer. He knows a small hindrance today will turn into a huge obstruction tomorrow. A real parent deals with their children by not ignoring those areas they know are conflictive to their character (2 Chronicles 7:14). We must turn from our manipulative ways.

We are given the capacity to judge, knowing right from wrong for a reason. If we did not have the acute ability to judge, there would be no laws to prevent harm. We learn at an early age that certain circumstances will injure us. As we grow, we learn wisdom to discern the difference between an egregious lie versus the truth.

> *"Come near me and listen to this: "From the first announcement I have not spoken in secret; at the time it happens, I am there." And now the Sovereign LORD has sent me, endowed with his Spirit.*

> —Isaiah 48:16, NIV

God invites us to look at our failings maturely. We have witnesses around us who see and observe us from afar. Some people use God's blessings as tactically diverse from His standards. They may be ignorant of the covenant banner of measure. His people are not excused from knowing God's expectations. We have the entire Bible to show us the way, truth, and the light. The Holy Spirit is our guide to that truth.

> **But it is from Him that you have your life in Christ Jesus, Whom God made our wisdom from God,** [revealed to us

a knowledge of the divine plan of salvation previously hidden, manifesting itself as] **our Righteousness** *[thus making us upright and putting us in right standing with God],* **and our Consecration** *[making us pure and holy],* **and our Redemption** *[providing our ransom from eternal penalty for sin].*

—1 Corinthians 1:30, AMP, emphasis added

Mystery Revealed

And to make all men see what is the fellowship of the mystery, which from the beginning of the world hath been hid in God, who created all things by Jesus Christ.

—Ephesians 3:9, NKJV

God's Kingdom came to Earth bundled up in an obscure way. It was hidden from Herod the baby killer who caused many mother's to cry out in anguish and dismay. Jesus was unearthed in meek surroundings tucked away in the hills. Christ came to us a tiny defense package. Then, when the time was right, Jesus blew the doors off of religiosity. Every kingdom must bow to Him now or in eternity; it's a matter of time.

For this reason I, Paul, a prisoner for Christ Jesus on behalf of you Gentiles—assuming that you have heard of the stewardship of God's grace that was given to me for you, **how the mystery was made known to me by revelation**, *as I have written briefly. When you read this, you can perceive my insight into the mystery of Christ, which was not made known to the sons of men in other generations as it has* **now** *been revealed to his holy apostles and prophets by the Spirit.*

—Ephesians 3:1-5, emphasis added

Paul, as God's messenger, was under Roman imprisonment. He didn't consider it a place to escape, even as they chained him at night. He thought himself a prisoner of Jesus Christ. He was there because his voice favors the Gentiles (non-Jews). God had a plan for us in the Old Testament but it is now being realized.

A mystery is something kept secret and remains unknown, as a puzzle that eludes our understanding. It is translated from the Greek *mysterion,* which is interpreted as something that was previously hidden, but now full disclosure comes out in the open. This is the revelation of God given to Paul upon completion of the cross.

> *But we impart a secret and hidden wisdom of God, which God decreed before the ages for our glory.*
>
> —1 Corinthians 2:7

In the Old Testament, Isaiah 49:6 tells us, "*I will make you as a light for the nations, that my salvation may reach to the ends of the earth.*" Light has the same inference as spreading the message of the good news of Christ to all the Earth.

Paul wants all to SEE, to envision the *fellowship of the mystery* from the beginning of the ages that had been hidden in God who created all things through Jesus Christ. He's calling the Gospel what it is and who it was intended for—His worldwide church body. Paul is displaying the mystery as a truth and a reality! It's not a smokescreen.

What was not made known to the sons of men before time has now been revealed to us. Salvation had already been prophesied, but this is an all-inclusive revelation. The mystery was the joining together of the Jews and Gentiles into one Body of one church of the Lord Jesus Christ. The separating partition period is over. No one group has preferential standing or treatment as we are all identified in Christ's glory.

> *There is one body and one Spirit—just as you were called to the one hope that belongs to your call—one Lord, one faith, one baptism, one God and Father of all, who is over all and through all and in all.*

> —Ephesians 4:4-6

Gentiles are full partakers in all of God's promises. There are no more divisive lines of superiority, demarcation, or rejection. There are no private country club churches for the rich and famous of prestige, power, fame, and fortune. We are all active participants in equal standing. We are bound together in the richness of Christ, "*as a plan for the fullness of time, to unite all things in him, things in heaven and things on earth*" (Ephesians 1:10).

> *[God] has kept this secret for centuries and generations past, but now at last it has pleased him to tell it to those who love him and live for him; and the riches and glory of his plan are for Gentiles, too.* **And this is the secret: Christ in your hearts is your only hope of glory.** *So everywhere we go we talk about Christ to all* **who will listen,** *warning them and teaching them as well as we know how. We want to be able to present each one to God, perfect because of what Christ has done for each of them. This is my work, and I can do it only because Christ's mighty energy is at work within me.*

> —Colossians 1:26-29, TLB, emphasis added

Incoming Revelation

Acts 17:30-31 tells us that the times of ignorance, or the days before Christ paid for the captivity of our souls, is complete.

Jesus fully paid that once in a lifetime debt. For the single price for our deliberate transgressions of every act, we need only repent of this waywardness as we accept Him to rule and reign in all the affairs of our life. Don't retreat back into the deep recesses of darkness. The mystery has been revealed!

Three White Columns Dream, 7.19.14

I was awakened early in the morning hearing the voice of instruction speak to me. I saw myself walking with a man as we went up to three separate white columns. Each column was designated by a name and purpose.

The first column was called "fellowship of kindred koinonia."

Koinonia comes from a Greek word meaning communion or joint participation. It is sharing anything one has in the contribution of a gift. It's the embodiment of fellowship and team ship. This is a vital key to the movement we are entering.

The Holy Spirit took me to the second column, calling it "reform" in relationship to the church. It is how churches relate in exchanges with one another. There can be no violating or diminishing this reform for empowerment and vitality to thrive.

The third column was of utmost importance. As I saw the dark haired man stand by the pillar and touch it with his right hand while facing me, he said, "This is called the, 'knowledge of cooperation.'" It will widen the spreading movement as people move hand in hand.

The Holy Spirit continued speaking on caveats that I needed to notice: (1) submission to the Lamb is the only way. (2) Creative expressions of the Holy Spirit are being released in a new way. (3) Supernatural speed in things getting done; things that used to take a long time will seem to change instantly. (4) Overgrowth in an abundance of provisions. (5) Outplaying of distributions going right where they were needed.

As these kindred spirits worked together in unified teams, different aspects of ministries were coming together as if on their own. The Holy Spirit was working and enhancing these unions. As the rifts of previous disassociations stopped Him, this time they were working for the churches exponentially, happening right before our very eyes.

Displays of gestures of His love continued to move things right along without delays, as if on a conveyer belt. There would be agreements of every kind as our biblical birth right of inheritance was being revitalized. As our wills were submitted, the bills were being paid. Breakthrough medical technology was coming to benefit mankind without harm. Divine knowledge was being sprinkled everywhere in holy tandem.

A new type of warring cantor (instructor of worship) style will immerge with people echoing musical verses with congregational response. According to Wikipedia,

> *A cantor must be competent to choose and to conduct the vocals for the choir, to start any chant on demand, and to be able to identify and correct the missteps of singers placed under him. He may be held accountable for the immediate rendering of the music, showing the course of the melody by **movements of the hand(s)**.*[7] (Emphasis added)

I see it as a type of worshipping powwow with a drum beat.

There will be no "messing" with the gifts of the Spirit, as an act of purification has poured out to consecrate those gifts. People will not be puppets of manipulation, but the Lord will use His servants virtuously. There will be no profane thing to stop its course.

The dragon will duck his head out of these places of revival, as the full swing of God's manifestations will dominate there exhibiting His Holy majesty, signs, wonders, and magnificent exploits.

But whoever lives by the truth comes into the light, so that it may be seen plainly that what they have done has been done in the sight of God.

—John 3:21, NIV

Top Secret

Your kingdom come, your will be done, on earth as it is in heaven.

—Matthew 6:10

Future Up-Station Dream

I was allowed to see into a very important operation in a dream detailing future plans. A building was in the process of being constructed, which was to serve multiple purposes. The wooden (effort in humility) beams and walls went up above ground along with other compartments.

Many people were involved in this operation, busy and very focused with their tasks. It was clean and organized. I was allowed to take this tour, but it was top secret. It seemed to have a technical side or use.

I was shown a disguised compartment to the upstairs. It seemed as if the building was three stories. Two were visible, while the third was accessible by the hidden and collapsible stairs.

While on the stairs, a child appeared who was being instructed on the uses and dangers of the stairs. The little girl fell down a wooden plate used over the floor to activate the stairs. She fell down the stairs but landed on cushiony positioned pillows. It was there on purpose for catching people. She was being shown the proper place where she should land and not get hurt.

The top "up-station" was for private use, as if for securing well hidden people in living quarters with many useful functions available to them. The lights were kept low at this time interval. The downstairs section had a kitchen with good capacity for dual functions. One side was for professional usage while the other side was for mass feeding. The business side was for legitimate purposes; prolifically state of the art. It was a prototype for operations in the last days.

Instead of underground, it was above ground. It appeared highly inventive, with an abundance of technological and multifunctional purposes.

I believe this outstanding design is a place of protection and provision for the preservation of God's people. This multifunction fortress has usefulness for the world's needs while dually taking care of those under God's watchful eye during a time of persecution and famine.

As the people came together in one place, in one accord, brilliant minds were united to transform one building into varying, functioning spaces. Each part was extremely important on its own while existing under one covering (Christ).

> *Immediately after the tribulation of those days the sun will be darkened, and the moon will not give its light, and the stars will fall from heaven, and the powers of the heavens will be shaken. Then will appear in heaven the sign of the Son of Man, and then all the tribes of the earth will mourn, and they will see the Son of Man coming on the clouds of heaven with power and great glory. And he will send out his angels with a loud trumpet call, and they will gather his elect from the four winds, from one end of heaven to the other.*
>
> —Matthew 24:29-31

Our Father's Intimate Plan

Dear friends, you always followed my instructions when I was with you. And now that I am away, it is even more important. Work hard to show the results of your salvation, obeying God with deep reverence and fear. For God is working in you, giving you the desire and the power to do what pleases him.

—Philippians 2:12-13, NLT

When we're in a loving and intimate relationship, we share our deepest secrets, yearnings, and desires. We experience transformation and transparency as the relationship grows and builds together. This is exactly as Christ would have it. He wants us to have that same kind of established relationship.

Jesus wants to know us; He wants us to know Him. It is in the knowing that people allow themselves to become close. We share our likes and dislikes, tastes, favorite things, movies, Bible verses. Jesus' disciples knew Christ as a friend who shared everything He could with them in an intimate, personal way. He took time for communion and fellowship.

God has something for His people! All of our lives He has been building inside of us His best purposes. If we kept track of them in a journal, as I have shared, there would be a huge trail of evidence to follow. His design has meaning; His adventures have purpose. We have a powerful destiny ahead *if* we step into and work it as a weapon.

Allow me to share a word of confirmation for my life's call. I hope it brightly encourages someone's faith walk, anointing, and ministry function. The Body of Christ must work together in a group effort to fulfill the next huge assignment. No one will get the credit except Christ.

Word of the Lord, 11.90

Those who are wise will shine like the brightness of the heavens, and those who lead many to righteousness, like the stars forever and ever.

Daniel 12:3, NIV

I am developing a weapon of warfare not used by you before and also very unique for you. It will be very powerful at destroying the roots the devil has used in people's lives. It will be a high powered and aggressive anointing. It will also be used to cleanse out impurities in people's lives; to bring smoothness to the rough places as I sweep through with wind and grind out the layers of darkness they have stored there. And they shall end up "*shining*" for My glory.

As you lay hands on the sick they shall be free, delivered. As you use your new gift, you shall be discovered to bring deliverance to the captives, to set at liberty those that have been bound, battered, and bruised. As you bring liberty to my people, the salvations shall follow you everywhere you set your feet to.

Help set My people free. I have called you to this very house and thanked you for helping feed the poor. My love goes out to you.

Father

I am the true vine, and my Father is the vinedresser. Every branch in me that does not bear fruit he takes away, and every branch that does bear fruit he prunes, that it may bear more fruit. Already you are clean because of the word that I have spoken to you. Abide in me, and I in you. As the branch cannot bear fruit by itself, unless it abides in the vine, neither can you, unless you abide in me.

—John 15:1-4

We are cleansed by the washing of the Word of God. Breathe it in and speak it out! The Word brings changes we can't always see; and then sometimes we do. Either way, the Word of God was here first bringing life to our planet. It created our universe and everything in it. It's what we use to transform negative darkness to brilliant light. We bring life out of death's sting.

God's tree has no caves, rotten branches, or spoiled fruit, so get connected to His rock solid root system. Do His plan, and then persevere to overcome. Proverbs 12:3 tells us, "*No one is established by wickedness, but the root of the righteous will never be moved.*" Our deep, strong roots are utterly fixed under the shadow of the most high. We are sturdy and stable.

> *But be doers of the word, and not hearers only, deceiving yourselves. For if anyone is a hearer of the word and not a doer, he is like a man who looks intently at his natural face in a mirror. For he looks at himself and goes away and at once forgets what he was like. But the one who looks into the perfect law, the law of liberty, and perseveres, being no hearer who forgets but a doer who acts, he will be blessed in his doing.*

—James 1:22-25

A List of Benefits to "Hide"

Hiding God's Word in Our Heart

> *I have thought much about your words and stored them in my heart so that they would hold me back from sin.*

—Psalm 119:11, TLB

Hiding His word within us prevents sabotage later, preparing us by faith.

Giving in Any Dimension

> *Beware of practicing your righteousness before other people in order to be seen by them, for then you will have no reward from your Father who is in heaven. Thus, when you give to the needy, sound no trumpet before you, as the hypocrites do in the synagogues and in the streets, that they may be praised by others. Truly, I say to you, they have received their reward.*

—Matthew 6:1-2

To be seen giving brings no reward with it.

Service to the Lord

> *Rendering service with a good will as to the Lord and not to man.*

—Ephesians 6:7

> *Whatever you do, work heartily, as for the Lord and not for men, knowing that from the Lord you will receive the inheritance as your reward. You are serving the Lord Christ."*

—Colossians 3:23-24

Serve the Lord in a private, heartfelt way, not to be noticed by it.

Devotional Times

> *And your Father, Who sees in **secret**, will reward you in the open.*

—Matthew 6:6, AMP, emphasis added

Rewards that last come from heaven; earthly rewards pass.

Fasting

*"Why have we fasted, and you **see it not**? Why have we hum-bled ourselves, and you take no knowledge of it?" Behold, in the day of your fast you seek your own pleasure, and oppress all your workers. Behold, you fast only to quarrel and to fight and to hit with a wicked fist. Fasting like yours this day will not make your voice to be heard on high. Is such the fast that I choose, a day for a person to humble himself? Is it to bow down his head like a reed, and to spread sackcloth and ash-es under him? Will you call this a fast, and a day acceptable to the LORD? Is not this the fast that I choose: to loose the bonds of wickedness, to undo the straps of the yoke, to let the oppressed go free, and to break every yoke? Is it not to share your bread with the hungry and bring the homeless poor into your house; when you see the naked, to cover him, and **not to hide yourself from your own flesh**?*

—Isaiah 58:3-7, emphasis added

Yet even now," declares the LORD, "return to me with all your heart, with fasting, with weeping, and with mourning."

—Joel 2:12

So that your fasting may not be noticed by men but by your Father, Who sees in secret; and your Father, Who sees in se-cret, will reward you in the open.

—Matthew 6:18

Be humble in fasting. It's not for show and tell; it's for last-ing results.

Boasting

*A [self-confident] fool's lips **bring contention**, and his mouth invites a beating.*

—Proverbs 18:6, AMP, emphasis added

He who guards his mouth and his tongue keeps himself from troubles.

—Proverbs 21:23, AMP

As it is, you boast in your arrogance. All such boasting is evil.

—James 4:16

Our mouth, by and large, is the most detrimental weapon we possess capable of shooting arrows of pain, rejection, and degradation to mankind. It is the same weapon that can relieve hurting hearts with the cleansing brought from a fountain of forgiveness. Don't use the tongue foolishly. Protect its use while motivating others by delivering peace.

Take Refuge

*You take me out of the net they have **hidden** for me, for you are my refuge.*

—Psalm 31:4, emphasis added

***Hide** me from the secret plots of the wicked, from the throng of evildoers, who whet their tongues like swords, who aim bitter words like arrows.*

—Psalm 64:2-3, emphasis added

Jesus is our refuge in times of trials.

Forgiveness

> *He who covers and forgives an offense seeks love, but he who repeats or harps on a matter separates even close friends.*

> —Proverbs 17:9

> *Hatred stirs up strife, but love **covers** all offenses.*

> —Proverbs 10:12, emphasis added

I used to believe that we were supposed to cover up secret matters about those we love. But the use of "cover" has to do with forgiveness, not secretiveness. There are issues in life that must be dealt with. Aversive behaviors, lies to distort others' well being, and detrimental or even scandalous acts benefit no one. However, forgiveness by faith as an act of our will in obedience (not feelings) is the only way. Surrender to God, as answers will follow. Our lives will line up in the way they should.

God Cares

> *Why do you **cry** out over your hurt? Your pain is incurable. Because your guilt is great, because your sins are flagrant, I have done these things to you. Therefore all who devour you shall be devoured, and all your foes, every one of them, shall go into captivity; those who plunder you shall be plundered, and all who prey on you I will make a prey. For I will restore health to you, and your wounds I will heal, declares the LORD, because they have called you an outcast: "It is Zion, for whom **no one cares.**"*

> —Jeremiah 30:15-17, emphasis added

In this descriptively significant scripture, the Jews sorrowfully acknowledge their "leaven" of overflowing sins. Their conjured up iniquity has lasted for such a prolonged period that a just judge would bring punishment. In this *second temple* built by the Romans there is *no hope* left, only incurable pain.

Helplessly, every effort to heal themselves is as a bottomless pit. They are left to their own despair while suffering justly. This people group is unable to fix their situation intelligently or otherwise. No one is there to recover them in their turmoil; no one but One.

Our turnaround God is nearby as He lifts the yoke of bondage in deliverance style. There has been a seventy-year empowerment exercised over the Jews by the king of Babylon. In God's perfect timing, His character will judge their oppressor.

For those Jews accepting Jesus as Messiah and Lord, there is a promise of liberty and restoration. They're a privileged people knowing the kind of God whom they serve has never truly abandoned them. They needed to desperately seek Him again.

There was a season in my life when I heard people continuously use the phrase, "I don't care," which grieved me instinctively. It went against the grain of what I knew; yet people would say it so flippantly. God lovingly cares for each of us without end (1 Peter 5:7).

It's hard to imagine in this life anyone not suffering in some area of conflict. It may be physical, mental, social, or financial. There are so many ways in which life is not fair, even cruel at times. We get the short end of the stick in a momentary setback. But it is just temporary; it is not a holding place or fixed jail cell.

This is a time for calling out what needs to be shaken loose, so we are not taken by dire, impending circumstances. Let's equip our voices unanimously to break the atmosphere loose of all destructive barriers. Be impactful. Radical change is in the air, so don't despair. The Light is calling all to arise with healing in His wings (Malachi 4:2).

God wants us to be RESTORED completely, as we are SUP-PORTED by Him, while being STRENGTHENED through it. He accomplishes this by putting us on His firm foundation; not the world's flaky, shaky, sand-filled sinkholes.

> *But all who listen to me will live in peace, untroubled by fear of harm.*
>
> —Proverbs 1:33, NLT

Gigantic Inflated Caterpillar Balloon Dream, 4.2.15

> *"For in him, we live and move and have our being." As some of your own poets have said, "We are his offspring."*
>
> —Acts 17:28, NIV

I saw an enormous glistening and translucent caterpillar balloon flying over the USA, just like the one's used in helium balloon parades. It had many tiny false legs and true legs grouped on either side of its body that were lit up with various little colored twinkle lights. This was being sent via the Heavenly host on a lookout. It was in the skyline at the same level as tall buildings. It was searching the scenery below looking for places upon which to spread its glory.

It arrived at an unnamed metropolitan city gracefully weaving in and out of any obstructions it might incur. The caterpillar was looking carefully, watching what was happening below, and trying to catch those upon which it could descend and impart its goodness.

This metamorphosis movement is GROWING and AD-VANCING upward.

Caterpillar facts that I believe relate wholly to what is being imparted on the Earth at this instant. It has twelve eyes, six on each side arranged in a semicircle. The purpose of the eyes is to help it differentiate between light and dark. It moves its head from side to side to help judge depths and distances.[8]

It hatches from an egg rich in protein for strength allowing a nutritious, rich start. The next stage is all about growth as it increases its body mass by 1,000 times or more; this would require tremendous energy. It grows exponentially being pliable and molts, shed's its external skeleton, multiple times as it grows larger and heavier.[9] In between the molts is a stage called an *instar*, a Latin word meaning "form, likeness."[10]

A caterpillar has three pairs of true legs and up to five pairs of prolegs that help it to hold onto surfaces and to climb up limbs and branches. They may have up to 4,000 muscles of which seventy control each body segment. (Seventy symbolizes spiritual order carried out in power). Their movement is wavelike from back to front.[11]

Caterpillars use unique, creative strategies not to be consumed by their enemies. Some advertise their toxicity by their bright colors. They will protect themselves from predators by using toxins taken from plants they have set apart in their bodies.[12]

I believe God is giving us a roadmap to follow in the move that's coming by reading the signs and strategies of the caterpillar and how it functions. It's intended for massive energy and enormous growth as it reproduces itself with many sons and daughters. It is waving about in a resilient and flexible pattern as it pulls the hind legs forward then extending its front half. Obstructions do not hinder its motion forward as it moves past them easily. It is lit up within, transparently lighting the way as it goes. It will embody a unified strength and richness to proceed or there will be struggles along its pathway.

We are to shed any old, dead skeletons from past methods of thinking, managing, or operating. It's imperative for new growth as a stentorian (loud and powerful) spiritual form takes shape before large crowds. We are to take on the likeness of Christ and His image as the stages change in process. We can remain liberated from getting stuck in the mud and safe from the toxic affects of intruders. We operate best with the inflating of the Holy Spirit and not ourselves.

As confirmation, the next day I heard a newscaster on television speak of an invasion of caterpillars in the city of Houston, Texas. The following day I read about a big, powerful caterpillar engine while reading a book.

The power of the Holy Spirit is on the move with splendid lights distinctly appearing out of the blue. I pray it descends and then spreads in cooperation with the Body of Christ on every city, town, and community in our nation.

> *And God hath raised up the Lord, and will also raise up us by his own power.*
>
> —1 Corinthians 6:14, KJV

Unstoppable

> *I know that you can do all things, and that no purpose of yours can be thwarted.*
>
> —Job 42:2

One time a pastor spoke to me about the coming year 1997 as being my year. He said that many mighty things would happen. Many prayers would be answered even to a greater capacity than what I'd thought. There were those who had tried to stop me, but I would not be stopped. This is still as true to this day as a fixed attitude of course.

> *Call to Me and **I will answer you**, and I will tell you great and mighty things, which you do not know.*

—Jeremiah 33:3, NASB, emphasis added

I've been asking God for more, more, MORE; bigger, bigger, BIGGER; greater, greater, GREATER! STAND BY! Matthew 19:26 tells us what is possible, "*And looking at them Jesus said, With people this is impossible, but with God all things are possible*" (NASB).

In Genesis 24:15-67 we read Rebekah's story, one of oppression and the blessing of an unselfish woman. It is a lesson in the way God provides surprising rewards for His servants. It was her will to wait for her family's blessing before accepting the invitation to leave for a marriage to Isaac, who was a wealthy prince.

What should our stance be to stand unstoppable despite the adversities we face? First Peter 5:8-11 below describes it best. It's what we know that helps us go. We mustn't let ignorance hold us back. We must position ourselves so that everything we desire is unavailable to the devil's plotting devices.

> *Keep a cool head. Stay alert. The Devil is poised to pounce, and would like nothing better than to catch you napping. Keep your guard up. You're not the only ones plunged into these hard times. It's the same with Christians all over the world. So keep a firm grip on the faith. The suffering won't last forever. It won't be long before this generous God who has great plans for us in Christ—eternal and glorious plans they are!—will*

have you put together and on your feet for good. He gets the
last word; yes, he does.

—1 Peter 5:8-11, MSG

To reiterate: we are to stay cool in tribulations. We are to stay alert with what is going on around us by keeping informed. We must not depend on others but go after and dedicate our time to what is going on in the world naturally and spiritually. We want the devil paralyzed, not ourselves.

We need to get up, awaken, and get our guard intact. We must hold firm to our faith by believing our virtue is wrapped up in Jesus' blood. This is a temporary turn of events: THEY HAVE PASSED. The NEW has come! We are to put our feet to good use spreading colorful, energized, and visible flames to penetrating practice first, then use exciting words of glory. This will allow our voices to have noticeable credibility. God has it all together as He is showing Himself vividly through the Holy Spirit. An eternal scope is spreading wide.

This is not a time to judge this new move in motion or it may sweep by those that do as a tidal wave.

Judge not, that you be not judged. For with the judgment you
pronounce you will be judged, and with the measure you use it
will be measured to you.

—Matthew 7:1-2

Prayer: "The Shema"

A simple prayer for those wanting to hear God's voice can be:
As your child, Lord, let me hear your voice LOUDLY, CLEARLY,
AND UNAVOIDABLY! There can be no mistaking my Creator's
voice above all other voices. He made me; He knows me, and I
can identify His highest voiceprint on the Earth as it is in Heaven.

Hear, O Israel! The LORD is our God, the LORD is one!

You are the One [echad] and only One creating unity in diversity.

Today, because of the mystery, we are all together one—Jew and Gentile.

The mystery unifies the Body of Christ, according to God's eternal purpose,

As one holy church body under the jurisdiction of Jesus Christ our Lord.

The transparent veil has revealed to all principalities and powers in the heavenly places

We are no longer ashamed, fearful, or disconnected because of the revelation of God's redemptive work on the cross.

We have equal access to the throne in all boldness.

We do not lose heart during any tribulations that we endure as good soldiers.

We are all part of the same family in Heaven and in Earth.

We are granted the riches of His glory, to be strengthened with might through His Spirit in our inner man.

That Christ may dwell in our hearts through faith by obedience

Being rooted and grounded in love.

We can comprehend with all the saints the width, length, depth and height of the love of Christ that passes all understanding.

We may be filled with the fullness of God.

Open our ears to hear the Spirit and obey You as we listen for Your voice!

Lord, open our eyes that we may see. (2 Kings 6:17)

Jeremiah 33:2

Thus says the LORD who made the earth, the LORD who formed it to establish it—the LORD is his name: Call to me and I will answer you, and will tell you great and hidden things that you have not known.

CHAPTER ELEVEN

Hope of Restoration

Remember not the former things, nor consider the things of old. Behold, I am doing a new thing; now it springs forth, do you not perceive it? I will make a way in the wilderness and rivers in the desert.

—Isaiah 43:18-19

Hopelessness Kills Faith

Hope deferred makes the heart sick, but a desire fulfilled is a tree of life.

—Proverbs 13:12

Symbolically trees describe people, and Jesus is our tree sustainer. Out of His abundance He gives us the rain, sunshine, and nutrient soil we need. The winds blow away old debris that collects on it. He is our ultimate resource for all we need as our roots dig deeply in His Word. The fruit is the byproduct of that fulfillment. Revelation 2:7 exhorts us: "*He who has an ear, let him hear what the Spirit says to the churches. To the one who conquers I will grant to eat of the tree of life.*"

When we experience a series of failures mixed with rejection and abandonment, the propensity is to look backwards and examine everything introspectively and hopelessly. All we may see are shackles of defeat, how we weren't good enough. It's about attitude! Faith and attitude are synonyms of one another, so choose what to believe.

> *I have told you these things so that you won't abandon your faith.*
>
> —John 16:1, NLT

> Failing is one of the greatest arts in the world. One fails toward success.[1]
> —Charles Kettering

> Walt Disney was fired by a newspaper editor because "he lacked imagination and had no good ideas."[2]

> Failure provides the opportunity to begin again, more intelligently.[3]
> —Henry Ford

> John Milton wrote Paradise Lost 16 years after losing his eyesight.[4]

Hopelessness is a heart killer poisonous to our health. It paralyzes our thinking as it undermines our future forward call. Don't stand for this; expect all hope in Christ. First Corinthians 15:1-2 tells us, *"Now I would remind you, brothers, of the gospel I preached to you, which you received, in which you stand, and by which you are being saved, if you hold fast to the word I preached to you—unless you believed in vain."*

If we spend too much time dwelling on the past, we're overdue to get a new vision because that old one is dead and gone. It can't be changed, but the future can. Leave those disappointments in

God's all consuming hands as He disposes of them. His hands are more than sufficient to handle anything. It's time to start something fresh and alive. Psalm 92:4 reiterates: *"For you make me glad by your deeds, LORD; I sing for joy at what your hands have done"* (NIV).

God's grace and mercy are new to us every day. Don't let the enemy deliver spoiled milk to our doorstep. Empty that vile container like the rancid spoilage that it is. Yesterday can't deliver tomorrow's delights. Let us dedicate our life, plans, and future to a pro—He's the best event planner ever. Expect His marvelous miracles for your life as God delivered His utmost precious possession, His Son, as a mystery gift to us all.

Faith feeds us! It builds up our most holy person. Take the initiative towards God's plan for that which will never waiver. Hebrews 11:6 says, *"And without faith it is impossible to please him, for whoever would draw near to God must believe that he exists and that he rewards those who seek him."* We have full confidence and assurance of His promises.

> *Therefore, brothers, since we have confidence to enter the holy places by the blood of Jesus, by the new and living way that he opened for us through the curtain, that is, through his flesh, and since we have a great priest over the house of God, let us draw near with a true heart in full assurance of faith, with our hearts sprinkled clean from an evil conscience and our bodies washed with pure water. Let us hold fast the confession of our hope without wavering, for he who promised is faithful.*
>
> —Hebrews 10:19-23

Don't ever settle for the enemy's promotional opportunities, because they are fake and temporary; fading fast as they do not last. Satan's bag of goodies is filled to overflowing with contempt, hatred, bitterness, and bondages deluxe. They are the counterfeit of Jesus; the substitute of Christ's love and restorative blessings.

With trees, the leaves are the receptors of the water to help them sustain life. Leaves grow where the branches are thirsty. If we are going through a trial, leaves are fixing to be birthed there. Healing is in the leaves just as water represents the Holy Spirit. If we are in a low place in our life, we must remember water seeks the lowest level.

> *The steadfast love of the LORD never ceases; his mercies never come to an end; they are new every morning; great is your faithfulness. The LORD is my portion," says my soul, "therefore* **I will hope in him.**"

—Lamentations 3:22-24, emphasis added

Restoration Abounds

> *And the **ransomed** of the LORD shall return and come to Zion with singing; everlasting joy shall be upon their heads; they shall obtain gladness and joy, and sorrow and sighing shall flee away.*

—Isaiah 35:10, emphasis added

According to *Merriam-Webster Dictionary*, *ransomed* means "a consideration paid or demanded for the release of someone or something from captivity."[5] Many stories and illustrations in this book speak of those in captivity, including myself. We are never to stay in that place, just push through it to be released from its tentacles.

At the end of the year in which my first husband left us, I was served divorce papers. Holding those papers at my front door was surreal. It was time to handle the business at hand. The Lord gave me a little ditty of a poem of promise He would provide for me in my future:

Someone New,
Someone True,
Someone Faithful,
Someone who will love you!

A female friend prayed that God would be my husband in fulfillment during this interim period of being a single mother. Then she prayed that God would go throughout the entire Earth and send me a best friend and prayer partner.

My faith had reached an all-time low mark! I wasn't able to ask or pray for anything regarding another relationship in a man to fill a father's and a husband's shoes. Who would want the role of raising another man's children? Then, in steps my then seven-year-old son, who started to pray every night. He asked the Lord to send me a kind, gentle, and loving man. Specifically, he requested a large home with his own bedroom. He wanted a family filled with children, boys or girls. Did this son get everything he asked for? Oh, yes!

I had a mini-dream about this time called,

My Father Knew Dream

My father and I were walking down some steps. My mother was close by, but not in the scene. Dad and I were talking about who I'd marry, and he said he already knew. This surprised me because we never talked about it before. I told him a prophet told me the same thing: that "my Father knew." My heavenly Father did know and that was encouragement enough.

*Son of dust, the people of Israel say, "His **visions** won't come true for a long, long time." Therefore say to them: 'The LORD God says: **All delay has ended!** I will do it **now**!"*

—Ezekiel 12:27-28, TLB, emphasis added

Cut Loose Vision, 8.8.98

(Three 8's = triune covenant of new beginnings.)

The word of the LORD came to me: "Son of man, you dwell in the midst of a rebellious house, who have eyes to see, but see not, who have ears to hear, but hear not, for they are a rebellious house.

—Ezekiel 12:1-2

I prayed to the Lord to open His vision for me concerning our next step together. After praying, I was brought back to a vision I'd had years ago inside a house.

It had at least three stories (three represents trinity) with many different areas to it, as well as rooms and corridors. It seemed to be under renovation on the bottom floor, but still contained cobwebs and dust, etc.

The second floor seemed newer and nicer. The third floor was very mixed with evil and good. It contained a central door leading outside. I was very eager to go outside the door, as if for a breath of fresh air.

I noticed an oval shaped designated area that I walked towards and stood within. Suddenly, a chain (like on a bicycle) came down from the ceiling attached to a cylinder. It came towards me in order to grab my neck and "*shock* me to death."

The chain failed to grab my neck, but it did snatch my hand pulling me up off the floor so that I'd lose my foundation (spiritually speaking). The chain handler was trying to strangle that area of my body. (My hand represents my writer's hand.)

Noticing my hand; it looked as if it were in *shock* and ready to explode from the intense pressure. Then the chain turned a few turns tighter! The enemy always oversteps his boundaries! Something happened above me as the chain seemed to lose its grip and dropped down with some slack, thus allowing a loosening. I heard the chain snap and break from the top.

Shock is a military term used during wartime in order to dismantle the proposed enemy's security by overwhelming and then overtaking them. In Hebrew the word would be *gadiysh*, meaning "to heap up," as in the analogy of a "tomb." Mark 16:8 says, "*So they left the **tomb** and ran away, overwhelmed by **shock** and astonishment. They didn't say a thing to anyone, because they were afraid*" (ISV, emphasis added).

Since there were three floors, it is easy to illustrate that the bottom floor is our past, the middle floor is our present, and the top floor is our future destination. God's ways are always higher as the chain got anointed by an angel and it slipped loose. The Lord set me free in advance of an incoming invasion of the enemy to prohibit my future.

> *He will direct the **shock of his battering rams** against your **walls**, and with his axes he will **break down your towers**.*
>
> —Ezekiel 26:9, emphasis added

I fell to the ground in a wilted heap. I felt no strength; it knocked the life out of me. I felt completely limp, unable to walk or move. This was satan's plan to destroy me and the ministry for my life—to be able to write and tell of God's plans and purposes.

God came towards me and began to breathe life into my soul again! He took me by my hand to restore my walk and life. He breathed and breathed on me.

I did not like the house, after all! (This represented my previous marriage.) What the enemy meant for evil, God was now going to turn around with abounding good.

God had a new house in store for me. It was better, more equipped (in Christ) and suitable for me. It was cleaned up, too. It smelled good—fruity! It was wrapped in a special package and had my name on the front door; the door knocker.

Ask, and it will be given to you; seek, and you will find; knock, and it will be opened to you. For everyone who asks receives, and the one who seeks finds, and to the one who knocks it will be opened.

—Matthew 7:7-8

It was special delivery from God Almighty. It had a big red bow around it and a yellow one, representing a "gift of God." My husband's favorite color is yellow. The red is the covenant blood of Jesus Christ that would not be stolen. How wonderful! Wow!

This is a Poem of Promise God gave to me:

Trust and Faith
Trust and Faith
Trust and Faith
Like on the face of the opposite pages in a book.
God is building these as companions in your walk.
No trace will be left of the counterfeit race.
It has been shaped and will not be erased.
No enemy can take what I have allowed to take place.
Together with thee or two or three I will be.
As I work together—as leavening rises in a mixture to
enliven the whole.

This will create a form not of the norm.
And I will enter into the picture **three** times stronger
than before.

*I have heard your prayer; I have seen your tears. Behold, I will heal you. On the **third** day you shall go up to the house of the LORD.*

—2 Kings 20:5, emphasis added

Son's Prince Dream, 10.22.96

This is as my eight-year-old son spoke it to me at that time. I wrote it down in my journal, asking him to repeat it over and over.

We lived where we are now. Then Mom got married to a new dad in Colorado. The man came from Nevada. We all lived in Colorado for one year until I [my son] was twelve. Then we moved to Washington until I [my son] was fourteen. Then we moved to Oregon for one year. We were tired from traveling when I was fifteen and we finally moved to California when I was sixteen. [Phew!]

We went to Nevada for vacation a lot. We stayed along the coast because our new dad liked the water. He liked the Pacific Ocean mostly.

We went to a courthouse to get married. There was me, my younger brother, a new dad, and a brother and sister.

The new dad preached in Austin, San Francisco, Seattle, Salem, Carson City, and Utah. In Nevada, he had a ranch. He liked to go fishing and there was a lake with a pier all the way around it.

He had tan skin, different colored eyes like hazel color. He was wearing blue jeans, a white shirt with black socks, and boots. He had light hair and it was straight, it looked neat. He had no beard or mustache. He was tall and lean.

At the wedding he looked like a prince. It looked weird. Mom's honeymoon was in Washington. We (the boys) flew to Colorado with new dad's friend.

All I can say is we did take our sons on a lot of traveling trips including Colorado. The preaching is on the horizon. But the description of my new husband to be was almost perfect! About one year from my son's dream is when my future husband and I started to spend committed time together.

Song of the Lord

> *He put a new song in my mouth, a song of praise to our God. Many will see and fear, and put their trust in the LORD.*

> —Psalm 40:3

Never Look Back Vision

I had a vision of a woman at a creative Christian meeting. She came up behind me and started to sing a song of the Lord. She used her finger on my face to illustrate her song. The music was unusual, in a sweet, renaissance style. These were her words to me continuing to use her finger to emphasize her message:

"You don't have to go around the corner [she drew a curve around my cheekbone]. You don't have to go around the bend. You don't need to tell a neighbor or even a friend. All you need to do is go straight to Jesus [she drew a straight line up my nose from the bottom to top]. And you'll never look back again!"

> *Oh sing to the LORD a new song; sing to the LORD, all the earth!*

> —Psalm 96:1

Dove Tail

The definition of *dovetail* is a tight interlocking joint; to connect precisely and harmoniously, to interlock into a unified whole, fitted into a corresponding mortise.[6] God was going to dovetail my union with a man from our church smack-dab on his front doorstep.

Lamentations 3:22 says, *"The steadfast love of the LORD never ceases; his mercies never come to an end."* The word that means mercy in Hebrew is *hesed*, which means "covenant love" or "steadfast love." It is linked to four areas: compassion, truth, faithfulness, and goodness. This was God's gift to me.

When everything else, including our own abilities, is gone, *hesed* remains. When all hope seems to have vanished from sight, God's *hesed* is still very much alive and real! Psalm 103:1, 4 confirms this: *"Bless the LORD...Who redeems your life from the pit, Who crowns you with lovingkindness and compassion"* (NASB).

I had just resigned from a job position that required I work weekends. The Lord blessed me with a Monday through Friday civil job that allowed me to join a single parent cell group that met on weekends. The fellowship was so great during my first cell group meeting that I thanked the Lord beneath my breath.

During our closing prayer, we held hands. A special man took mine. He was holding my hand so warmly, with compassion. It seemed he almost didn't want to let go! We prayed until tears came. I listened to his heart prayer.

Then I prayed quietly to the Lord:

Why am I attracted to this fifty-year-old country cowboy type with two beautiful boys? If it is You, I want complete confirmation from You—Your way. Lord, let there be assuredness firm and strong on Your part concerning this man and my heart.

And now my head shall be lifted up above my enemies all around me, And I will offer in his tent sacrifices with shouts of joy; I will sing, yes, I will sing praises to the LORD....I would have despaired unless I had believed that I would see the goodness of the LORD In the land of the living.

—Psalm 27:6, 13, NASB

Concerns

Trust in the LORD, and do good; dwell in the land and befriend faithfulness. Delight yourself in the LORD, and he will give you the desires of your heart.

—Psalm 37:3-4

The month of September had truly "lit up," as I saw a small fire start to grow. As Jeremiah 20:9 says, "*There is in my heart as it were a burning fire shut up in my bones, and I am weary with holding it in, and I cannot.*"

While I was speaking about this special man to my spiritual mentor, she prayed asking the Lord what needed to be broken off from a past failed relationship and present condition. We prayed he would be sensitive to the leadings of the Lord and not to turn to the left or the right while focusing on Him. "*Lord, confirm with him what you've already told him. Let him not be led down rabbit trails.*" (He was considering moving away.)

We bound off false busyness, pretentions, false preoccupations, and trepidation. We asked the Lord to help him not reflect over past fears, worries, sorrows, and anger. "*Let him **not** be turned inward, but outward to You. His will is loosed to abundant life.*"

Then I added: "*Lord, let him hear Your voice. Jesus, let him be sure and confident and help him make right decisions. Help me to be content. Let the waiting stop. I want a friend for life. Lord, don't leave me out. I want a happy, healthy relationship. I want a real gentleman!"*

Next Prayer

I have seen his ways, but I will heal him; I will lead him and restore comfort to him.

—Isaiah 57:18, NASB

My mentor exhorted that he is carrying false guilt over the demise of his past marriage. It is self-projected. He is blaming himself. Pray for him. He is very responsible. He is gracious, it can even be said he is noble of character.

He is deeply bruised over the failure of his prior marriage. This makes him cautious with women. He does know how to treat a woman; and even has insights many men do not.

He does take his responsibilities seriously, and it makes him feel overwhelmed at times. The self-rejection from the dissolution of marriage has created a "blockage" emotionally and spiritually. It keeps him from reaching out in his anointing and calling. It needs to be prayed over and broken-off.

He is consecrated to the Lord. He needs reassurance on the faithfulness of the Lord. He needs to be admired as a strong man. This was stolen from him because of the mourning and grief over his divorce.

Just like David in the Bible with his son, he needs to wash his face and go on! Let it be dead and buried. His prior spouse did not appreciate all he was as a man or could have been.

He needs to hear from the Lord concerning this possible move and not do it just out of responsibility to his mother. The Lord wants him to trust Him completely.

He does have spontaneity in him. It's been hidden some because his potential has been stifled. There is really great exuberance on the inside of him, and it needs to be released to fulfill what God's called him to do."

Then she directed her prayer to me.

There is healing in your hands for him, for his soul. The relationship will enrich both of your lives. The relationship is two-sided and because of your faithfulness, too. It is okay to think about him. There will be a mini-transfusion (spiritually a transfer) between us.

There is restoration regardless of where the relationship will go. There is peace about it. God is going to gift you with the ability to discern the needs of a person through a photo or picture. This will allow you to pray specifically for their needs."

God wants you to savor (taste or enjoy with zest, to relish, quality of exciting interest) the relationship with David. Proverbs 18:12: "Hope deferred makes the heart sick, But when the desire comes, it is a tree of life" (AKJV).

The lines have fallen for me in pleasant places; indeed, I have a beautiful inheritance. I bless the LORD who gives me counsel; in the night also my heart instructs me. I have set the LORD always before me; because he is at my right hand, I shall not be shaken.

—Psalm 16:6-8

Still Worth It

And your ancient ruins shall be rebuilt; you shall raise up the foundations of many generations; you shall be called the repairer of the breach, the restorer of streets to dwell in.

—Isaiah 58:12

Nothing worthwhile comes easy. The truth of love was Jesus' ministry being the hardest one on Earth. No one else could have fulfilled it but Him. He is our Prince of Peace. He makes the crooked places straight and the rough ones smooth.

He sacrificed His whole life. He enveloped twelve relationships with His very soul, only to be abandoned by all! He still felt they were worth it, just as we are to Him now!

Prophecy by CS

Seeking the will of God: Wanting to know God's will is better than anything. When you want God's will, you're in God's will. How could it be any other way?

Things you've been committing unto Him, He appreciates; but the Lord wants me to tell you the enemy has sought to burden you at times with issues that have not really been on His heart. They're things the enemy trumps up in order spoil your relationship of joy with Father. Reclaim the joy of friendship like you have never known.

The Lord wants you to renounce false guilt and things that are behind. He wants you to see Him in all of the light of His radiant greatness. You are no longer to be trampled upon. You are going to be a mighty conqueror, on top of situations and them not on top of you.

You have been shuttling (like a taxi-cab) children, investing in those not yours. You are not being used, you are being filled with an anointing to touch other lives and redeem them. He's going to give you a 100-fold return for it. Hide behind Jesus. Be free from false responsibilities then pray about it. You are asked favors a lot, but ask the Father first.

You will be one like on a mighty stallion, riding on a horse, your hair flying in the breeze. You will be a great blessing in a classroom situation. The Lord is going to cause you to minister to teachers and educators in the educational system. Laws are going to be changed that are going to bring blessing into the lives of people.

You are going to fast and pray. You will see people's lives turned around. Hang in there and let God do His thing!

Encouragement

The LORD your God is in your midst, a mighty one who will save; he will rejoice over you with gladness; he will quiet you by his love; he will exult over you with loud singing.

—Zephaniah 3:17

By now it was October and I was finding out more about my husband to be. This is what I was finding out as revealed by the Lord through my spiritual mentor:

Small things have real meaning to him. He's a tremendous giver. To get him to do something means it is important. Inner healing will come to him.

He is able to treasure and cherish because he is a man that has been robbed. He is a man, a real man! He is a leader and will be an example to men. Respect him and see things in him. Things in your heart are the same as his.

Ex: A tractor cultivates the land as it plows and plants. They are dug out in rows to bring healthy growth.

There are similarities; there are things in him you need. Things in him cultivate you. The things that are similar to your heart bring new growth. Same soil, but gets dug down deep to let oxygen in and keeps weeds out—enjoy!

He really cares to the soul of his feet. The guilt is starting to disperse and break up.

Within a week, the gray skies will see blue. By next Sunday, little clouds of guilt will have left. He has a trust and confidence in you and in the Lord that is being restored. In the next seven days, God will enable you to lie at the feet of Jesus to reach inside of your expectations and fears. You will pour out yourself before the Lord. A real cleansing will come, purging the old stuff.

Within six days, there will be a clear plan concerning your car. Do not put off credit report papers today. Make a separate file for old separation and divorce stuff.

Sort things out—big paper clips and folders. Move out the old things in a place not viewed much. Don't make it nice, put it aside. God is moving out all the if's and maybe's in your vocabulary permanently concerning your past spouse. It will be final in the next seven to ten days. God is making things black and white.

There is real victory for you. An open heaven for my sister, Lord. The next thirteen days things will be tied up neatly; **the fourteenth day** the sun comes up!

Betah Rakem, "my trusted friend"

For anyone amused by such things, I did make out a list of husband/daddy qualities that I desired. I'm a list girl; what can I say? These are quite different from the ones I'd made out in my twenty something years. Men, take notice! This below is as I wrote them down:

1. *Betah Rakem* means trusted friend. Trust = Confidence.
2. Proverbs 13:12: "A desire fulfilled is a tree of life." He's my tree of life.
3. *Akela*—a good leader.
4. Excellent steward of finances.
5. Helps facilitate a loving, accepting blended family.
6. All children respond with respect to the new father/mother relationship.
7. Cherishing of old and new combinations.
8. Obedient son/servant of God.
9. Gentle, kind-hearted man.
10. Committed covenant keeper.
11. Responsible to family, church, and job.
12. Creates divine family order in home.
13. Wants to be a protector and provider.
14. God's appointed marriage.
15. Receive each other as one.
16. Faithful father.
17. Romantic.
18. Sensitive to the female role.
19. Dual helper in the home.
20. Priest, prophet, and minister with a heart to serve.

Two can accomplish more than twice as much as one, for the results can be much better. If one falls, the other pulls him up; but if a man falls when he is alone, he's in trouble. Also, on a cold night, two under the same blanket gain warmth from each other, but how can one be warm alone? And one standing alone can be attacked and defeated, but two can stand back-to-back and conquer; three is even better, for a triple-braided cord is not easily broken.

—Ecclesiastes 4:9-12, TLB

Reflection

...as he did for the people of Esau, who live in Seir, when he destroyed the Horites before them and they dispossessed them and settled in their place even to this day.

—Deuteronomy 2:22

I entered our single adult Bible study a little late and sat in the back by myself. Our leader Jack said that wasn't acceptable and David stood to let me sit by him.

We walked to the main service together as we spoke of the night before. In service our oldest sons came and sat by us. David said he felt they should have stayed in their youth Bible class, asking what I thought. Without answering, I asked him what he felt about it. The thought of knowing that he cared about my opinion was refreshingly insightful.

After service we walked to the communion table; he served me and I served him the elements. He prayed and we took the symbolic bread and wine together. He took my sons home while I had to drive to work.

After our cell group later that night, I told him there was a special place in my heart for him. We stood very close and hugged. It seemed so natural and a bit scary all at once. I could have stayed in his arms all night.

We had both walked through the dreary dungeon of darkness before and now we were getting the power over it. We were coming out of the pit holes into the palace. We can take hold of the olive pits or reap plentifully from the wine press.

God was bringing healing and growth to us. I was struggling to be natural. I was cautioned not to do anything less than a friend would. We agreed for the opportunity for a real date.

My mentor prayed that God would give David the opportunity to make decisions on his own! She said, "He needs a wife! Salt him with your words to make him more seasoned. There is a real comfortableness between you because you complete each other. God reserved you for one another."

God was removing David from slumbering in his self-preserving habits he had used in order to survive. God was drawing him out of his safety zone and ruts of the past. He wasn't able to be objective with his past marriage—that's how bad it really was. "God is going to melt away the tin man inside of him."

I started to visualize a glacier melt away to nothing. Then I saw a closet full of old clothes of what he used to be. There were cobwebs of "old draining words" covering it all. I prayed them away and they became drenched in water. They fell down to the ground. God was going to send out new clothes for him.

God was giving us a new vision with new conversations. He gave David an "urgency" to get on with the business of living. God showed him how young he is with a future to fulfill! The heat I felt around David was God's confirmation it was Him and His anointing.

Warning

> *Return to your stronghold, O prisoners of hope; today I declare that I will restore to you double.*

> —Zechariah 9:12

I was warned; from this point on, "don't chase him!" This meant not to put any pressure or drive for him to progress in the relationship.

The Lord knows what he can take. It's David's move. When the Lord says it's okay, then don't hesitate. Continue to pray every day for mental and emotional ties and habits to be broken that he's allowed his ex-wife to do. David will never be in the same bondage he was in.

He was receiving deliverance and healing. My prayer was he would see these allowances he'd made as disgusting. He would gird up his loins against any tactics or ways that harmed and damaged his emotions. God would protect David's significance and manhood. David's eyes would be open to motives or from anything that would divert his attention.

Journal:

David, you are so easy to enjoy! What a pleasure to spend real moments...to talk and taste, to hear and see. What a treasure in life to be so comfortable with someone. To delve into any and every subject together. I cherish the memory. Thanks for the bubbles, too!

By the end of the year, David would come over for visits. We talked for hours then would agree when he should go. He put on his jacket, and we both got quiet! I stood against the wall, and we looked at one another.

I spoke up first, "Yes, you can." He asked how I knew what he was thinking. We kissed. David said he felt as young as I looked. He said if he'd married me twelve years ago we'd have twelve children. Well, good luck with that; but I got his point.

David said he had been so empty that he couldn't get full. Not yet! He felt we would be good together. Finally saying it felt so right. It was too good to behold.

Many a man claims to have unfailing love, but a faithful man who can find? The righteous man leads a blameless life; blessed are his children after him.

—Proverbs 20:6-7, NIV

Engagement

By Christmas, David started to hint about becoming engaged. Unbelievably, with his suggestion, I knew I wasn't ready. As much as I had longed for this occasion, my emotions had not caught up yet. I was nervous about it all.

Even so, the creative instincts in me took over and I began to draw a wedding ring. By the second attempt, I knew I had it. When the time was right, I showed it to my David. He knew a wholesaler at church that assisted him in picking out the center cut—a trillion cut. It's the shape of a triangle with beveled edges; this represented Christ as the head of the home. There were two smaller trillions on each end that represented David and me.

We then added three round diamonds on each side to represent the two separate families we were adding together to our formation of six people in our new family. We added four baguette cut diamonds on each side representing the number eight for new beginnings.

On Valentine's Day we had dinner at an Italian restaurant where I was presented with a red rose and a pearl necklace. This was more out of fear on his part because he chickened out on the proposal over dinner. We left the restaurant to pick up his sons. While waiting at a stoplight he took a pink, heart-shaped, velvet box and proposed. I opened the small box to find the center trillion cut diamond for my wedding ring.

We both knew the date of the wedding. It would be the day we met in his home on Mother's Day in May. We decided since God brought me to his doorstep as a gift to him, that was the place we would marry as well.

Reverse Surprise

I am the LORD; I have called you in righteousness; I will take you by the hand and keep you; I will give you as a covenant for the people, a light for the nations, to open the eyes that are blind, to bring out the prisoners from the dungeon, from the prison those who sit in darkness.

—Isaiah 42:6-7

Although not required for marriage in our state, my fiancé had a complete physical done since it had been awhile since his last one. He called me that evening with an uneasy voice. He didn't want to tell me. I told him whatever it was we would face it together.

The doctor asked David if he had prostate cancer in his family. David told him, "No, why?" The doctor informed him his prostrate was enlarged. The doctor did a PA test coming up with a rating of seven. David was scheduled for a biopsy a few days later, which tested positive.

David told me over the phone that he could not hold me to our engagement. He couldn't tell me what the future would hold. He understood if I wanted our relationship to end. That is when I reigned in every ounce of faith I ever knew and then some. I told him the enemy could not have him and we were going to fight.

I called the strongest people of faith I knew to pray over my fiancé. Our group of believers stood and prayed a long time until we had a complete release that it was taken care of in advance.

His surgery was scheduled rather quickly; the sooner it was done the better chance of a good outcome.

Everyone who met my fiancé told me he was a keeper. I got thumbs up from family and friends, as I wanted to know for sure. No skeletons in the closet. On our first date, David showed me proof of his past divorce certificate. He wanted me to know for certain he wasn't a married man playing games as he'd seen other men do.

The day of his surgery he called me at work to tell me the angels were singing over him. I said, "What?" He explained that he had prayed for a nurse while on his hospital bed awaiting surgery. That attendant left to get all three of her nurse friends to meet the patient that prayed for her needs instead of his own.

All four nurses got one corner of his hospital bed while wheeling him down the hallway to the operating room singing, "Victory in Jesus." When the doctor opened up the prostate area to remove the cancer tumor, he found it to be completely solidified, rock solid. David was told if the surgery had been delayed even a month the cancer would have spread.

After several follow-up appointments and tests, he was declared to be completely cancer free. That has been many years ago. He has had other health issues to conquer, and each time the Lord has helped him overcome with medical, nutritional, and spiritual support.

The doctor who performed his surgery came self-invited to our wedding. He told David he was his star patient, bouncing back quicker and healthier than any other patient he'd ever seen from this type of surgery. David was ready for our honeymoon.

And they came, bringing to him a paralytic carried by four men. And when they could not get near him because of the crowd, they removed the roof above him, and when they had made an opening, they let down the bed on which the paralytic lay. And when Jesus saw their faith, he said to the paralytic, "Son, your sins are forgiven."

—Mark 2:3-5

Baby Delivered Dream, 1.8.10

Or if they ask for an egg, do you give them a scorpion? Of course not!

—Luke 11:12, NLT

I had already had two previous pregnancy dreams in which I was almost ready to deliver but there was no doctor (authority) available. Now, with this third dream, that was about to change.

I was very pregnant while walking with two friends who wanted me to go somewhere with them. But I was starting to feel tired from my condition. The sidewalk we were traveling was the direction which faced **west** (toward the Lord).

*So they shall fear the name of the LORD from the **west**, and his glory from the rising of the sun; for he will come like a rushing stream, which the wind of the LORD drives.*

—Isaiah 59:19, emphasis added

I collapsed in a bowing position on all fours with both my hands and knees. One of the women came beside me and put her hand on my back. I felt as if I was going to break my water (the Holy Spirit being released). Unexpectedly, a very large, oval hard-boiled egg came out of me and broke in two pieces except for the center yolk.

The yellow yolk normally seen inside an egg was replaced by a human baby boy. I took him home directly because I was concerned he may have gotten hurt by coming out so fast. I carefully observed his head (Christ) to make sure there was no bruising. Since the egg white broke in two, it did not allow a lot of time for cushioning or catching him.

At home, I took the infant to the baby's room. I began to bundle, clean, and secure him. After this, the baby began to "speak to me" fluently with great wisdom as he was giving me instructions. The "spirit of wisdom" was speaking as I listened. Right at this moment, you are reading from that wise baby boy!

Proverbs 19:27 tells us, *"If you stop **listening** to instruction, my child, you will turn your back on knowledge"* (NLT, emphasis added).

An important fact about albumin is it helps move many small molecules through the blood which helps one to absorb nutrients.[1] In eggs (egg white) it contains four (God's creative works) altering layers of a whitish liquid fortified with forty (generational/completed rule) different proteins (strength).[8] These accomplished works will be passed to future generations giving them Godly fortified strength.

The number two has been used twice in this dream—two friends and two separate portions of the egg white. This means it would be used for double the multiplication of His purposes. I believe this generational birthing will pass down as a completed fixture of righteous ruling in strength. The white egg and egg white confirm the Spirit of the Lord is involved all the way through to its completion.

A fourth dream of the same context was given to me 1.15.04 that I titled,

Encampment Dream

To confirm the dream above, I added this one that included my husband and a team who had stopped at an encampment. To my surprise, I was told I was pregnant while at that instant I delivered a 10 pound, 12 ounce baby boy (10 = journey, 12 = government/united/joined). This would be a united journey established of the Lord.

Before I could tell my husband I was pregnant, the large and mature baby was in my hands. The head (position of authority) flopped noticeably, having some discoloration of a blue tone (anxiety). I held the baby securely, especially holding the head in place for protection.

I told the nurse we had no baby items as I'd given them all away. I asked my husband to get some basic needs like powder, diapers, and an outfit. I told him to get it NOW! Then I looked at an apparatus that rolled into our room that was fully equipped with baby essentials (all needs were met instantly). I noticed a baby brush to comb the baby boy's hair (brushing in wisdom).

Buried Underground Dream, 4.23.12

If you come across a bird's nest in any tree or on the ground, with young ones or eggs and the mother sitting on the young or on the eggs, you shall not take the mother with the young.

—Deuteronomy 22:6

I stood observing a plane flying low over an asphalt **two**-lane road that appeared to be in an open rural area with a mountain in the far distance. The plane came so close to the **highway** that it **divided** it in **two** on the inbound side closest to a hedge of **green** grass.

I looked beneath the black roadway, which had revealed a nest of exposed pastel colored eggs. Pastel embodies colors in our emotional area of feelings, thoughts, and passions. There were many eggs layered in a bundle on top of one another. I believe these represented the heart chapters of my life. The nest had been buried underground, as if secret hidden treasures.

In the distance I saw a long, heavy commercial eighteen-wheeler truck driving toward my direction. I became distressed at the situation not wanting any of the eggs to be harmed. I could not allow the truck to destroy my newfound discovery.

I rapidly tried to think of ways to prevent a collision of devastation. I did not know if the driver would skirt to the side of the eggs or see that I was trying to signal him to move over to the next lane.

Instead, I decided to pick up all the eggs and put them inside a safe container. It is important to protect our future vision. Selah.

Clues: (1) *Asphalt* is brownish black solid (bitumen) material used for surfacing roads and waterproofing.[9] (2) *Egg* as a transitive verb means to encourage or incite to action as was required in this dream.[10] An idiom for many eggs is "all of one's eggs in one basket," which means risking everything on a single venture.[11] (3) Protect means to keep from harm, attack, or injury—guard.[12] (4) The eighteen-wheeler is significant because the number eighteen means established blessing or judgment—A blessing will overtake (wheel) her.

*I have robbed their **nests of riches** and **gathered up kingdoms** as a farmer **gathers eggs**. No one can even flap a wing against me or utter a peep of protest.*

—Isaiah 10:14, NLT, emphasis added

No resistance was given by protesting parent birds, except for pitiful cries. They flew away without clinging to their eggs with warm protection. There was no chirping sound, striking of their bill in protest, or fluttering of their wings to warn predators of their precious hatchings. It was an easy steal by the enemy's hand. No one cared or dared to make a sound. Not even a word.

Isaiah 10 gives a harrowing reminder to God's people. Assyria had become a godless nation. The pompous Assyrian ruler, King Sennacherib, acted out of his own desire (see 2 Kings 19). This was an idolatrous king with greed and ambition under his wings. He had the power to undo nations and strip them naked. He mocked the God who gave him the rulership for this position. He was able to accomplish the defeat of Samaria and resolutely expected to conquer God's people next.

When we experience pain, distress, and losses, we are not alone to save ourselves. Jesus learned obedience through what He suffered (Hebrews 5:8). I pray the Lord gives us the precise clarity to see and hear. *In Jesus' name all dullness, ambiguity, obscurity, unsanctified noise, and paralyzing waxes has melted from our lives.* I ask the Lord for the maximum "pellucidity" (passage of light without diffusion or distortion)[13] that allows His translucent light to pour through us at the highest range possible.

We are reminded of the one true God who can deliver us from our afflictions as we come in the power of agreement to His will. As an eighteen-wheeler looms over the horizon to wipe us out, we have the opportunity to cry out with His righteous voice inside out. We must desire a humble posture that allows us to catch His secure covenant promises. Jesus is not stingy!

Hebrews 5:7 says, *"During the days of Jesus' life on earth, he offered up prayers and petitions with **loud cries and tears** to the* *one who could save him from death, and he was heard because of his reverent submission"* (NIV, emphasis added). I pray we are like Jesus as devoted sons and daughters who recognize the time and seasons. Let's not allow one tear to be wasted because of a lack of Godly fear and submission.

Marauders had infiltrated the bird's nest. Let's identify with God as He draws us closer while He is moving closer to us. We must undergird one other with the broken chains that once held us back. Connect those ropes and chains together like a scarlet cord of prayer that leads us to the Promised Land as our holy Lord puts the enemy to flight. There is no maneuvering that can blind us to the reality of who God is. Just as the Assyrian army was slain by the angel of the Lord, never to rule in darkness again, we are free to reign in the light of Christ today!

The king who blasphemed Jerusalem and its people proved to be a coward:

> *The angel of the LORD went out and put to death 185,000 men in the Assyrian camp. When Hezekiah's army awakened in the morning—there were all the dead bodies! King Sennacherib **broke** camp, **retreated, returned** home to Nineveh, and remained there. Later, while he was worshiping in the house of his god Nisroch, his sons Adrammelech and Sharezer **cut him down** with swords and escaped to the land of Ararat. Then Sennacherib's son Esar-haddon reigned in his place.*

> —Isaiah 37:36-38, ISV, emphasis added

Two Silver Trumpets

The LORD spoke to Moses, saying, "Make two silver trumpets. Of hammered work you shall make them, and you shall use them for summoning the congregation and for breaking camp."

—Numbers 10:1-2

The two sons of Aaron, as priests, each blew their signal trumpet as an ordinance by God throughout all generations (v. 8). If one trumpet blew it was for the leaders to gather before the people, whereas other specific trumpet calls directed the people in the movement of the camps (vv. 4-7).

When both silver trumpets were blown simultaneously, all those in the assembly (about 2,500,000) would gather themselves in the tent of meeting (God's mobile residence) (v. 3). Silver represents redemption. As these trumpets blew, the pure silver components gave off a shrill, recognizable sound.

The sanctified trumpets sound an alarm of military style warfare. They are proclaiming prayerful liberty to the captives and slaves of sin. The advancing, worshipful sound of war is being released today with enhanced intensity. It's being sent to the heavenly realm at the helm of God.

Numbers 10:9 tells us, *"When you go into battle in your own land against an enemy who is oppressing you, sound a blast on the trumpets. Then you will be remembered by the LORD your God and rescued from your enemies"* (NIV).

It's time for the army of God to mobilize into positions of spiritual authority to the nations.

As we blow our voice trumpets with authority, our enemy's maneuvers will be exposed as they spiral downward. Let's lift our marching voices in unified prayer to defeat all perpetrators against the glorious Gospel.

Blow the trumpets in times of gladness, too, sounding them at your annual festivals and at the beginning of each month. And blow the trumpets over your burnt offerings and peace offerings. The trumpets will remind your God of his covenant with you. I am the LORD your God.

—Numbers 10:10, NLT

The Body of Christ is being encouraged as never before with our impending jubilance. Our enemy wants us to believe we're defeated forever. Those that have come against our land, its people, and our nation are vanquished by triumphant trumpets. We are coming into a rejoicing liaison with God as a salute to our freedom in Christ, deliverance from oppressive laws, and relational reconciliation.

*For the Lord himself will descend from heaven with a **cry of command**, with the **voice of an archangel**, and with the **sound of the trumpet of God**.*

—1 Thessalonians 4:16, emphasis added

Confetti and Confirmation Vision, 8.1.01

*At the end of every seven years you shall grant a **release**. And this is the manner of the **release**: every creditor shall **release** what he has lent to his neighbor. He shall not exact it of his neighbor, his brother, because the LORD's **release** has been proclaimed.*

—Deuteronomy 15:1-2, emphasis added

During a time of evening intercession at church, I began to see a visible colored confection of confetti. This rainbow array represented released prayers falling from heaven to earth over the people during our service time.

In response, I saw some people taking out their front shirt tails and collecting these heavenly prayer answers. Then I saw another group of people who were jumping on a mini-trampoline with radiant joy beaming from them while they reached out for these blessings.

But for you who revere my name, the sun of righteousness will rise with healing in its wings. And you will go out and **leap** *like calves* **released** *from the stall.*

—Malachi 4:2, NIV, emphasis added

This group, extended themselves farther to catch the increase with their hands, and then quickly released them back into the heavenly realm. (This upward movement of **release** is what brought a great increase to the church body.) The confetti began to **double** in its content while floating directly above our heads all around the room.

Confetti originated during the nineteenth century as candy or *confetto* thrown during lively festivities. They originally used Bon-bons, literally meaning good-goods as a DOUBLE compound, to throw. The word confetti comes from the Latin word *confectum*, which means something prepared. Today, it is used symbolically as small pieces of colored paper thrown from a height to enhance the event. This can occur during a celebration such as a wedding.[14]

Does anyone get the idea a wedding feast is being prepared for us right now? We are in celebration mode. The church is being released for astounding answers as we prepare our hearts for a ripened harvest. It's about release! Don't hold back and don't hold onto the blessings. Release, release, RELEASE!

*Then Moses commanded them: "At the end of every seven years, in the year for canceling debts, during the **Festival of Tabernacles**."*

—Deuteronomy 31:10, NIV, emphasis added

This is our season of release, "our appointed time" from every nightmarish form of sinister evil, addiction, dark filters, and every chain-style compulsion. This time of release is the transparent gift of the Gospel of grace which is acceptable to the Lord. We have received our pardon from jail. We are set free in liberty. As we release those things holding us back, increase will come upon us.

We are released from treachery, strangulation, fear, shame, defenses, oppression, and domination. Now freely release the good-good things that belong to God. It's the time of double, so expect double as we let go of blessings to receive vaster ones. They will hover above us all as one unified design. We can release gifts, ownership, resources, ministries, debts, enemies, dreams and visions, encounters, gateways, solutions, promises, power, praise, and joy.

Some churches are stagnant and not growing because they are holding on instead of letting go. Let go of past ways of thinking, manipulations, or organizations that stifle by control. It's the same for an individual, corporation, or institution. We must quit trying to protect what is not truly ours. We need to bless everyone with uplifting promise confessions, and not judge as an inmate but release all for the collaboration of the majestic harvest.

We are on the winning side of joy. Magnify God's goodness; let our hearts be filled with radiant praise and gratitude. His gladness has taken away sorrows and signings. His benefits are overtaking us, so rejoice in His holy name. This is a time for rejoicing, so proclaim it loudly.

If you listen to these commands of the LORD your God that I am giving you today, and if you carefully obey them, the LORD will make you the head and not the tail, and you will always be on top and never at the bottom.

—Deuteronomy 28:13, NLT

Confirmation #1, 8.2.01: The Lord knew I needed firm confirmation from the vision the day before, even though I received it by faith. I drove to work that morning taking a different route than normal. While driving I spotted a new store by the name of "Confetti's." What a sweet confirmation.

Confirmation #2, 8.3.01: I picked up some underclothing while at the lingerie area of a department store. During my checkout, I glanced around at the displays, and then focused on a pretty arrangement of polka dotted bras. As I semi-realized the connection, the saleswoman spoke up and said, "Yes, we like to call them our confetti bra!" Of course, Jesus! He can confirm Himself anywhere, during any activity of our lives.

Confirmation #3, 8.4.01: My husband and I made a weekend trip to the beach staying at a hotel. I began to read a book in our hotel room then looked up to see a beach towel hanging outside on our patio. Upon focusing more closely, I noticed the multi-colored bright background over-laid by vivid round circular dots. Again, confetti!

For the LORD your God will bless you, as he promised you, and you shall lend to many nations, but you shall not borrow, and you shall rule over many nations, but they shall not rule over you. If among you, one of your brothers should become poor, in any of your towns within your land that the LORD your God is *giving you, you shall not harden your heart or shut your hand against your poor brother, but you shall **open your hand** to him and lend him sufficient for his need, whatever it may be.*

—Deuteronomy 15:6-8, emphasis added

*Do not be mean-spirited and refuse someone a loan because the year for canceling debts is close at hand. If you refuse to make the loan and the needy person **cries out to the LORD**, you will be considered guilty of sin.*

—Deuteronomy 15:9, NLT, emphasis added

Waterfall Conclusion

*And I will give them **one heart** [a new heart] and I will put a new spirit within them; and I will take the stony [unnaturally hardened] heart out of their flesh, and will give them a heart of flesh [sensitive and responsive to the touch of their God].*

—Ezekiel 11:19, AMP, emphasis added

What can we possibly *disguise* that our Abba Father could not detect? Our Creator created us inside and out. He is all *penetrating* to our core.

No *secret* can linger that Jesus can't *uncover*. Time is not a factor. He's the here and present Abba Father, knowing all things about us. Even as frail as we are, He loves us just the same.

He loves us enough He doesn't want our sins to carry us into death. That is why our expression of repentance is so valid and real. It gives us the chance we need to be free. We can start all over again, afresh and new! The old things do pass away permanently.

I asked the Lord to show me what it looks like to "*cast all our sins into the depths of the sea*" (Micah 7:19). The concept of forever lost sins was completely overwhelming to grasp. Where did they really go?

Whirlpool Vision

Deep calls to deep at the roar of your waterfalls; all your breakers and your waves have gone over me.

—Psalm 42:7

I began to envision a huge circular whirlpool with a black, vertical tube sunk in the center. There were multiplied waterfalls on the top, stacked side by side all the way around the upper rim of the whirlpool. The water tumbled voraciously from above as if over cliffs. The cascading water gathered all the floating filth and debris at the bottom. It siphoned everything downward into a permanent drainage tube away from the surface, never to be seen again. Lost forever!

Confessing our sins isn't for God's benefit; it's completely for ours. It has lasting effects for us, those around us, and the next generation who carry on *without guilt or shame. Uncovering* our sins in order to be rid of them permanently is a believer's natural course. We need to know God is ready to take them off our hands as soon as we let them go. We were not designed to hold iniquities unto ourselves.

Sin isn't a *disguise* we wear. It shows up in our attitudes, our emotions, and our peace of mind or lack of it. It shows on our face, making us look older. When free from unnecessarily hidden guilt trash cans of the soul, we can even appear younger, revitalized, and fresh. We are free of all regrets!

The root of disturbing *secrets* always finds an outlet of expression! Unfortunately, if not dealt with, it can fester as new growth spurts as new avenues open up to it. God's love puts the "want to" in getting the sin out of us, giving us a right standing before Him. I recommend a tidy bowl flushing daily! We are sanctified (cleansed) daily by the washing of the Word.

Ephesians 5:26-27 (emphasis added)

*That he might sanctify her, having cleansed her by the washing of water with the word, so that he might present the church to himself in splendor, without spot or wrinkle or any such thing, that she might be holy and **without blemish**.*

Isaiah 35 (emphasis added)

*The wilderness and the dry land shall be glad; the desert shall rejoice and blossom like the crocus; it shall blossom abundantly and rejoice with joy and singing. The glory of Lebanon shall be given to it, the majesty of Carmel and Sharon. They shall see the glory of the LORD, the majesty of our God. Strengthen the weak hands, and make firm the feeble knees. Say to those who have an anxious heart, "Be strong; fear not! Behold, your God will come with vengeance, with the recompense of God. He will come and save you." Then the eyes of the blind shall be opened, and the **ears of the deaf unstopped;** then shall the lame man leap like a deer, and the tongue of the mute sing for joy. For waters break forth in the wilderness, and streams in the desert; the burning sand shall become a pool, and the thirsty ground springs of water; in the haunt of jackals, where they lie down, the grass shall become reeds and rushes. And a highway shall be there, and it shall be called the Way of Holiness; the unclean shall not pass over it. It shall belong to those who walk on the way; even if they are fools, they shall not go astray. No lion shall be there, nor shall any ravenous beast come up on it; they shall not be found there, but the redeemed shall walk there. And the ransomed of the LORD shall return and come to Zion with singing; everlasting joy shall be upon their heads; they shall obtain gladness and joy, and sorrow and sighing shall flee away.*

Notes

Dedication
1. "Gladys Broun Stern Quotes," *ThinkExist.com*, http://thinkexist.com/ quotation/silent_gratitude_isn-t_much_use_to_anyone/10824.html (accessed March 25, 2015).

Preface
1. "Lily of the Valley," *Learn the Bible*, http://www.learnthebible.org/ the-lily-of-the-valley.html (accessed March 4, 2015).
2. WritesEverything, "What Does Motor Oil Do for Your Car?" *HubPages*, http://writeseverything.hubpages.com/hub/What-Does-Motor-Oil-do-for-Your-Car (accessed March 25, 2015).

Introduction
1. "Henry Maudsley," *BrainDash*, http://www.braindash.com/quotes/ henry_maudsley/the_sorrow_which_has_no_vent_in_tears_may_ make_other_organs_weep/ (accessed March 25, 2015).
2. Charles Spurgeon, "Morning November 3," *Morning and Evening* (Peabody, MA: Hendrickson Publishers, 2007), 616.

Chapter One: Inside the Circle
1. "Loneliness and Social Isolation Are Just as Deadly as Obesity, Study Finds," *Publichealthwatch*, https://publichealthwatch.wordpress. com/2015/03/17/loneliness-and-social-isolation-are-just-as-deadly-as-obesity-study-finds/ (accessed March 26, 2015).
2. "C.S. Lewis Quotes," Christian Quotes, Telling Ministries LLC, http:// www.christianquotes.info/quotes-by-author/c-s-lewis-quotes/ (accessed March 26, 2015).

Chapter Two: Hide and Seek
1. *TheFreeDictionary*, s.v. "restitution," http://www.thefreedictionary. com/restitution (accessed March 26, 2015).
2. "Dental Caries (Tooth Decay)," *Dental Health Foundation*, http://www. dentalhealth.ie/dentalhealth/causes/dentalcaries.html (accessed March 26, 2015).
3. Richards Dicensoon, "Body Acidity—Problems Caused When Your Body Is Too Acidic," *Shapefit.com*, http://www.shapefit.com/health/

body-acidity-problems.html (accessed April 20, 2015).

4. *Merriam-Webster Dictionary*, s.v. "acid," http://www.merriam-webster.com/dictionary/acid (accessed April 20, 2015).

5. Tyler Wolfe, "A," *ChrisianDreamSymbols, com*, http://christiandreamsymbols.com/alpha/a.html (accessed April 20, 2015).

6. "Dental Cavities (Dental Caries)," *MedicineNet.com*, http://www.medicinenet.com/cavities/article.htm (accessed April 20, 2015).

7. "Cockroach," *Wikipedia*, updated March 20, 2015, http://en.wikipedia.org/wiki/Cockroach (accessed March 26, 2015).

8. *Merriam-Webster Dictionary*, s.v. "spoiler," http://www.merriam-webster.com/dictionary/spoiler (accessed March 26, 2015).

9. John Paul Jackson, "Bad Things, Good People," Streams Ministry International, http://www.streamsministries.com/resources/discipleship/bad-things-good-people (accessed March 4, 2015).

10. See John Paul Jackson's website at http://www.streamsministries.com/.

Chapter Four: The Escape—His Voice

1. *TheFreeDictionary*, s.v. "escape," http://www.thefreedictionary.com/escape (accessed March 27, 2015).

2. Ibid.

3. *Dictionary.com*, s.v. "sense," http://dictionary.reference.com/browse/senses (accessed March 27, 2015).

Chapter Five: Shame Hides

1. *Wordnik*, s.v. "shame," https://www.wordnik.com/words/shame (accessed March 27, 2015).

2. "Sabotage," *Wikipedia*, last modified March 12, 2015, http://en.wikipedia.org/wiki/Sabotage (accessed March 15, 2015).

3. *TheFreeDictionary*, s.v. "presumption," http://www.thefreedictionary.com/presumption (accessed March 27, 2015).

4. *Merriam-Webster Dictionary*, s.v. "blockage," http://www.merriam-webster.com/dictionary/blockage (accessed March 27, 2015).

5. Maria Finn, "Step 2: Nori/Lavar (Porphyra)" in "How to Wildcraft Nori, Wakame and Other Seaweed," *Instructables*, http://www.instructables.com/id/How-to-Harvest-Seaweed/step2/NoriLavar-Porphyra/ (accessed March 27, 2015).

6. *TheFreeDictionary*, s.v. "laden," http://www.thefreedictionary.com/laden (accessed March 27, 2015).

7. *Merriam-Webster Dictionary*, s.v. "compromise," http://www.merriam-webster.com/dictionary/compromise (accessed March 27, 2015).

8. *TheFreeDictionary*, s.v. "compromise," http://www.thefreedictionary.com/compromise (accessed March 27, 2015).
9. *TheFreeDictionary*, s.v. "reproach," http://www.thefreedictionary.com/reproach (accessed March 27, 2015).

Chapter Seven: Linen Girdle

1. Bill Johnson quote from a sermon. Used by permission.
2. "Stainless Steel—Corrosion Resistance," *Vinmay*, http://www.vinssco.com/news/11.html (accessed March 18, 2014).
3. *Oxford Dictionaries*, s.v. "latent," http://www.oxforddictionaries.com/us/definition/american_english/latent (accessed March 28, 2015).
4. "Glitch," *Wikipedia*, updated March 18, 2015, http://en.wikipedia.org/wiki/Glitch (accessed March 28, 2015).
5. "Snake Anatomy and Physiology," *Doctors Foster and Smith*, http://www.peteducation.com/article.cfm?c=17+1831&aid=2974 (accessed March 28, 2015).
6. "Snakes Have 'Heat-Seeking vision,'" *The Telegraph*, March 14, 2010, http://www.telegraph.co.uk/news/earth/wildlife/7441002/Snakes-have-heat-seeking-vision.html (accessed March 28, 2015).
7. Terry Dunn, "Small Mammals: Black Howler Monkeys, *Smithsonian National Zoological Park*, http://nationalzoo.si.edu/animals/smallmammals/exhibits/howlermonkeys/loudestanimal/ (accessed April 22, 2015).
8. "Howler Monkey Facts," *Buzzle*, http://www.buzzle.com/articles/howler-monkey-facts.html (accessed April 22, 2015).
9. "Handling Monkey Aggression," *Monkeykisses.com*, http://monkeykisses.com/monkeyinfotidbits/monkeysandaggression.html (accessed April 22, 2015).
10. Ibid.
11. "C'est La Vie: French Expressions Analyzed and Explained," About Education, *About.com*, http://french.about.com/od/vocabulary/a/c-est-la-vie.htm (accessed March 28, 2015).

Chapter Eight: The Black Veil

1. *TheFreeDictionary*, s.v. "lure," http://www.thefreedictionary.com/lure (accessed March 28, 2015).
2. "Carnival," *Wikipedia*, last modified March 20, 2015, http://en.wikipedia.org/wiki/Carnival (accessed March 20, 2015).
3. *Dictionary.com*, s.v. "circus," http://dictionary.reference.com/browse/circus (accessed March 20, 2015).
4. Ibid.
5. *TheFreeDictionary*, s.v. "carnival," http://encyclopedia2.

thefreedictionary.com/Carnival (accessed March 20, 2015).

6. Ibid.

7. Ibid.

8. "Tammuz (deity," Wikipedia, Last modified March 3, 2015, http://en.wikipedia.org/wiki/Tammuz_%28deity%29 (accessed March 20, 2015).

9. *Dictionary.com*, s.v. "disguise," http://dictionary.reference.com/browse/disguise (accessed March 20, 2015).

10. John Paul Jackson, Dream Card can be found at http://www.streamsministries.com/store/product_info.php?products_id=99.

11. Jeff Benner, "The Goat Hair Tent," *Ancient Hebrew Research Center*, http://www.ancient-hebrew.org/33_tent.html (accessed March 22, 2015).

12. Ibid.

13. "Color," *Jewish Encyclopedia*, http://www.jewishencyclopedia.com/articles/4557-color (accessed April 22, 2015).

14. Bill Johnson, quote from sermon. Used by permission.

Chapter Nine: Investigate My Life

1. "The Lord Is My Shepherd," *sheep101.info*, http://www.sheep101.info/sheepbible.html (accessed April 22, 2015).

2. K.M. Kendrick, "Sheep Senses, Social Cognition and Capacity for Consciousness," *Cornell University*, http://people.psych.cornell.edu/~jec7/pcd%20pubs/Kendricksheep08.pdf (accessed April 22, 2015).

3. "Sheep," *Onekind*, http://www.onekind.org/be_inspired/animals_a_z/sheep/ (accessed April 22, 2015).

4. Joseph Asher, "Sheep Move Towards Center of Group When They Face Threat," http://www.natureworldnews.com/articles/15/20120729/sheep-move-towards-center-of-group-when-they-face-threat.htm (accessed April 22, 2015).

5. "Follow the Leader," *sheep101.info*, http://www.sheep101.info/flocking.html (accessed April 22, 2015).

6. Richard Cobb, "An Introduction to Sheep Behavior," *Illinois Livestock Trail*, http://livestocktrail.illinois.edu/sheepnet/paperDisplay.cfm?ContentID=1 (accessed April 23, 2015).

7. "Sheep," *Wikipedia*, updated March 29, 2015, http://en.wikipedia.org/wiki/Sheep (accessed April 23, 2015).

8. Wanda Embar, "Sheep," *Vegan Peace*, http://www.veganpeace.com/animal_facts/Sheep.htm (accessed April 23, 2015).

9. "Sheep Behavior," *Follow Your Dream Farm*, http://www.followyourdreamfarm.net/sheep-behavior (accessed April 23, 2015).

10. Kendrick, "Sheep Senses, Social Cognition and Capacity for Consciousness."

11. "The Lord Is My Shepherd,"*sheep101.info.*

12. Ibid.

13. *TheFreeDictionary*, s.v. "cork," http://www.thefreedictionary.com/Cork (accessed March 22, 2015).

14. *TheFreeDictionary*, s.v. "inflammation," http://www.thefreedictionary.com/inflammation (accessed March 22, 2015).

15. *Merriam-Webster Dictionary*, s.v. "hardness," http://www.merriam-webster.com/dictionary/hardness (accessed March 22, 2015).

16. *Oxford Dictionaries*, s.v. "practise (US practice)," http://www.oxforddictionaries.com/us/definition/english/practise (accessed March 28, 2015).

Chapter Ten: God's Revealed Secrets

1. "The Blue Whale," *American Museum of Natural History*, http://www.amnh.org/exhibitions/permanent-exhibitions/biodiversity-and-environmental-halls/milstein-hall-of-ocean-life/the-blue-whale (accessed March 23, 2015).

2. "7 animals that Can Be Heard for Long Distances: 1 Blue Whale," howstuffworks, *InfoSpace LLC*, http://www.howstuffworks.com/animal-facts/7-animals-that-can-be-heard-for-long-distances5.htm#page=1 (accessed April 23, 2015).

3. "The Blue Whale," *American Museum of Natural History*.

4. *TheFreeDictionary*, s.v. "uncover," http://www.thefreedictionary.com/uncover (accessed March 28, 2015).

5. Kevin Martin, *Hypoxia: Causes and Symptoms* (Riverside, CA: RC Educational Consulting Services, Inc., n.d.), 15, http://www.rcecs.com/MyCE/PDFDocs/course/V7004.pdf.

6. Ibid., 5

7. "Cantor (church)," *Wikipedia*, last modified March 2, 2015, http://en.wikipedia.org/wiki/Cantor_%28church%29 (accessed March 23, 2015).

8. Debbie Hadley, "10 Fascinating Facts about Caterpillars," about education, *About.com*, http://insects.about.com/od/butterfliesmoths/a/10-Cool-Facts-About-Caterpillars.htm (accessed April 23, 2015).

9. Ibid.

10. *AllWords.com*, s.v. "instar," http://www.allwords.com/word-instar.html (accessed April 23, 2015).

11. Hadley, "10 Fascinating Facts about Caterpillars."

12. Ibid.

Chapter Eleven: Hope of Restoration
1. "But They Did Not Give Up," *University of Kentucky*, http://www.uky.edu/~eushe2/Pajares/OnFailingG.html (accessed March 23, 2015).
2. Ibid.
3. Ibid.
4. Ibid.
5. *Merriam-Webster Dictionary*, s.v. "ransomed," http://www.merriam-webster.com/dictionary/ransom (accessed March 24, 2015).
6. *Dictionary.com*, s.v. "dovetail," http://dictionary.reference.com/illus/illustration.html/ahd4/dovetail/doveta (accessed March 24, 2015).
7. "Albumen—Serum Test," *Blood + Work*, http://www.bloodwork.com/albumin-serum-test.html (accessed March 25, 2015).
8. "Yolks Vs Whites," *North Carolina Egg Association*, http://ncegg.org/egg-nutrition-center/yolks-vs-whites/ (accessed March 25, 2015).
9. *TheFreeDictionary*, s.v. "asphalt," http://encyclopedia2.thefreedictionary.com/Bitumen+feedstock (accessed March 25, 2015).
10. *YourDictionary*, s.v. "egg," http://www.yourdictionary.com/egg (accessed March 25, 2015).
11. Ibid.
12. *TheFreeDictionary*, s.v. "protect," http://www.thefreedictionary.com/protect (accessed March 25, 2015).
13. *Merriam-Webster Dictionary*, s.v. "pellucid," http://www.merriam-webster.com/dictionary/pellucid (accessed March 25, 2015).
14. *TheFreeDictionary*, s.v. "confetti," http://www.thefreedictionary.com/confetti (accessed March 25, 2015).

List of Dream Titles

Contact the Author

Karen Wright
P.O. Box 500
Hitchcock, TX 77563-0500

Phone: 409-739-5953
Email: wright.kw.08@gmail.com
Linkedin: Light Exposure by Karen Wright